Russian Strategic Thought toward Asia

Strategic Thought in Northeast Asia
Gilbert Rozman, Series Editor

Russian Strategic Thought toward Asia
Edited by Gilbert Rozman, Kazuhiko Togo, and Joseph Ferguson

Japanese Strategic Thought toward Asia
Edited by Gilbert Rozman, Kazuhiko Togo, and Joseph Ferguson

Strategic Thinking about the Korean Nuclear Crisis: Four Parties Caught between North Korea and the United States
By Gilbert Rozman

Korean Strategic Thought toward Asia
By Gilbert Rozman, In-taek Hyun, and Shin-wha Lee

Chinese Strategic Thought toward Asia
By Gilbert Rozman

Russian Strategic Thought toward Asia

Edited by
Gilbert Rozman, Kazuhiko Togo,
and
Joseph P. Ferguson

First published in 2006 by
PALGRAVE MACMILLAN™
175 Fifth Avenue, New York, N.Y. 10010 and
Houndmills, Basingstoke, Hampshire, England RG21 6XS
Companies and representatives throughout the world.

PALGRAVE MACMILLAN is the global academic imprint of the Palgrave Macmillan division of St. Martin's Press, LLC and of Palgrave Macmillan Ltd. Macmillan® is a registered trademark in the United States, United Kingdom and other countries. Palgrave is a registered trademark in the European Union and other countries.

ISBN-13: 978-1-4039-7554-6
ISBN-10: 1-4039-7554-X

Library of Congress Cataloging-in-Publication Data

Russian strategic thought toward Asia / Gilbert Rozman, Kazuhiko Togo, Joseph P. Ferguson, eds.
    p. cm.
Includes bibliographical references and index.
ISBN 1-4039-7554-X
    1. Asia—Foreign relations—Russia (Federation) 2. Russia (Federation)—Foreign relations—Asia. 3. National security—Asia. 4. National security—Russia (Federation) I. Rozman, Gilbert. II. Togo, Kazuhiko, 1945– III. Ferguson, Joseph P.

DS33.4.R8R88 2006
355'.033047—dc22   2006041843

A catalogue record for this book is available from the British Library.

Design by Newgen Imaging Systems (P) Ltd., Chennai, India.

First edition: December 2006

10 9 8 7 6 5 4 3 2 1

Printed in the United States of America.

Contents

Acknowledgments

This volume is the first in a series on Strategic Thought in Northeast Asia. With support from the Princeton Institute of International and Regional Studies (PIIRS), directed by Miguel Centeno, the overall project began in 2004 and is expected to continue until 2009. Without encouragement from PIIRS this project would not have been possible. Former Japanese diplomat, Kazuhiko Togo, after serving as director-general for European Affairs in the Ministry of Foreign Affairs and as ambassador to the Netherlands, came to Princeton to work with Gilbert Rozman, professor of sociology, on both Russian and Japanese strategic thought toward Asia. Joseph P. Ferguson also arrived in the fall of 2004 as a post-doctoral fellow expert on both Japanese and Russian foreign relations. Together the three of us organized a conference in Moscow in March 2005, where each of the six Russian authors presented an initial version of his chapter and critiqued an early draft of the overview. We are grateful to the East Asian Studies Program at Princeton, directed at the time by Martin Collcutt, for providing additional support for the two visitors to Princeton and the conference. We also want to thank the Moscow Carnegie Center, led then by Andrew Kuchins and including authors Dmitri Trenin and Vasily Mikheev, for supplying the venue for the conference. A number of specialists who attended the conference or joined the organizers at workshops in Princeton also played a role in shaping the contents of this volume.

Production of this volume was facilitated by Anthony Wahl at Palgrave. The sharp eye of an anonymous reader led to more comprehensive and systematic coverage. We are thankful to all at Palgrave who have contributed to this publication.

CHAPTER 1

Overview

Gilbert Rozman, Kazuhiko Togo,
and Joseph P. Ferguson

When Russians face east, they see a region vital for their country's security and development. If matters of security have lately been associated with troubles to the south and today, as historically, the question of development draws attention to the west, we should recognize that the eastern vector is rising rapidly in significance. Our study examines how strategically Russian leaders over the past two decades have viewed Asia, especially Northeast Asia. We identify criteria for strategic thinking, assess how well they were met across four periods (the Gorbachev era, the first term of Yeltsin, the second term of Yeltsin, and the Putin era through 2005) and separately focus on China, Japan, and the Korean peninsula, as well as providing a broad look at linkages to Central Asia, India, and Southeast Asia, and emerging prospects for regionalism in Asia.

It is essential to avoid the pitfalls of judging what is strategic through the frame of preferred relations with one or another country. For some, positive strategic thinking is linked to associating Moscow with the United States and the West; for others, it means more actively opposing them. Our criteria are independent of such choices. We ask to what extent was thinking targeted at making Russia and, specifically, the Russian Far East and Siberia, more secure and developed. Additionally, we consider to what degree was it directed toward reassuring the Russian public rather than arousing them, solving recognized problems instead of postponing or exacerbating them, and putting in place a process of careful deliberation at home and consultation abroad. These criteria stress the pursuit of long-term aims, balancing the expansion of Russian influence with success in winning greater trust abroad and avoidance of excessive dependency with recognition of the need for increased interdependence.

Evaluations of what constitutes strategic thinking should be able to agree on certain noncontroversial indicators. Even if there may be a sharp break with past reasoning, we can look for a new pattern of consistent thinking rather than chaotic conceptualizing. Ideas should be sustainable, not quickly reversed. With long-term objectives in mind, ideas should be clearly prioritized instead of expedient. Thinking about different countries and aspects of foreign policy should be coordinated, not spontaneous without due consideration to other approaches to Northeast Asia. Moreover, in place of utopian thinking, we regard strategic calculations as realistic in terms of what is possible and can bring the desired results. It is not just results that serve to judge the extent of strategic thinking; it is also the process that thinkers have in mind for advancing toward their goals.

Over two decades with three leaders at the helm, calculations in Moscow toward Asia changed dramatically, but, comparing the beginning and the end, we find some important continuity. The same set of factors had to be taken into account. To what extent was the West, including the United States and its main allies in Europe, considered threatening, and could respite of some kind be found in Asia? Was there danger gathering to the south, especially from Islamic fundamentalists organized in Afghanistan with backing from Pakistan, and could that be countered by policies toward other states active in Asia? Did the exposure of the distant appendage of the Russian Far East to Asian states cause anxiety, and if so, would an adjustment in Asian foreign policy strengthen security? Finally, did the flux in great power relations in dynamic Northeast Asia offer a window of opportunity for an increase in Russia's influence? These considerations fluctuated sharply from 1985 to 2005, and so did the responses of the leadership in the Kremlin, as well as the political elite in ministries and institutes across Moscow. Our interest is in the reasoning that shaped policy decisions by the leaders—Mikhail Gorbachev, Boris Yeltsin, and Vladimir Putin—and the assumptions by those who managed these policies or played an important role in explaining them.

We do not consistently identify the actor who is doing the strategic thinking, but we have in mind three levels that usually overlap. The process in the Kremlin vests an enormous amount of authority in a single national leader. When possible, it is the logic of this leader that we emphasize. Often it is the foreign minister, leading figures in the Ministry of Foreign Affairs, or other ministers of state who have the authority to speak for the president. This is the second level. Finally, reading the explanations by Russian experts and journalists, claiming to decipher or influence central policies, we gain deeper awareness of the calculations behind policy decisions, which are sometimes affected by the thinking of politicians, business representatives, and regional leaders. This is the third level. Prioritizing these separate levels, we aim for a composite picture of why policies toward Asia evolved as they did over twenty years. For expediency, we often refer to a unitary national actor, reflecting the central reasoning in Moscow and paying little heed to regional voices and to those to the Right and the Left expressing disagreement.

In the chapters that follow, claims to causality are not in most cases explicitly set forth. We do generally accept a sequential process in which changes in strategic thought mold policy outcomes. At the same time, we recognize that there may be other reasons for policy outcomes—for instance, economic benefits to particular actors or personal preferences of leading figures—that produce shifts in strategic logic as a kind of rationalization after the fact. Concentrating only on the strategic thought, we do not pursue questions of causality, however much they may be of interest to policymakers. Instead, our overriding objective is to identify and evaluate the changes in strategic logic and their application to particular areas in Asia. We do not have to argue that top-down reasoning guides all decisions, but only that grasping the calculus used to explain foreign-policy decisions shines a light on how and why Moscow's policies in Asia were evolving. Combining chronological and geographical approaches, we aspire to an overall view of the strategizing about an entire region.

Looking back from the foreign policy of Vladimir Putin in 2005, we find four contrasting explanations for recent changes. One, some blame the United States and to a lesser extent the countries of NATO and the EU for aggressively expanding their presence in the former Soviet Union, arousing alarm among Russians and obliging them to search for countermeasures. Two, others point to Putin and his associates as heirs to the security obsession in Soviet times and consider their thinking about Asia to be a reflection of their domestic strategy for comprehensive political control from above and restricted foreign investment and integration with the outside world. Three, still others trace Russian responses to the contrasting approaches of the major powers in Asia, above all to Japan's rigid stance that alienated Russia's political elite and China's sustained wooing of Russian leaders. Four, there is also the view that national interests were decisive in the face of objective conditions across Asia, and the choices made by Putin were the natural ones for any leadership as limited as Russia's was. In the following chapters, you will notice references to all four of these explanations, with each given some credence.

The contributors to this volume are not of one mind in assessing the performance of the leaders as strategic thinkers toward Asia. The main disagreement is over how to place Putin. That said, the three authors of this overview agree with Evgeny Bazhanov that Gorbachev deserves rather high marks. Gorbachev deserves credit for radically reorienting a disastrous foreign policy and laying a foundation for a realistic one. If he may not have given enough priority to Asia or found a region-wide approach, he deserves high marks for realism and problem solving in this region. He made tough decisions toward China, North Korea, and South Korea, and started a hopeful process toward Japan.

We consider with Alexei Bogaturov that Boris Yeltsin in his first term deserves quite low marks. Early Yeltsin brought Russian indifference to Asia to its extreme, while allowing ideology to overwhelm realism and starting on a path that resolved little and soon had to be drastically turned around. He let ties to first North Korea, then China, later Japan, and finally South Korea deteriorate before scrambling for effective responses. In between Gorbachev and Yeltsin's first term, we place Yeltsin in his second term. While late Yeltsin made progress in rebuilding in all directions, his approaches lacked coordination or were not pursued vigorously.

Putin's five years in office rank above Yeltsin's two terms. Putin established a more consistent course and reestablished Russian influence, but he was playing a weak hand and may have committed Russia in ways that will prove harmful or fail to leave a sustainable path for economic development and integration into the region. If favorable opportunities are weighed against strategy for the economic development of the Russian Far East and Siberia, we must agree with Dmitri Trenin that there is some disappointment with what has not been accomplished. Given the high priority on not becoming overly dependent on China and not becoming closely identified with North Korea's desperate tactics, we also share Vasily Mikheev's concern that policy toward North Korea is ambivalent. At the same time, we recognize the arguments of Aleksander Lukin and Aleksander Panov that circumstances have left Putin with good strategic reasons to draw closer to China and to delay on Japan. Yet, any overall verdict on how Putin's Asian policy deserves to be evaluated cannot neglect two serious concerns: (1) a dearth of globalization; and (2) over reliance on China and on Central Asian leaders who are failing to take advantage of opportunities. We do not discern an agenda for overcoming severe problems of governance or a strategy for development that reduces heavy dependence on energy. Ever more sophisticated arms sales to China carry the danger of backfiring on Russia. We detect no evidence of a substantive debate about ways to achieve a balanced, long-term regional approach. Instead, reliance on China and even North Korea hark back to cold war reasoning that may reassert Russia's voice without laying a foundation for future benefits and stability. Critical decisions about the future of Northeast Asia lie ahead; it would be premature to rank Putin above Gorbachev with the evidence at hand.

Chronological Overview

The Gorbachev Era

During the Brezhnev era and the brief tenure of Andropov and Chernenko, Soviet leaders took for granted that the eastern half of Asia was a dangerous arena that must be approached with military strength and diplomatic toughness. They narrowly defined strategic thinking to exclude arguments that could lead to compromising Soviet power and influence, but in the process saw their country isolated from the dynamism of East Asia and become increasingly criticized for its military buildups and aggression. Already in the late Brezhnev years some officials and academics were searching for outlets to question the evidence used to justify strategic arguments and at least to hint at alternative conclusions. Yet, even when traces of these debates filtered out, they gained little publicity and made little impact on policy. The legacy of an era of "stagnation" was to define strategic thinking so rigidly that it failed to accept genuine strategizing about a rapidly deteriorating environment.

The Soviet tradition of strategic thinking had driven Moscow into a corner in Northeast Asia. In 1960 the decision unilaterally to abrogate the 1956 treaty with Japan that had acknowledged the need to return two islands at the time a peace treaty was signed came at a time of rapidly deteriorating relations with China. Only a decade after communist expansion had made it appear that all of continental East Asia would come under Moscow's tutelage, the danger of isolation was growing. In 1973, when Prime Minister Tanaka Kakuei visited Moscow, common interests in natural resource development and the extension of détente could have produced breakthrough negotiations, but Soviet officials soon insisted that Brezhnev was just clearing his throat and not agreeing that a dispute over four islands existed. From mid-decade, Japan abandoned hope in talks and the two sides entered a decade of frozen relations. In 1976–79 the response to the long-awaited death of Mao Zedong and then the unexpected reform program of Deng Xiaoping could have been an initiative to woo China toward some sort of equidistance with the United States, but instead the go-ahead for Vietnam's invasion of Cambodia and then the dispatch of the Red Army to Afghanistan set relations back by a decade, remaining obstacles to normalization after talks had begun. Denying the rising dynamism of the region and its promise for economic integration, Moscow increasingly narrowed its options. The strategic reasoning at the root of the problem could not be easily dislodged.

In the mid-1960s China was isolated from the world and convulsed with radical class struggle. Two decades later it had solidified strategic ties with the United States, launched wide-ranging reforms, and opened its doors to trade and investment. Yet, apart from belatedly agreeing to start normalization talks, Moscow had simply continued to build its military juggernaut on the border with China without any decisive strategic response. Over the same two decades Japan's economy had become an industrial giant, and in its wake the little tigers of South Korea, Taiwan, and Hong Kong had become exporters on an ever-larger scale. The Soviet Union had only the dinosaur economy and military paranoia of North Korea with which to ally; yet, experts who urged a new strategy for China aimed at quick normalization, a new priority with Japan to achieve normalization, or some balance on the Korean peninsula including possible normalization with South Korea, could not make their voices heard. Even as internal discussions intensified, censorship left strategy to those who rejected change.

Despite lingering censorship, three messages were starting to emerge by the time Gorbachev took power. First, there was a call for realism that takes into account the actual situation in Northeast Asia without continuing to distort the truth. Second, there was urgency for advancing normalization with China above all, but with Japan as well. Third, there was a growing call to open the Russian Far East in order to partake of a dynamic region. Only months after "new thinking" became the guidepost for foreign policy, the July 1986 Vladivostok speech by Gorbachev brought together ideas that had sprouted from years of concealed venting within the government and the Communist Party of dissatisfaction with foreign policy in the region. In 1986–88 officials responsible for stifling sprouts of new thinking were ousted—first for China, later for Japan and Korea—amidst optimism that a sudden change of course would bring dramatic results.

Openness to new ideas and talk of pragmatism are necessary but not sufficient conditions for strategic thinking. In the critical middle years of the Gorbachev era there was no genuine regional strategy toward

Northeast Asia. One reason was that the overarching priority was the West, especially the United States. Even the name given to the region to the east, the Asia–Pacific region (APR), highlighted the U.S. role there. Both Beijing and Tokyo would have welcomed a strategy in Moscow that put them on the fast track, rather than leaving them as an afterthought. Another reason was that the proclaimed regional strategy for the development of the Russian Far East in 1987 was a grandiose wish list for luring massive investment into industry and infrastructure that was in no way prepared, quite the opposite of the systematic opening through special economic zones that propelled China forward. Moreover, there was little recognition of the real weakness of the Soviet Union in the region. The United States had little interest in striking any deal covering security in this region, and Japan expected little economically or even strategically, despite its desire for four islands. Moscow was holding a weak hand.

Gorbachev separately pursued normalization with the three countries actively wooing him, whose goals would not be easy to reconcile. The challenge was to figure out a balance among the three. While adhering to its priority for "peace and development," China eyed geopolitical objectives, seeking a revival of the strategic triangle with itself at the pivot between the United States and the Soviet Union. Although Gorbachev eliminated its "three obstacles" to normal relations, which also met the interests of other countries, he did not make common cause in "reform socialism" or geopolitical balancing. The Chinese option was not pursued in parallel with the rush to draw closer to the United States, limiting Moscow's strategic options. Yet, it was pressed before ties to Japan, foregoing regional balance.

Japan was preoccupied with the territorial question. At the price of four islands Gorbachev could have established a partnership with considerable possibility for solidifying the Soviet Union's place as part of a regional triangle with China. Even if the geopolitical consequences had been unappealing to China, it would have had little choice but to accept the arrangement. Whether Tokyo was too inflexible in its demands or Moscow too dismissive of its significance, the result was a second strategic option left unrealized. Lacking a "Japan card," Gorbachev had little flexibility in the region.

South Korea made a stronger pitch than Japan, giving assistance in return for normalization while seeking leverage to press North Korea into talks and, eventually, reintegration. Gorbachev agreed, angering North Korea without taking steps to reassure it as Beijing was doing. Within a few years Russians would look back on this abandonment, carried further by Yeltsin, as a mistake. Even without alienating Pyongyang,

Moscow had a good chance to secure similar benefits from Seoul. Another option was forsaken. If leaders in Moscow were indeed intent on forging a close partnership with the United States and opening their country's economy ever more, and were correct in expecting that the Russian people and local elites would accept this, then a global strategy may have dictated the kind of regional approach that was taken. With such a global strategy having little chance, however, the shortcomings of the regional strategy could not long be concealed.

By the time Gorbachev left office he had established a foundation for improved ties in the region, but he had done little to position his country to take advantage of the expected rise of this region and its uncertain balance of power. Vladivostok, the gateway to the Russian Far East, remained closed until after the demise of the Soviet Union. Nearby Nakhodka, the port designated as Russia's first free economic zone, remained mired in red tape and conflicting legislation. Chinese, Japanese, and North Koreans all blamed Gorbachev for missing strategic opportunities and leaving Russia without the partnerships in the region that it should have had. Soon Seoul decided that Moscow's loss of leverage over Pyongyang lessened its strategic value as well. While the shift from the Soviet Union to the Russian Federation meant no loss of territory in Northeast Asia, the decline in influence was more rapid and far greater than it needed to be. Saving money and avoiding any threat were not enough.

Given the difficult starting point he inherited and the contradictory strategic needs of working with the five states active in the region, Gorbachev's limited achievements in normalization deserve some positive acknowledgment. His situation was made more difficult when after June 4, 1989 he faced a China under international sanctions. North Korea's extreme reactions made it hard to find balance on the Korean peninsula. Setbacks that delayed his trip to Japan until April 1991 could be blamed on Japan as well as the Soviet Union. While pointing to the lack of wide-ranging strategic thinking toward Northeast Asia under Gorbachev, we recognize that the circumstances were not easy.

Gorbachev's primary goal was to strengthen the Soviet Union, but his policies resulted in its destruction and a debilitating legacy for its principal successor state Russia. Asian leaders in Beijing, Tokyo, and Seoul all beckoned to him, and he sought to develop an Asia–Pacific strategy that would serve his overall objectives. Instead, he normalized relations with China after four years and just as that country was becoming an international pariah that made closer ties difficult; he failed to achieve a breakthrough with Japan when it reigned as the world's capital-rich, manufacturing powerhouse with the potential to assist Russia; and he reached a deal with South Korea that brought loans of about $2 billion that were largely wasted while throwing off-kilter Moscow's regional influence. Despite speeches in Vladivostok in July 1986 and Krasnoyarsk in September 1988 that set forth regional priorities and came closer to a strategic overview for a region than any other speeches he made on Asia, Gorbachev was unsuccessful in reaching beyond the most apparent gaps in Soviet policy. In his final three years of leadership, he never again articulated a regional approach. Yet, he accomplished a great deal after inheriting policies that had left his country deeply isolated.

The Yeltsin Era: 1992–95

The demise of the Soviet Union and the creation of Russia brought about the period of "Atlanticism" in Russian foreign policy. The internal logic that Russia had forsaken totalitarianism and a socialist economy, and that it would create a new democratic and market-based economy, was reason to draw Russia very close to "Western countries" such as Europe and the United States. Although criticism was raised early on that Russia must pay more attention to the former Soviet Republics, until October 1992 when Yeltsin made an open request to implement foreign policy based on national interest at a Ministry of Foreign Affairs conference, there was little enhancement of relations with the states in the new Commonwealth of Independent States (CIS).

Even after Yeltsin's October statement, Asia in general was kept as a low priority during this period. By far the more important task was to rebuild relations with the CIS, and from the perspective of NATO eastward expansion, Europe and the United States were at the center of attention. In the New Year Address to the Russian Congress in 1994, Russian foreign policy priorities were given in order as: the CIS, America and Europe, Central and Eastern Europe, and finally Asia. In 1995 it was shifted to the CIS, Central and Eastern Europe, Europe, America, and finally Asia. Atlanticism was gone by the end of 1992, and there was talk of "Eurasianism," but Asia was marginal.

This period also reveals striking confusion in the Russian Far East. After the total opening of the society, considerable interest emerged in all neighboring countries—including China, Japan, and South Korea—to let the Russian Far East engage in more dynamic economic activities. But the collapse of the previous socialist order, the total inability to create an orderly market, and the resulting chaotic situation where mafias played an omnipotent role in transactions, all amplified by the remoteness of this region from Russia's European center, combined with substantial weakening in border controls, became conspicuous phenomena of the era. The authorities' belated reactions often looked powerless.

Thus, Yeltsin's Northeast Asian policy during his first term in office was largely a co-efficient of Russia's overall external policy and the deteriorating internal situation. It was remote from any autonomous, coordinated, long-term strategic thinking. Nevertheless, within the limits of this overall framework, important developments took place with respect to Japan, China, and South Korea.

At the height of post-Soviet Atlanticism, the first Asian country to which Russia directed its attention was Japan. Its position as a "West in Asia" gave compelling reasons for that. An historic opportunity emerged to resolve the territorial issue, which had separated them for nearly half a century, but Japan failed to grasp it and relations suffered considerably by Yeltsin's cancellation of his planned visit in September 1992. Yeltsin's renewed visit in October 1993 brought back relations to where they had stood before the cancellation, but the Duma elections in December, which saw the abrupt rise of communists and nationalists, crushed hopes that Japan–Russia relations could be placed at center stage in Yeltsin's foreign policies. Japan did not appear again at the forefront of Russian Asian policy until 1997. Meanwhile, in the Russian Far East, rising Japanese interest in small- and medium-scale business after the demise of the Soviet Union soon was replaced by thorough disappointment that emerging profits were grabbed by local mafias. Lack of effective border controls resulted in a sharp rise of "illegal" Japanese fishing around the four islands, further damaging ties.

The country that drew Russian attention after Japan's eclipse was China. This shift coincided with the change from Atlanticism to national interest policy. Immediately after the demise of the Soviet Union, relations with China were tense. Chinese sympathy for the August 1991 coup did not please Yeltsin, and Yeltsin's initial Atlanticism did not please China. But Yeltsin's visit in December 1992 made a new opening, marked by a Joint Declaration that referred to the necessity of developing friendly relations despite the difference in social structure, and to anti-hegemonism, enhancement of military–technology cooperation, and security cooperation in Asia. The Duma elections at the end of 1993 further enhanced Yeltsin's pro-China policy, Jiang Zemin reciprocated Yeltsin's visit in September 1994, and the two countries signed an agreement to demarcate the western border.

This period was noteworthy for the efforts made by the two administrations to overcome two difficult issues: a perceived Chinese demographic threat and the settlement of the eastern border. In 1992 and 1993 there was a rapid rise in the number of Chinese crossing the border—many as petty traders who overstayed their visas—, and Evgeny Nazdratenko, the governor of Primorskii krai, began waging a strong public campaign. Nazdratenko was also not silent in expressing his dissatisfaction on the border agreement concluded between Gorbachev and the Chinese leadership in May 1991 for having abandoned important territories to China, in particular, in the area of Lake Khanka, Ussuriisk, and Lake Khasan. Only with effort did Moscow officials bring back some order to the border control and to resolving the border demarcation issues, although problems lingered until at least 1998.

As Japan fell and China rose in Russian Northeast Asian policy, South Korea for a while took the role of a "West in Asia" instead of Japan, at the expense of exacerbating relations with North Korea. Yeltsin did not lose time in compensating for his cancelled visit to Japan in September by visiting South Korea in November 1992. He went so far as to call South Korea the leading partner in the region, and even discussed defense cooperation. Kim Young-sam reciprocated his visit in June 1994. However, economic relations did not prosper as much as Russia had expected, partly because of Russian inability to pay interest on Soviet loans from 1990. A compromise was reached in August 1994 to include Russian weapons transfers to Seoul as payment for Soviet debt, but the South Koreans riled Moscow by not continuing the loan package and dismissing its lack of influence in the region.

The continued reliance on the South infuriated North Korea, and relations that had already been strained in the Gorbachev years hit their bottom in the first half of the 1990s. Russian military cooperation with South Korea might have been a triggering factor in inducing North Korea to embark on its brazen nuclear armament program in 1993–94, and to Russia's humiliation, it was excluded from the settlement of that nuclear crisis, and from the four-party talks which were proposed in April 1996.

The Yeltsin Era: 1996–99

At the beginning of 1996, Yeltsin had as his paramount political agenda the election to take place in the summer of that year. All his efforts to stabilize the country, particularly its economic situation, to give minimal satisfaction to the impoverished sectors of the population, to bring back security and political order in the society, and to defuse the war in Chechnya should be judged in the light of the coming election. In foreign policy, Yeltsin sought an image of strong leadership in the face of still unresolved problems. Mostly these were matters tied to the CIS, including Russia's relations with Ukraine, Belarus, and Central Asian countries; but they also included finding a way to show resistance to the eastward expansion of NATO, which had become an irreversible trend by this time, and proving that Russia was making headway in Northeast Asia.

At the beginning of 1996, Yevgeny Primakov was appointed foreign minister. His emphasis on multipolarity in international relations and on Russia taking an omnidirectional foreign policy, combined with the political weight that he carried in Russian internal politics, was instrumental in boosting Yeltsin's foreign policy image. In fact, Primakov's efforts quickly helped to enlarge the scope of Russian foreign policy in Asia even more than in other parts of the world.

Even acknowledging Primakov's special role, one cannot but observe that foreign policy was very much a presidential matter. Real achievement could only be associated with Yeltsin's direct participation, if not his active leadership. Although there were important developments in relation to China and the CIS, Yeltsin was largely preoccupied with his election campaign in the first half of 1996. After his victory in the July election, his heart attack virtually incapacitated him from presidential duties until March 1997. Thus major foreign policy events are concentrated in the short period between March 1997 and the fall of 1998, after which Yeltsin's health again declined, making foreign policy less active once again in 1999.

The first major achievement of this short 1997–98 period was Russia's final agreement with Ukraine to settle the fate of Crimea and Sevastopol. An important treaty framework was established with Belarus as well. After the Oslo summit with President Clinton in March, Russia also accepted the modality with which Poland, Hungary, and the Czech Republic joined NATO, and NATO's eastward expansion was promulgated at the Madrid NATO summit in August 1997. With these developments, Russia finally concluded the post-cold war security structure in the trans-Atlantic space. The conclusion of the trans-Atlantic security structure at Madrid gave Russia breathing room and incentive to direct its attention elsewhere. The deep psychological scar that it had to swallow the unwanted expansion of NATO eastward was an impetus to turn its eyes in the opposite direction, to Asia.

Russia–China relations kept their momentum. Even before the election Yeltsin visited Beijing in April and the two countries declared a strategic partnership. In same month, the leaders of five countries

(Russia, Kazakhstan, Kyrgyzstan, Tajikistan, and China) met for the first time in Shanghai and agreed on troop withdrawals from the border. The gathering of the five leaders had already played a useful role in demarcating the so-called western border between the four and China, but from this time onward, such meetings became institutionalized as the "Shanghai Five," continuing to enhance mutual trust without raising Russian alarm about Chinese inroads into Central Asia.

After Yeltsin's return to active presidency in March 1997, Jiang Zemin immediately visited in April and joined in a Joint Declaration on the multipolarization of the world. Furthermore, at Yeltsin's visit to Beijing in November 1997, the two sides had at last agreed to the eastern border demarcation, except for the question of three islands, two near Khabarovsk. Events in 1999, such as NATO's bombardment of Kosovo, a new U.S. approach to missile defense, and Western criticism against Russia's operation in Chechnya, drew Russia closer to China. Yeltsin's visit to China in December 1999 highlighted this convergence of immediate interests between the two countries.

Japan made the most of the window of opportunity opened in 1997–98. Ryutaro Hashimoto, who had his first harmonious meeting with Yeltsin at the nuclear summit in April 1996, continued to attract Yeltsin's attention at the Denver G-8 summit, and with his July 1997 Eurasian speech succeeded in opening Yeltsin's heart. His strategic thinking on the two countries' shared geopolitical interest in strengthening relations and his readiness to propose an attractive economic cooperation program gave further momentum to the relationship. In November 1997 Yeltsin proposed to conclude a peace treaty by 2000. Then in February 1998 a fishery agreement was successfully reached to put any "illegal catch" around the four islands under control. In April the Japanese side made a concessionary proposal on the four islands issue, postponing the time when any transfer would occur. But from the summer of 1998, Yeltsin's health began to fail, and his counterproposal in November did not attract Japanese attention to lead to a breakthrough. Momentum between the two countries weakened in 1999.

After serious difficulty in its relations with North Korea, Russia tried to regain a more balanced position on the peninsula. Losing influence over North Korea was not in Russia's interest because it was South Korea's expectation that Russia would help to soften North Korea's erratic and irrational behavior. Efforts were made in high-level official visits to Pyongyang by Georgy Kunadze (1993) and Alexander Panov (1994), and in the Russian proposal to conclude a new Treaty of Friendship and Good Neighborly Cooperation (1995). The new treaty was initialled in March 1999, but the actual signing was delayed until Putin became acting-president. Relations with South Korea were strained by a spy incident in July 1998, but the two sides made efforts to overcome it. In May 1999, Kim Dae-jung visited Moscow and Russia openly declared support for his sunshine policy. With the United States entering an election year and no real political agenda with Europe, Kim's visit was, perhaps, the most important summit to take place in Moscow in 1999. But clarification of the overall thrust of policy toward the Korean peninsula had to wait until the emergence of a new leader in the Kremlin.

The Putin Era: 2000–05

Vladimir Putin became president of the Russian Federation at a time when its geopolitical strategy was somewhat adrift. Relations with the United States and Europe were increasingly strained by the conflict in Yugoslavia and the bloody quagmire in Chechnya. Relations with Japan—which had held such promise for a short time—seemed stagnant once again by 2000. Russia was thought by some to be leaning heavily on China as a strategic partner by the end of 1999. There was a question over whether this strategy would actually result in a solid partnership due to China's increasingly global economic profile, and its growing trade turnover and investment links with the developed economies. The one region where Russia seemed somewhat more assured of its standing by 2000 was Central Asia, but this was due more to the increasing frustration of the United States and the West about the progress of democratization and human rights in this region than to any concerted Russian effort to restore its paramount position there. The after-effects of the August 1998 financial crisis were still being felt, and Russia's long-term financial and economic health was still in doubt.

In spite of the obstacles that Putin faced as he was sworn in on New Year's Eve 1999–2000, he proved to be a good study and quickly grasped a fundamental understanding of Russia's limitations and strategy needs. The period 2000–01 was a time of consolidation politically, economically, and diplomatically for Russia. During this period Putin reached out to all of Russia's neighbors and "partners" to establish a balanced diplomatic initiative that could shore Russia up strategically. The period 2001–03 saw Russia move firmly behind the United States in the global war on terror, but it also witnessed attempts by Moscow to maintain cordial relations with all nations, including those in East and Southeast Asia. The period 2004–05 was a time for recalculation for Russia, due to events in Eastern Europe and Central Asia, which left many strategic thinkers in Moscow wondering how far strategic cooperation with the United States should be carried, especially in Central and East Asia.

2000–01

Within his first few months in office leading up to the March 2000 presidential election, debate raged in the West over what Putin was like and how his policy might be formulated. Eventually, Putin came to be seen as a pragmatist, and to have a "Western" outlook, due to his training in the KGB and his experience of having lived in Germany during the Gorbachev years. People such as Tony Blair and Gerhard Schroeder were quick to pronounce Putin "a man we can do business with." George W. Bush, upon meeting Putin in Genoa in 2001, was said to have looked into his soul and established a rapport.

Although some in China (and perhaps elsewhere in Asia) were initially taken aback by Putin's supposed penchant for leaning toward the West, Putin quickly demonstrated his flexibility and his desire to work with Russia's Asian partners by embarking on a series of trips to the region during his first six months in office after the March 2000 presidential elections. Putin's trip to Beijing and Pyongyang on the way to the G-8 Okinawa summit in July of that year was viewed as a tremendous breakthrough for Russia, which was increasingly becoming marginalized in Northeast Asia. Putin obviously hoped to use his trip to the DPRK as a tool not only to heighten Russia's profile in the region, but also as an attempt to thwart the U.S. drive to abolish the ABM treaty and develop regional and national missile defense systems (due to the United States using the North Korean missile program as a rationale for such a system). Although Putin was unsuccessful in persuading the North Koreans to abandon their ballistic missile development programs, he did succeed in mending the Russian–DPRK relationship. Putin also succeeded in assuaging the fears of his Chinese hosts that Russia would throw itself blindly into the Western camp. Although leaders in Beijing would have liked to have seen a more spirited Russian opposition to the abrogation of the ABM treaty, they came to accept this fact as their counterparts in Moscow had done later in 2001.

In September 2000, Putin made a trip to Tokyo and pleased his hosts by presenting himself as a man of his word, and demonstrating that he had a decidedly less mercurial disposition than did his predecessor. Although no immediate breakthrough in relations occurred, the two sides understood that a genuine discussion would ensue over the coming months. As this occurred, diplomats from both nations were encouraged by their leaders until the spring of 2001 to find a shared path forward.

Putin and others in Moscow understood the dire situation they faced in the Russian Far East, which was rotting under the weight of corruption and economic stagnation due to tremendous political, legal, and infrastructural impediments. Russian leaders understood the need for a multidirectional strategy and diplomatic effort in the Asia–Pacific region that would help contribute to the economic revitalization of Russia's Far East and Russia's decidedly weakened political profile in the region. Internally, Russia was consumed with political consolidation (and centralization) and economic revitalization after the disjointed Yeltsin years. The primary focus, of course, was the war in Chechnya. As the months dragged into years, Russia found itself having to defend its actions more and more to the West. Meanwhile, many nations in Asia (especially China) took a sympathetic view of Russia's plight. The expansion of the Shanghai Five to include Uzbekistan and the subsequent formation of the Shanghai Cooperation Organization (SCO) in June 2001 was a confidence-building measure for all sides, and it was also another indication that Putin wanted to broaden Russia's political and diplomatic profile in the face of the impending charge toward globalization led by the United States. Jiang Zemin's visit to Moscow in July 2001 was a clear signal that Putin looked to play as many cards as his hand would allow. The dramatic events of September 11, 2001 gave Putin the rationale and wherewithal to forge a closer bond with the United States. Although some of Russia's Asian partners were initially put-off by the newfound Russian–American strategic partnership, Russia soon made it clear that it had no intention of abandoning the drive to up its political profile in the APR.

2002–03

The war on terror gave Russia the opportunity to legitimize its operations in Chechnya, while moving closer to Washington. In return, however, Moscow acceded to the United States a special political, military, and economic role in Central Asia and the Caucasus. Soon U.S. troops and bases would be scattered from Kyrgyzstan to Georgia, and a multinational coalition of forces would topple the ruling Taliban in Afghanistan and launch elections to bring democracy. In Northeast Asia the threat of a U.S. attack to topple the DPRK regime re-energized Russia to assume a more active role, and in 2003 Moscow would be rewarded with a seat at the six-party talks. The diplomatic initiative with Tokyo that offered great promise for progress in bilateral relations failed due to political infighting in Japan. Great hope for a revitalized role in Northeast Asia was subsequently placed in burgeoning energy relations across the region. This went hand in hand with the rise in world oil prices, which was a boon to Russia's economic situation. Although China warily viewed Russia's cozying up to Washington, Putin and Chinese President Hu Jintao paid reciprocal visits in late 2002 and May 2003, which cleared the atmosphere to some extent. Nevertheless, in spite of Putin's eagerness for all-around engagement, maintaining a balance proved a tall order.

Increasingly warm relations with Washington proved problematic for Moscow. As mentioned, Moscow was forced to accept the heightened U.S. political and military profile in Central Asia and the Middle East. If Russia was able to benefit from a positive image in Western business and financial circles, thanks in large part to Washington's blessing and anticipated WTO membership as well as a permanent place at the G-8 (and, hence, globalization) table, concern was spreading that its political position was becoming further marginalized. Historically high energy prices gave leaders in Moscow greater confidence, while a weakened political position in the CIS and assertive U.S. policies such as the war in Iraq made it more alarmed. These conditions raised the stakes for pursuing an active foreign policy in Asia that would not allow the United States to consolidate its hegemonic position.

Energy offered the greatest promise in terms of increasing Moscow's clout in Northeast Asia during this time frame. Large-scale energy projects in progress in Sakhalin and plans for future projects and pipelines from Siberia were drawing the interest of more than a half-dozen nations, including China, Japan, India, and South Korea. The appearance of Sino-Japanese friction over an oil pipeline route gave Russia a renewed sense of its importance, and both sides continued to evince interest in large-scale investment in Russia's Far Eastern energy complex through 2005.

Political relations with China were strengthening again by the end of 2003 and paved the way for increasing economic interaction; not the least of which was the significant amount of high-tech weaponry that Russia increasingly sold to the PLA. Political relations with Japan were stagnant, but Japanese business concerns were increasingly taken with opportunities that the Russian market provided. Though the lion's share of the interest was in the energy sector, investment opportunities were eyed in other areas, as well. The year 2003 also saw a major initiative by Moscow to begin discussions on a trans-Korean railroad initiative that would link the major trading centers of East Asia with Europe, via the Trans-Siberian Railroad. If this fanciful vision was problematic given the North Korean situation, it tied in well with the grand vision of large-scale energy and infrastructure projects that Russia hoped to use to revitalize the Russian Far East. If Korea could not help in Russia's economic resurgence, at least the six-party talks offered Russia some increased political clout.

2004–05

Russian concerns about the overbearing nature of the Bush administration, though latent from day one, came to the surface with the invasion of Iraq in the spring of 2003. Moscow voiced its displeasure with the U.S. actions, but it did not come out nearly as strong in opposition as some of Washington's closest allies in the West. By 2004, clashes over foreign policy as well as Putin's increasing drive to centralize authority across Russia led to the exposure of fissures in the relationship with Washington. U.S. attention was somewhat distracted by the troubling situation in Iraq and the presidential election, but notice was taken of Putin's seeming authoritarian bent. What drew more attention was not so much the crackdown on civil liberties and the free press or the decision to annul gubernatorial elections throughout the Federation in favor of presidential appointments, but two particular events that transpired in late 2004: the conviction of the oil magnate Mikhail Khodorkovsky (the head of the oil giant YUKOS) and the presidential election in the Ukraine. Khodorkovsky was seen in the West as a champion of the free market and globalization in Russia. He also claimed to be the champion of democracy in Russia, and however true those claims may have been, it endeared him to many in the West. The Ukrainian presidential elections at the end of 2004 were, perhaps, the most damaging event for bilateral relations: the Kremlin felt that the United States was meddling in the area most vital to traditional Russian influence.

By 2005, Washington's heightened presence in Central Asia had created considerable strategic discomfort in Moscow. Putin actively began maneuvering to balance against the U.S. presence and to reassert Russian political influence. This included the reactivation of old Soviet bases in Uzbekistan and Kyrgyzstan. Newly strained ties between the United States and Uzbekistan over human rights allowed Moscow to rekindle the relationship with Uzbekistan, which had been strained throughout the 1990s. Moscow also cooperated with China to heighten the political role of the SCO, and to rescue the foundering CIS. Although Russian leaders were prepared to admit China's role in the region and to cooperate more closely on energy, the Sino-Russian relationship remained a double-edged sword, both in Central Asia and in the Russian Far East. In 2004–05 Sino-Russian relations were advancing on many fronts despite misgivings.

The two primary levers of Russian influence are energy and arms sales. Each has drawn China closer while making close ties with the United States less likely. As Moscow has increasingly granted Beijing its requests, these two forces have privileged bilateralism over regional balance. Yet, arms sales to India and Southeast Asian states as well as solidified military alliances in Central Asia indicate Putin's broader objectives. On energy, the pursuit of Japan for a pipeline and related infrastructure and extraction financing as well as repeated discussion with South Korea about long-term projects suggests that Putin is looking beyond China. Regardless of strategic intentions, there is a danger for Russia that the Chinese connection will so predominate that no balance occurs.

Putin's centralizing tendencies did bring about a unified voice in foreign policy, particularly in the Far East, where in the 1990s recalcitrant governors and local political leaders had done their best to frustrate Russia's relations with China and Japan. His ability to push through a final territorial agreement with Beijing in October 2004 is a clear indication that Putin was able to silence, or at least mollify, local opposition. His offer to return two islands to Japan in late 2004 also speaks to this unified voice on regional policy. It should be noted that one of the first governors to be appointed under Putin's new system of central nomination of regional governors was Sergei Darkin of Primorskii krai, who asked for Putin's support in February of 2005. Although Darkin is known for corruption, he is seen as a pillar of political support for the Kremlin administration in the Russian Far East, something that could never be said of his predecessor Nazdratenko.

By the end of 2005 Putin's strategic thinking had become clearer. He would tighten ties with China and continue to strengthen the SCO, while waiting for new opportunities. Toward Japan he would dangle economic incentives without showing any interest in territorial talks, at least until Tokyo changed its position. Lacking much influence on the Korean peninsula, Putin would keep a low profile in the six-party talks and wait for others to find some kind of resolution while striving for balanced and forward-looking ties with both South and North. Meanwhile, Russia sought a seat at the new East Asian Summit, seeing this both as a gateway to rebuilding influence in Southeast Asia and as a venue for working to bring Beijing and New Delhi together in a broader framework of regional security cooperation. Many policy decisions appeared to counteract U.S. positions, above all in Central Asia, but also in solidifying the alliance with Japan and taking a firm posture toward North Korea. Putin's desire to gain leverage without becoming dependent on

China and to boost Russia's influence in Asia in the absence of an understanding with the United States and Japan is undoubtedly a daunting task.

Geographical Overview

China

Moscow made serious strategic mistakes in its approach to China prior to the late 1980s, but it has been most consistently forward-looking in its approach since 1988, and, even more so since 1996. We see both extremes of Moscow's strategic thinking over the past quarter century of managing relations with China. Over this period, China has represented three things, above all. First, it has stood in a global great power context as a force linked to the extension of relations with the United States beyond bilateral ties. Even when the concept of a "strategic triangle" was not favored or when India and the EU entered into multipolar thinking, China had special significance as a balance to the United States. Second, China stands at the center of Moscow's interest in establishing a favorable grouping of powers in the area around the Russian Far East, usually referred to as the APR. As China's rise has become more obvious, its impact on the strategic balance in this region has risen in Russian calculations. Third, China's growing involvement in Central Asia as well as Mongolia and cross-border relations in the Russian Far East and Eastern Siberia raises its profile as a neighboring state capable of shaping the security environment inside the borders of the former Soviet Union and even the Russian Federation itself. This third area of significance has been rising in priority, even as the other two areas have remained of great concern.

With respect to China as a global power, we observe the depths of Moscow's miscalculation in the late 1970s with less serious miscalculations through the late 1980s and early 1990s. From 1994 to 2005 Moscow was very attentive to China's role as a balance to the United States, although oscillations suggest that it was at times overvalued without adequate consideration for its growing regional power. Given the three distinct security contexts in which China's power operates, Moscow has faced a complex challenge of weighing their relative importance.

In the period of the Brezhnev era, impatient ideologues, confident that they grasped the big security picture, insisted on an exaggerated image of China as a threat and a state impervious to realist foreign policy calculations. In the years 1967–72 they failed to await China's emergence from the peak of the Cultural Revolution and its provocative border incursions as the United States searched for a way to mitigate its failed strategy in Vietnam. In the wait for Mao's death and its aftermath through the late 1970s, Soviet leaders and ideologues did not prepare for a pragmatic leadership ready to open China's economy to the world and to cast aside charges of revisionism as they looked to normalize relations with the Soviet Union and establish equidistance with the United States. Then, at the start of normalization talks in 1982 there was insufficient urgency to reducing military pressure along China's borders. Instead, the strategy remained to rely on Soviet power alone and on states under Soviet control or intensely hostile to the United States. This approach left Moscow overexposed and isolated from the dynamism in Asia, while preventing rapprochement with the one power eager to use it as a balance in global relations.

The period 1986–95 saw many improvements in relations with China and efforts to prevent new problems (distrust between Deng and Gorbachev in 1989–91, resentment of China for being on the side of the abortive putsch in August 1991, and Yeltsin's poor start with China in 1991–92) from setting back relations sharply. Moscow made strategic concessions to China: for normalization and a demarcation agreement, for the sale of aircraft, and in December 1992 for friendly ties with a message to the United States and Japan not to take Russia for granted. Yet, Moscow could have gained more leverage in international relations by advancing ties more quickly and boldly at several junctures. Gorbachev's delay in normalization and removal of the "three obstacles" left him more vulnerable to the United States without any balance of power. His hesitation after June 4, 1989 failed to take advantage of increased Chinese isolation and need for partners. And Yeltsin's neglect of China in his first year as Moscow's top leader added to the impression that his foreign policy created a one-sided dependence. The years of concentrating on the United States without seeking some balance from China were premised on assumptions that were later proven incorrect to those looking at declining power globally, regionally, or bilaterally.

Beginning with his visit in December 1992 and accelerating in 1994 and again in 1996, Yeltsin turned to China as a balancing force. This interest, labeled a strategic partnership in April 1996, served to stabilize a long and exposed border, while it also became the prime factor in resuming its regional role, however diminished. No less importantly, it provided some satisfaction to many who resented U.S. assertive behavior as the remaining superpower pressing its advantage along Russia's borders. There was a cost in the sale of arms to a rising power that was feared to seek advantage in the Russian Far East. Yet, Russian hesitation toward solidifying the partnership in 1997–99, except for a time during the Kosovo War, reflected both awareness of this downside and strategic wavering without a well-defined set of priorities.

China assumes a large place in Russian strategic thinking toward Northeast and Central Asia. Upgrading ties has been driven by strategic objectives. Russia has not been disappointed by China's reactions. On the territorial dispute, not only did China show flexibility and understanding in reaching and implementing demarcation agreements, but it took a constructive approach in later agreements that resolved all differences. In the formation of the SCO and its early meetings, Russia was satisfied that China deferred to its greater political influence in Central Asia. As Putin positioned his country to gain a role in disputes involving North Korea, coordination with China proved useful. After the Bush administration launched its war against terrorism Putin found it easier to offer his support, knowing that the strategic partnership with China was stabilizing. Later, as he soured on U.S. policies, the China connection was further upgraded.

In the first half of 2000 and again after 9/11, doubts were raised over whether Putin valued a special partnership with China as much as Jiang Zemin prized Russian relations. At both times, Putin signaled strong interest in boosting ties with the West, especially the United States. With the sudden arrival of a new Russian president and later with the new conditions of the war against terror, some feared that the momentum of closer partnership in the first half of 1999 and of the friendship treaty of July 2001 could be slipping. Putin was slow to arrange a summit with China in 2000 and was preoccupied with boosting cooperation with Bush in the fall of 2001. Yet, the message of cooperation with China in power balancing was reinforced each time, and it has been trumpeted in 2004–05.

After a surge of emotional arguments about China, driven by anger over the United States or alarm at China's rise, the Putin era is characterized by sober reflections on how China serves the strategic needs of Russia. At the global level, it is accepted as a useful balance to U.S. hegemony, but only one of many and not as an alliance partner that would obscure the need to cooperate with the United States on some issues. On the regional level, China is regarded as useful in drawing Japan's attention and facilitating a role in the Korean peninsula, but the goal of keeping China from regional dominance is also evident. Putin continues to seek more regional balance. And at the bilateral level, Putin is most careful not to let China gain an advantage in economic integration or access to the Russian Far East that could later put Russian interests in jeopardy.

In comparison to thinking on other countries active in Northeast Asia, Moscow has shown over the past two decades the highest level of strategic orientation toward China and a learning curve that keeps boosting it. As long as Japan does not make Russian relations a priority and the Korean crisis does not end in a new regional framework, we should not expect much change in recent thinking toward China. The territorial compromise in October 2004 that saw Putin agree to transfer parts of two islands to China offered proof of a pragmatic leader seeking to put ties on a stable long-term foundation. The emotionalism toward China of the 1990s is receding. Although a quieter determination was evident early in Putin's tenure not to allow dependence to grow quickly, reliance on China has kept growing with uncertain consequences.

Japan

In Russian strategic thinking toward Japan from the Soviet era to date, there have always been two major factors: geopolitical interest in the APR and Japan's value in contributing to Russia's economic development. The content, emphasis, and nuances differed in time and in differing situations, but in essence, these two have always been the determining factors.

How was Japan perceived during the Soviet era? From the point of view of geopolitics, first, it was the days of the cold war. The United States was the arch-enemy, and Japan was a close protectorate and ally to it. The Soviet strategic objective was to drive a wedge in all possible circumstances between Japan and the United States, and draw Japan as close as possible toward its own area of influence. Second, it was a period of Sino-Soviet rivalry. The worst strategic situation for the Soviet Union was to face encirclement by the United States–China–Japan. Hence emerged Soviet interest toward Japan in the détente era and then mounting rigidity in the post-détente era when Japan–China relations began to take off.

From the point of view of economic relations, Japan became an important target to enhance trade and investment, particularly after the Japanese economy began to take off in the 1960s. Mutual efforts to foster trade and investment bore fruit alongside the development of political relations during détente. But from the latter part of the 1970s to the first half of the 1980s, Soviet policy became trapped by intransigency to treat Japan just as a follower of the United States, which was dangerously drifting toward China. The Soviet Union completely failed to grasp the importance of Japan with its rising economic power and emerging-proactive foreign policy, guided by Yasuhiro Nakasone from the middle of the 1980s.

When Gorbachev assumed power in 1985 and soon enlisted Shevardnadze as his foreign minister, probably the first task they had in mind was to mend the obvious mistakes committed by their predecessors. Thus Shevardnadze initiated an active policy at the beginning of 1986, reciprocated by his Japanese counterpart Abe in the middle of the year. But this initiative did not last long, and from the autumn of 1986 for nearly two years relations saw a nadir, comparable to the worst years of the 1970s or the 1960s. Why did it happen? What was the strategic thinking behind this deterioration? On the one hand, Gorbachev's interest was far more directed to major preoccupations such as Afghanistan, the United States, and Europe. In contrast to those pressing issues related to the cold war rivalry, Asia was a secondary consideration for the leadership. Even in his second major policy speech on Asia at Krasnoyarsk in 1988, Gorbachev saw Asia from the geopolitical perspective of countering U.S. military forces there. On the other hand, Japan's attitude of placing the territorial issue at the forefront in the relationship must have dropped its priority to the bottom in Gorbachev's Asia policy.

After this freezing of relations for about two years, relations began to warm up in the second half of 1988. But along with the Soviet underestimation of Japan as a secondary factor under the U.S. umbrella, Japan's persistence in placing the territorial issue as a prerequisite for developing bilateral relations brought back another chill in the first half of 1989. This chill resulted in a costly delay in Gorbachev's visit to Japan, which took place only in April 1991. Thus, Japan became Gorbachev's last priority in his new-thinking Asian agenda: his breakthrough visit to China took place in 1989 and resumption of diplomatic relations with South Korea in 1990. However, Gorbachev's visit to Japan revealed an interesting aspect of his strategic thinking toward Asia. On geopolitics, after the unification of Germany and with the conclusion of START I expected in the near future, Gorbachev did not have the need to look at Japan from the perspective of an American protectorate. Rather than trying to drive a wedge between Japan and the United States, Gorbachev proposed enhanced cooperation of the Big Five in Asia: the Soviet Union, China, Japan, the United States, and India. Japan was looked at as an independent actor playing a role in the newly emerging vision of Asia–Pacific cooperation. Through the process of negotiations on a joint communiqué, it also became clear that what Gorbachev expected most from Japan was dynamic development of economic relations. In the territorial negotiations, Gorbachev could make only limited progress. The delay in his trip to Japan cost dearly, not enabling him to make any audacious proposal.

This lingering situation was swept away after the failure of the August 1991 coup and the demise of the Soviet Union. During the brief period of euphoria in 1992, when Atlanticism and cooperation with the West became the key motive of Russian foreign policy, Japan became a natural representative of the West in Asia. From the point of view of both geopolitics and economic cooperation, Japan became unconditionally the best target. The initial months of Japan's response seemed to indicate that it understood this message and was prepared to move ahead. But when Russia apparently made an unprecedented compromise proposal on the territorial issue in the spring of 1992, Japan's response stopped there, and Yeltsin cancelled his visit to Japan in September. Relations were frozen and Yeltsin's visit to Tokyo in the fall of 1993 barely brought back the relationship to the level of the late Gorbachev days.

Thus, from the autumn of 1992 to 1997 Russia kept Japan outside its scope of strategic thinking. Some substantial progress was made in consolidation of security relations. Signs of greater efforts toward enhancing economic relations were seen. But Japan had not appeared as a serious objective for developing strategic relations. It was only after the Madrid summit in August 1997, where NATO's eastward expansion took its final shape, and by which time Ukraine and Russia settled the dispute over Crimea and Sevastopol, that Russia turned its eyes to Japan. An underlying sense of dissatisfaction incurred by NATO's expansion gave priority consideration for the Russian leadership to look East. China was an undeniable target, but results had already been seen. Japan appeared as a natural policy objective to strengthen Russia's geopolitical position in East Asia. Flows of investment and technical cooperation were another lure for Russia. Hashimoto and his team had sent consistent signals that they were prepared to develop relations with Russia in all dimensions. Yeltsin responded at Krasnoyarsk, proposing to conclude a peace treaty by 2000. It was a powerful message to indicate that Russia was willing to substantially move relations ahead. But Yeltsin could not follow his intention, because of his ailing health and the Russian financial crisis in the summer of 1998.

Putin succeeded Yeltsin in facing this unfinished agenda. The legacies inherited from Yeltsin (stalemate in relations with the United States in its election year on such contentious issues as missile defense and the ABM Treaty, hesitation from the Europeans in dealing with an unknown KGB president—except for Blair who capitalized on his personal friendship with Putin—, a sense of achievement already realized in China relations) gave room for Putin to direct his attention toward Japan. Surely, that attention proceeded in parallel with enhanced developments with both North and South Korea, but Japan's emphasis cannot be underestimated, as a country that might bring greater geopolitical and economic leverage by overcoming the "difficult issue" that had divided the two countries.

Mori Yoshiro and the Japanese team took initiatives with a determination not to miss any window of opportunity. Thus, Irkutsk in March 2001 brought the two countries to the verge of head-on negotiations to discuss the transfer of the two smaller islands and the sovereignty of the two larger islands. But reconsideration of Japan's position from May 2001 on peace treaty negotiations resulted in a substantial loss of interest for the Russian leadership. In geopolitics, Japan was no longer a threatening nuisance under the American wing. China had already established itself in the driver's seat of Russian Asian policy, and at least for the immediate to mid-term perspective, Russia had no reasons to hurry in its Japan's relations. Japan's economic potential after the "lost 1990s" was also not particularly seducing. Reasonable grounds for cooperation in the six-party talks and energy competition for East Siberian oil and gas helped to move relations forward, albeit slowly, befitting Russia's strategic position toward Japan. Putin's visit to Tokyo in November 2005 showed his optimism about Russia's energy position, but no sign of hope for a territorial compromise.

The Koreas

Russian management of relations with South and North Korea did not serve strategic goals well. In 1990 a deal was reached with South Korea that gave Moscow brief hope of a new type of regional influence as well as an infusion of cash. Yet, South Korean ties without Japanese ones or an American interest in a multilateral regional security framework were of little strategic value, and Moscow failed to find a way to keep North Korean ties active. In the fall of 1992 Yeltsin visited Seoul after hastily cancelling a trip to Tokyo, but this did not provide leverage over the Japanese or solve the deteriorating economic ties with the South Koreans. In 1993–94, Russians felt excluded from efforts to resolve the nuclear crisis created by North Korea. Troubled in the Gorbachev era until almost the end that close ties with the North were an albatross in the way of entry into the APR, Russian officials and academics not long after the start of the Yeltsin era became preoccupied with the opposite opinion that the deterioration of ties with the North had become a major barrier to being taken seriously in the region. The nadir in Russia's sense of acceptance into the area came in 1993–95 when ties with South Korea offered little political influence or economic optimism.

The second half of the 1990s was characterized by a search for regaining influence over the Korean peninsula. Strategic thinking started with the consensus that Russia required such influence and that improved ties with North Korea would be more productive than improved ties with the South. Indeed, the dual financial crises in South Korea and Russia coupled with the arrest of a Russian official for spying for the South set relations with Seoul back. There was little discussion of what steps should be taken to restore those relations and to make Seoul a closer partner in the region. Instead, talk ensued of a Sino-Russian strategic partnership working toward shared aims in resisting U.S. unipolarity and in resolving tensions on the Korean peninsula. Meetings with officials in Pyongyang grew more frequent in an effort to boost Moscow's influence in future talks over the peninsula.

Kim Dae-jung's sunshine policy gave Russia an opening for a new Korea policy. When Kim sought Russia's support in a great-power combination to bring both Koreas together, the result was full recovery in bilateral relations and an open door for pursuit of closer ties with the North. When Putin took office he carried this process forward, deciding to make personal ties with Kim Jong-il his unique contribution to Korean reintegration. In three meetings over two years with the North's leader he linked energy and transportation planning to the resurgence of Russia in the region. Not only would pipeline construction down the Pacific coast of Russia and the Korean peninsula bring the North much-needed oil and gas supplies and revenue as a corridor, it would give a powerful boost to development in the three territories of Primorskii krai, Khabarovskii krai, and Sakhalin oblast, which were vital to Russian security and regional ties. The notion of the "Iron Silk Road" suggested a parallel train corridor that would secure the position of the Trans-Siberian railway. Suddenly, Russia's future in the region became closely linked to the reintegration process on the peninsula. If it bypassed Russia, the resulting transportation and energy planning could marginalize the Russian Far East even as Russia's voice became insignificant on regional economic and security matters. If, however, Russia found the right strategic approach with understanding from both Korean states, then there could be a regional commitment to gradual Korean reintegration vital to Russia's interests.

The aftermath of the Korean summit of June 2000 raised hope that Putin had found a winning strategy. For two years it appeared that the sunshine policy would continue, although with difficulty, placing a premium on Putin's special bond with Kim Jong-il. Even as late as January 2003 Moscow's extravagant expectations that it could play a weak regional hand on the basis of a single personal bond led to a diplomatic mission to Pyongyang by Foreign Ministry official Aleksandr Losyukov to broker an agreement between George Bush and Kim Jong-il as the nuclear crisis was intensifying. Yet Bush regarded this mission as unhelpful, sending the wrong signal to Kim, and Kim dismissed Russia as having too little to offer. Over the next seven months Russian leaders scrambled against marginalization as the United States turned to China for three-party talks and then to Japan and South Korea for a trilateral path to combining dialogue and pressure. When Moscow succeeded in August in becoming part of the six-party talks, it was clear the primary reason was that Pyongyang sought its presence. Coordination with China became the principal means to exert influence on the process. Roh Moo-hyun, too, welcomed its presence. While the crisis put on hold any broad strategy toward the peninsula, Russia was cooperating above all with its continental partners in maneuvering toward an end-game.

Central, South, and Southeast Asia

The fall of the Soviet Union and its subsequent dissolution brought Central Asia to the forefront of international diplomacy and politics. A relative backwater in terms of the global strategic situation, Central Asia emerged overnight to grab the attention of strategic planners in the United States, in Europe, and across Asia. This, of course, has naturally affected Russia and strategic thinking among Russian leaders. Central Asia had been for more than a century under Russian, and then Soviet, domination. Suddenly this changed overnight. What did not change overnight was the Russian interest in the region, and the deep connections and influence that Moscow still wields over the five new nations in the region. Additionally, the independence of the Central Asian states has brought South Asia and its evolving political situation that much closer to Russia, and has forced strategic thinkers in Russia to consider this greater region in a much more complex way.

Russian activity and influence in Central Asia waned throughout the 1990s, as Yeltsin and his foreign policy advisors turned their attention to the West during the early years of his presidency. Although the five new Central Asian republics (Kazakhstan, Kyrgyzstan, Tajikistan, Turkmenistan, and Uzbekistan) became independent nations in 1991, in the early half of the 1990s they were still somewhat influenced by Moscow. The diminished role of Russia did not coincide with the high expectations for influence over the area.

Early in the 1990s, Moscow found itself having to respond to the deteriorating situation in Tajikistan, where civil war became almost an extension of the lawlessness and tribal warfare that marked Afghanistan throughout the 1990s. Russian troops had never left the Afghan–Tajik border after the Soviet withdrawal in 1989, but they were now much less capable and properly supplied to carry out their mission (of maintaining peace in Tajikistan) successfully. Nevertheless, there is a substantial Russian population that still resides in the region and counts close to ten million in number. Russia is a member of no less than half a dozen multilateral political, military, and economic groupings in Central Asia that vary in their influence and prestige. Russian troops still occupy bases in Kyrgyzstan and Tajikistan, the Russian government has recently negotiated with the Uzbek government to open bases there, and Russia has a bilateral defense treaty with Kazakhstan.

Although the sudden American interest in the politics and economics of Central Asia during the 1990s may have been a concern for Moscow, this quickly dissipated after the September 11 attacks and the U.S. invasion of Afghanistan, which was accomplished after the insertion of U.S. troops in Kyrgyzstan and Uzbekistan in December 2001 and the establishment of two U.S. airbases there. For the period 2001–03 U.S.–Russia relations seemingly prospered in the global war against terrorism. In exchange for Russian acquiescence to the new U.S. presence in Central Asia, Washington turned somewhat of a blind eye to Russia's actions in Chechnya.

In spite of the improved atmospherics in U.S.–Russian relations, there remained a good number of irritants, not least NATO expansion; arms control issues; and the issues of human rights, democracy, and civil society in Russia itself. In Central Asia, nevertheless, these issues were of minimal consequence and were subsumed by the greater strategic coop-erative effort aimed at eradicating terrorism and establishing a friendly regime in Afghanistan. Russia continued to maintain a prominent regional profile, as evidenced by the frequent state visits between the leaders of four of the Central Asian states (excepting Turkmenistan) and Putin, whose interest in the region manifested itself more than that of his predecessor, due, no doubt, in part to the war on terror and the con-tinuing morass in Chechnya. But by early 2004 it was clear that the U.S.–Russian strategic partnership was under immense strain, not because there was a diminution of the threat, but because U.S.–Russian relations—already tenuous—were dogged by election year politics (in both countries), and calls within the United States for the Bush admin-istration to take a more critical stand against Putin and his centralizing tendencies. Combined with the overwhelming U.S. strategic presence in

Central Asia, there is a sense that leaders in Russia (and Russians in general) have become weary of their "partner" the United States (perhaps the Bush administration in particular). The limits of this new partnership were reached first in Central Asia, especially when the second term of the Bush administration heralded an attempt to see through the recent promises by Washington to "promote" democracy and civil liberties across the globe. Central Asian leaders may be loathe to listen to Washington, and have moved closer to Moscow in an attempt to ward off U.S. pressures, should they come about (as unlikely as that may be as long as the United States maintains troops in Afghanistan and Iraq). Nevertheless, apart from the convenience and reassurance of a familiar face, what can Moscow offer the nations of the region? Sympathy and familiarity will only take a nation so far. China, and, perhaps, Japan can potentially offer these nations much more, but at what cost is unknown. Possibly another neighbor, India, can become a more positive influence in the region.

India could be a future key player not only as the leader of South Asia, but also in Central Asia, as well. But what is of more immediate interest is whether the triangular relationship between Beijing, Delhi, and Moscow can actually be formulated in a plus-sum, positive way. Moscow maintained a cordial relationship with Delhi throughout the 1990s, but this was driven more than anything by the sales that Russian arms manufacturers were able to push through with regularity (and still are able to do today). Russian leaders, especially Putin, strove to keep a warm relationship with Delhi. Putin visited New Delhi in November 2000 and again in 2004. During the June 2001 visit to Moscow by Indian Foreign and Defense Minister Jaswant Singh, the two governments agreed to a series of large-scale arms deals. Although the Indo-Sino-Russian "strategic triangle" that had been proposed by Foreign and Prime Minister Primakov in the late 1990s seemed a far-fetched idea, there is no question that the three nations began to see points of potential cooperation, especially in the form of anti-terror agendas in Central and South Asia, the bringing of order to Afghanistan, the need for stability in Pakistan, and growing concerns about the unilateralist U.S. global agenda.

The agenda of Putin's visit to New Delhi in December 2004 was again dominated by arms sales, but he and Indian Prime Minister Manmohan Singh also agreed to increase anti-terror cooperation, and Russian firms inked deals to construct two more nuclear power plants in southern India. India undoubtedly shares with Russia some concern about Chinese designs in Central Asia, something that prompted Indian observer status in the SCO.

Another area of great potential cooperation between Moscow and Delhi is energy. The Indian Petroleum and Natural Gas Ministry is reportedly keen to invest in Russia's oil and natural gas industries. Meanwhile, the Indian government also hinted that it would be interested in a gas pipeline linking Turkmenistan, Afghanistan, and Pakistan to India.

After the heyday of the Soviet-Vietnamese strategic partnership in the 1980s, the 1990s were a time of relative Russian inactivity in Southeast Asia. The long-standing Soviet support of Vietnam was drawn down, and eventually the Russian naval facility on Cam Ranh Bay was closed. In the 1990s, nevertheless, Russian arms manufacturers saw great opportunity in Southeast Asia, and new partners for arms deals were found in Indonesia and Malaysia. If Russia was marginalized strategically in Southeast Asia, even more so than in Northeast Asia, Putin took steps for Russia again to find its voice in the region through multilateral institutions.

Russia's strategic position in Central, South, and Southeast Asia has undoubtedly slipped since the days of the Cold War. But Russia is leveraging what tools it can—whether it be multilateral partnerships, arms sales, diplomatic forays, energy, or old political connections—to maintain an active role in the region that in the future could be translated into a role as an honest broker, or a balancer of the last resort as other nations jockey for political and strategic influence in the region. Moscow will now have to learn to deal with entrenched American power, Chinese thirst for energy, and India's attempt to become engaged in the region in order to stabilize that nation's northern flank.

Regionalism

Leaders in Moscow have also been beckoned by proposals for regionalism. At the start of the 1990s some in Japan called for a "Sea of Japan economic rim." From China came proposals for making a planned Tumen river delta development program the engine for regional growth. A decade later South Korea was suggesting that it become the hub of Northeast Asian regionalism. The six-party talks from 2003 also carried the seeds of a regional framework for both security and the integration of North Korea into a joint economic endeavor. At the same time, proposals for energy pipelines and new investments sometimes conceived of these as an agenda for regional economic integration. Each of these appeals and others posed a challenge to engage in strategic thinking about Russia's place in a newly emerging region; yet they also put a premium on finding balance in the region to pursue a program that holds great promise for Russian economic revival and global integration.

Through the 1990s there was great wariness in Moscow as well as in the Russian Far East about possibilities for regionalism. They posed a danger that distant outposts of a newly decentralized state would be turned away from Moscow toward neighboring states. Another concern was that rival cities or transportation routes would benefit, leaving the bypassed coastal corridor of the Russian Far East to wither away. The prospect also loomed that either Japan with its powerful world-class corporations, or China with its hordes of small-scale entrepreneurs would gain leadership in the region. If at times local officials drew attention and modest infusions of money by feigning an interest in discussions about regionalism, the reality was that both the center and the border areas had too little confidence that they could compete in a market environment or, perhaps, desire to do so in order to go forward. Strategic thinking was limited to ideas on the means for resistance.

Under Putin four things have changed that make it easier to contemplate Northeast Asian regionalism, but the process is complicated. First, at the initiative of Kim Dae-jung and then as a result of the showdown between George Bush and Kim Jong-il, North Korea emerged as a focus of both strategic and economic calculations for finding a multilateral approach. Second, a sharp rise in energy prices and a frantic effort by China and, to some extent, Japan to secure future supplies has given Russia, flush with cash and an image of sustained growth, a privileged status. Third, Putin has succeeded in reasserting central control over local authorities, overcoming the divisions that made coordinated policy toward Northeast Asian states difficult. Fourth, U.S. unilateralism and Putin's maneuvering to cooperate while searching for balance have raised the stakes for regionalism. Strategizing about Russia's important place in an emergent region no longer seems far-fetched.

So far, hopes for Northeast Asia have failed to focus realistically on persistent problems. The idea of Putin becoming a critical mediator because of his personal ties with Kim Jong-il floundered when it became obvious that Russia has few cards to play compared to any of the other participants in the six-party talks. Dreams of an "iron silk road" revitalizing the Trans-Siberian Railroad faced the stark reality that this is not the shortest distance across Eurasia and that Russia's investment climate is not reassuring to those interested in the oil industry or container shipping to Far East ports. In the July 2004 election for the mayor of Vladivostok and then the February 2005 reappointment of the incumbent governor of Primorskii krai, we see no sign of centralization as a means to tackle corruption and misadministration. Finally, the fact that China champions regionalism and could be poised to gain a dominant position may make Russians reconsider plans that they gain by limiting the U.S. role. Instead, strategic thinking should be preparing the way for finding an endgame in the Korean nuclear crisis, a jumpstart to South Korean interest in a regional approach to reintegration of the peninsula, and a renewed effort to win Japanese cooperation as well as that of international investors in risky, long-term projects essential if Russia is to use its energy as a springboard to regionalism.

Limiting strategic thinking to one country at a time is not an answer to Russia's exposed Far East and weak economic and demographic position in Northeast Asia. It should be a champion of some sort of regionalism based on an accurate assessment of long-term trends in the area. The appeal to join the East Asian Summit in December 2005 showed Putin's new interest in regionalism, but the prospects for entry were slim without a strategy to reassure more countries. Of course, with the region in great flux, including uncertainty over the North Korean nuclear crisis and a deepening divide between China and Japan, it is still early to test how Moscow may respond to the prospect of widening opportunities for balanced relations and region-wide cooperation.

PART 1

Chronology

CHAPTER 2

Soviet Policy toward the Asia–Pacific Region: The 1980s

Evgeny Bazhanov

A view exists, both in and outside Russia, that Russian foreign policy has always been dominated by its western direction, and Asia has been almost forgotten by the tsars and later communist leaders.[1] This view is hardly accurate. Let us recall: since the late sixteenth century, the time of Ivan the Terrible, and in the course of the following centuries, Russians have rapidly advanced eastwards. They quickly cultivated the unlimited spaces of Siberia and the Far East, which could easily accommodate several Europes. Then Russia gained a firm foothold in Manchuria and Korea, encountering Japan. New colonies were established in Alaska, California, and the islands of Hawaii. The tsar saved Siam from French and British claims. At the same time, the Russian Navy was so active near the shores of Australia and New Zealand that the local population imagined that Russians were striving to conquer them. Locals installed artillery guns all along the seashore against the Russian navy, and those guns are still there.

In the early years of the twentieth century, Russia fought Japan over domination in China's Northeast and Korea. Defeat in this war provoked an internal revolution, which nearly toppled the Russian tsar; however, the Russian empire continued to move into Mongolia, Xinjiang, Afghanistan, and Persia. The successful Bolshevik revolution did not alter Russia's interest in the East. On the contrary, the communist regime intensified the drive in the eastern direction looking for allies in the struggle against "world imperialism," trying to undermine Western domination and to test ideological recipes of transformation of world civilization there.

Though bringing large dividends, these actions triggered responses on the part of old colonial empires and new powers—the United States and Japan—as well as local elites. As a result of diplomatic scandals, clashes, and armed conflicts, Soviet Russia was forced to limit its goals in some countries and was altogether excluded from others. In World War II the Soviet Union actively helped the United States, China, and other states to fight Japan and directly joined the struggle itself in the conclusive stage of the war, liberating Northeast China and the northern part of the Korean peninsula. With the return to peace, the USSR did not reduce its participation in Asia–Pacific affairs. The world split into two camps— the Soviet and the American—or, to use the terminology of the recent past, into the communist and the imperialist camps. A ferocious global struggle developed between them into which other countries, peoples, movements, and parties were gradually drawn.

The first major battle between the camps erupted in China, where the communists won in 1949. The United States reacted to that defeat with an outburst of anticommunist emotions, lurching to the right not only in its foreign policy but also in its domestic life. A second battle immediately followed the first one, this time in the Korean peninsula. Blood was shed there between 1950 and 1953 before an armistice perpetuated the division of the Korean nation into two antithetical and mutually hostile regimes. Acts resulting from the great ideological confrontation of the second half of the century in the Asia-Pacific region (APR) followed one after another with kaleidoscopic speed. Soon the Soviet camp underwent a split. China withdrew from it and started knocking together its own bloc directed against Washington and Moscow. But it was no easy task to fight on two fronts, the more so as the Chinese camp had a significantly smaller potential than did the other two camps. Eventually China "shifted" westward in order to more successfully resist the enemy that appeared more dangerous. There emerged a Chinese–U.S. partnership. Relying on it, Beijing came into a conflict with its former Soviet ally, while Vietnam clashed with Pol Pot, China's protégé in Cambodia.

As the escalation of contradictions and clashes acquired an increasingly dangerous character, China was the first country to come to its senses and withdrew from the scene. In 1982 the PRC refused to continue its link-up with the West and set out to normalize relations and carry on mutually beneficial cooperation with as many states as possible. The USSR still pursued its former policy, mired in a war in Afghanistan. Power politics devoured immense resources, and exhausted the country without yielding any dividends: the threat to its security far from diminishing on the contrary increased; Soviet prestige was on the decline; the country's political positions were eroding; and the Far East of the USSR increasingly was turning into a backwater in a newly dynamic region. There was an urgent need to change course, and growing numbers of officials and experts in the Soviet foreign policy establishment realized it.

Evolution of Gorbachev's Strategy

At the Twenty-seventh Communist Party Congress in 1986, Gorbachev continued to promote the standard thesis on division of the world into two confronting camps, while also reiterating the aggressive nature of imperialism, the peace-loving essence of socialism, ideological struggles, the plight of young Third World states suffering under the hands of neo-colonialists, and the attraction of "the real socialism" represented by the Soviet Union and its allies.[2] At the same time, however, Gorbachev's speech differed from what had been said on such occasions by his predecessors. The new Soviet leader showed genuine determination to solve world problems by starting a series of far-reaching initiatives before the Congress convened, having already taken a number of practical steps toward other states. At the Congress, he went even further by introducing new proposals and advocating the urgent necessity of moving in international relations from confrontation to cooperation.

Not all of Gorbachev's ideas were welcomed by the outside world. Some of them had propagandistic undertones, while others sounded too idealistic and hasty. Certain initiatives were perceived in the West and in Asia as attempts by Moscow to gain unilateral advantages and harm the interests of opponents. In reality, the new Soviet leadership was attempting to free itself from outdated ideological dogmas, taking a more objective look at the outside world, and allowing a diversity of opinions in the foreign policy decision-making process. A gradual disintegration of the Kremlin's old and outdated foreign policy system began to take place. A new strategy and system painstakingly and carefully (though not always flawlessly) began to take its place. Substantial personnel reshuffling in the Soviet political leadership, Communist Party Central Committee staff, and in ministries and other organizations connected with the foreign policy decision-making process contributed to the spirit of perestroika.

Glasnost and democratization taking place within the Soviet Union had an ever-growing impact on Soviet strategies abroad. Genuine public opinion began to surface in the country and make its mark on politics.

Old taboos were being overturned, and a new world outlook was emerging. Economic difficulties played a role in the transformation of Soviet foreign policy. The burden of confrontation and the arms race against the West became impossible to sustain. The shift in Moscow's worldview also led to positive, if at times turbulent, changes spreading throughout the world in the latter half of the 1980s. Among them was improvement of the Soviet image abroad; advancements in the field of disarmament; and the dramatic disintegration of the Stalinist-Brezhnevite regimes in Eastern Europe. Gorbachev's new thinking launched the beginning of a process that sought to overcome the international system of confrontational blocs, while emphasizing human over class interests, across-the-board disarmament as an urgent goal, the construction of a common European community to include former socialist countries, and the creation of a global security system.[3]

New developments were also evident in Soviet strategy toward Asia and the Pacific. Right from the start the new leader emphasized the necessity to "instill dynamism" in Soviet policy in the region.[4] Gorbachev argued that the USSR, in terms of its geography, was not only a European but also an Asian country, and that it was in fact "one of the most important Asian powers."[5] Relying on the advice of his close assistants, the new Soviet leader was drawing attention to the fact that the Pacific region had developed into a center of gravity for the world economy and was increasingly turning into a center stage in world politics.[6] In order to assure its security, internal development, and leading role in the world, the Soviet Union, according to Gorbachev's thinking, had to overcome inertia and disagreements in relations with regional states and become integrated into the economic life of Asia and the Pacific.[7]

Chernenko, Andropov, and Brezhnev did not strike such chords even when they gave Asia policy speeches in the Asian parts of the Soviet Union. The fact that Gorbachev already traveled to Siberia and the Far East a year and a half after assuming office—a step which took Brezhnev fourteen years—should be seen in this context. In his depiction of the main directions of Soviet foreign policy at the Twenty-seventh Communist Party Congress, Gorbachev emphasized "the Asian and Pacific direction" together with the European as the most significant and as that "which continues to gain importance."[8] While Gorbachev's interest in the APR became immediately evident, the essence of Moscow's policies there, as of its overall strategy, remained for some time largely confined to the framework of the traditional communist ideology. The main thrust of Soviet activities was toward "strengthening international positions of socialism."[9] The Kremlin aimed at broadening the scale of military cooperation with the DPRK, joint Soviet–North Korean steps to liquidate American military bases in Korea, transformation of the Korean peninsula into a non-nuclear zone, and countermeasures against attempts to create a military axis of Washington–Tokyo–Seoul.[10]

Another goal was "to increase military aid to Indochinese states, to intensify support of their initiatives and proposals."[11] Certain experts objected, arguing that some of the above-mentioned steps and goals put additional barriers in the way of the settlement of old conflicts, provoking further mistrust, arms races, and confrontation. By conducting such policies, the USSR harmed rather than promoted the basic interests of the socialist states.[12] In connection with the goal of strengthening the position of the socialist states, the Kremlin saw the necessity of countering in the APR the "aggressive, hostile policies of the USA and its allies."[13] Opportunities were sought "to strike at the oriental flank of imperialism."[14] Among the proposed measures were: "activization of the DPRK's protests against militarization of Japan and the rise in Washington's military expenditures; broadening of the top-level dialogue with India; promotion of anti-nuclear sentiments in New Zealand; disruption of American plans to prolong the Pentagon's presence in the Philippines, utilization of the anti-imperialist potential of non-allied movement."[15]

The United States was blamed both in internal documents and public pronouncements for "further militarization of its policies in the Pacific, claims that the APR is the zone of American vital interests, creation of an aggressive axis with the participation of Tokyo and Seoul, linking ASEAN countries to the axis, forming an eastern front against socialism, resistance to settlements in Afghanistan and Indochina, ambitions to put under American control the most important communications in the APR, intensification of American–Japanese coordination in the nuclear field, working out projects of global struggle against socialism and national liberation movements, achievement of military superiority over the USSR, stealing resources of Asia, imperialist exploitation of young states, pressures and brutal interference in their internal affairs."[16] Such views in the initial stages of perestroika were not only the result of inertia in the thinking of Gorbachev and his close assistants, but also a reflection of resistance to change on the part of the huge, still powerful, and increasingly confused and divided party and government bureaucracy.

In April 1986, the Soviet government suddenly began an intensive campaign against "the Pacific Community," which was described as "an emerging new military bloc threatening to tip the balance of class forces in the region and to change conditions of the struggle between two opposing systems in their regional as well as global dimensions."[17] Asian leaders were still trying to figure out Soviet reasons for focusing on a very vague idea of "the Pacific Community," when Gorbachev three months later publicly stated that the above-mentioned idea "had never materialized, it had been in fact rejected."[18]

In July 1987, Moscow convened in Mongolia a consultative meeting of the Communist and Workers' Parties of Asia and the Pacific. At the meeting, close aides of Gorbachev, including former ambassador to the United States and at the time Secretary of the Communist Party of the Soviet Union (CPSU) Central Committee Anatoly Dobrynin, urged impotent Communist Parties of the United States, Canada, and Australia and microscopic illegal sects in Asian countries "to multiply their traditions of anti-imperialist struggle and utilize the experience of other countries in assuring security and promoting peaceful coexistence among states."[19] At the same time, the Kremlin advanced one after another initiatives aimed at easing tensions and promoting multilateral security and economic cooperation in Asia and the Pacific.

At first on May 21, 1985, Gorbachev presented the idea of an "all-Asia forum."[20] In 1986 he called for "a conference of the countries of the Pacific Ocean along the lines of Helsinki conference."[21] Immediately after, the Soviet leader began to champion the "creation of the negotiating mechanism for the Asia-Pacific region." Those were not different proposals; due to haste and lack of coordination the Kremlin was not always consistent. However, not much attention was paid abroad to these variations and nuances, since grandiose Soviet ideas were anyway rejected outright by most regional states. Despite the reaction, the Soviet bureaucracy—in the worst communist tradition—launched a large-scale campaign in support of an overall security system for the APR. Instead of trying to solve real problems, Soviet propaganda and its diplomatic machine were preoccupied with the task of "constantly, step by step, moving ahead and implementing the proposal of the system."[22] Inertia and disagreements in the ruling circles of the USSR were revealing themselves in Moscow's approaches to arms control and disarmament in the APR. Numerous initiatives to widen trade and economic and scientific ties with regional states were not supported materially and legally and looked ill-considered.[23]

Gorbachev's strategy in the East, following general trends in Soviet foreign policy and internal developments, was gradually freeing itself of ideological dogmas. It was becoming more and more flexible, striving for improvement of the overall international political climate and bilateral relations with individual states. The basic outlines of the new strategy can be found in the Soviet leader's speech given in Vladivostok on July 28, 1986. The ideas enunciated at Vladivostok were further elaborated in such documents as the Delhi Declaration on Principles of a Nuclear Arms Free and Nonviolent World (November 27, 1986), Gorbachev's answers to questions posed by the Indonesian newspaper *Merdeka* (July 27, 1987), and his speeches in Krasnoyarsk (September 16, 1988) and at the United Nations (December 7, 1988).

The newly emerged Soviet strategy had a number of directions. The first was aimed at balanced development of bilateral ties with all states within the region. The second was to put an end to the arms race and pursue disarmament. The third direction concerned settlement of conflicts. Finally, the fourth direction was the promotion of wide-scale and multinational economic, scientific, technical, and humanitarian cooperation in the APR and establishment of a multilateral security system. The agenda was enormous and, as time showed, to a large degree idealistic. It required a multitude of moves and initiatives on various issues and toward many states that were extremely difficult to correlate with each other.

Bilateral Ties

Prime importance was attached by the Gorbachev leadership to the normalization of relations with the giant neighbor—*China*. It should be noted that certain changes for the better in Soviet–Chinese relations began to appear in the early 1980s, before Gorbachev came to power. The reshaping of China's strategy in 1982 facilitated those changes. Beijing concluded that the pro-Western tilt in its foreign policy was no longer justified and hindered its modernization drive. It was decided that a limited rapprochement with the Soviet Union, entangled in domestic difficulties and at loggerheads with the West, would benefit China's national interests.[24]

The Soviet leadership's response to China's overtures was prompted by growing confrontation with the West, the dead-end in Afghanistan, and numerous other problems in the international and domestic arenas. More reasonable attitudes toward China began to prevail in the Kremlin after the replacement of Brezhnev by Andropov.[25] Yet, despite some progress in Soviet–Chinese relations in 1982–85, they remained far from normal. Beijing continued to regard the Soviet Union as the "main threat" to China's national security, and the Chinese leadership kept demanding that Moscow remove the "three obstacles," which allegedly were the cause of the "threat" and hampered the return to good-neighborly relations (the Soviet occupation of Afghanistan, Vietnam's occupation of Cambodia, and the Soviet military presence in Mongolia and on the Soviet–Chinese border).

A real breakthrough in Soviet–Chinese relations came as a result of perestroika. Gorbachev gradually made numerous concessions to China, among them: the USSR's consent to eliminate all intermediate-range missiles in Asia, reduction of the Soviet military presence on the border with China and in Mongolia, readiness to give up a naval base in Vietnam, acknowledgement that the Sino-Soviet border goes along the Amur river's fairway in accord with international custom, respect for China's independent foreign policy line and its interests in the West, and encouragement of the rapprochement between China and East European communist states. Moscow's efforts to break the Afghan and Cambodian deadlocks made an especially favorable impression on the Chinese leadership.[26] Changes in the overall Soviet strategy in the world as well as internal reforms in the USSR also convinced China's leadership that the moment had come for full normalization of relations.

In May 1989 Gorbachev made an historic visit to the PRC, which marked the beginning of a new stage in Sino-Soviet relations. The two sides agreed to promote all kinds of mutual ties based on the commonly recognized principles of peaceful coexistence and remaining independent of each other in taking any domestic or foreign political decisions. The May talks gave strong impetus to Soviet–Chinese ties. However, quite soon new negative factors clouded the improving atmosphere. On June 4, 1989, the army and young demonstrators clashed in Beijing with massive casualties. According to the Chinese leadership, the troops quelled a "monstrous counterrevolutionary rebellion staged by anti-socialist forces inside and outside the country."[27] Following the crisis, Secretary General of the Communist Party Zhao Ziyang and other liberal reformers were ousted from power and replaced by more conservative politicians, who had long sounded the alarm by warning against "infiltration of bourgeois liberalism" and "spiritual pollution."[28]

As a result, the ideological positions of the CPSU and the Chinese Communist Party (CCP), which had drawn closer in 1987–88, once again diverged. The differences were deepening as Soviet society progressed further from its old model. The leadership of China believed that the CPSU was pushing political reforms, letting loose antisocialist and nationalist elements and losing control over the situation. Fearing the negative influence of the Soviet example, the Chinese authorities reduced the flow of information from the Soviet Union, starting to censor news in order to publish only those stands of the CPSU which were consonant with the views of the CPC. Beijing was trying to avoid expressing support for the Soviet reforms. The new Soviet political thinking, which the Chinese mostly approved until the summer of 1989 because of its benefits for Beijing's foreign policy, was now regarded with suspicion. If internal Chinese publications had earlier been skeptical about the idea of the primacy of shared human values over class ones, construction of a common European home, and so on, now there was open apprehension of the harm that was occurring.[29] Despite such misgivings about Gorbachev's policies, Beijing managed not to return to polemics and quarrels. Instead it was decided in China "to try to help the Soviet Communist Party to retain power and prevent collapse of the socialist system and of the USSR, which could seriously damage China."[30]

Russia's relations with *Japan* were chronically bad or uneasy. After the last military conflict in 1945, Moscow and Tokyo did not succeed in normalizing their relations through the 1980s, despite formal establishment of diplomatic ties in 1956. When Gorbachev began the process of reexamination of Soviet policy toward Japan, the importance of this economic giant was finally appreciated fully and the goal of overcoming differences with it was set. Tokyo was much slower in adjusting its attitude toward the USSR. Japan had used the cold war set-up, which allowed the island-nation to build up its economic muscles while staying away from international cataclysms, and found that the improved superpower relations posed new challenges. Would the United States retain strategic interest in Tokyo? Would it take a tougher, vengeful attitude to defeats in economic competition?[31] Soviet–Japanese dialogue was focused on the first visit ever of a Soviet (Russian) top leader to the Japanese islands, which finally occurred in 1991.

Four sets of problems were on the agenda: a territorial settlement; other historical differences and complaints; the military-strategic confrontation; and economic cooperation. Previous Soviet leaders refused to admit the existence of the territorial question in relations with Japan. As for Japan, this question had turned into a kind of idée fixed. No political figure could afford to ignore the issue. Tokyo tied progress in bilateral relations to the satisfaction of the territorial claims: the return of four islands administered in Russia as the Southern Kuriles and labeled in Japan the "northern territories." Perestroika raised Japanese hopes. Experts began to advance various compromise formulas for the solution of the territorial issue, including resettlement of Soviet citizens at Japan's expense, joint exploitation of the four islands, and so on.

However, Gorbachev, due to the resistance of conservatives, especially among the military, was not ready for real concessions.

At the 1991 summit the territorial issue was central. While confirming the existence of this issue in bilateral relations, Gorbachev refused to satisfy Japanese demands. The Soviet leader did not even dare to take such a step as recognition of the 1956 treaty. Instead he suggested developing the whole complex of Soviet–Japanese relations, thus building a proper foundation for tackling "a painful problem" in a better atmosphere.[32] Among other historical grievances, Japanese mentioned at the negotiations Soviet entry into the war in 1945 in violation of the neutrality treaty, forced resettlement of the Japanese population on the islands, and the often-lengthy incarceration of Japanese captured by Soviet troops in August 1945. Yet, Gorbachev did not discuss the POWs taken to the USSR to the annoyance of Japanese. The Soviet Union had its own complaints: Japanese intervention during the Russian Civil War, border provocations in the 1930s, and the de-facto anti-Soviet alliance of Tokyo with Hitler in World War II. During Gorbachev's visit the two sides agreed to leave behind these historical grievances, taking measures to respond to mutual complaints (care of military graveyards, exchanging documents on POWs, etc.).[33]

The third "knot" in Soviet–Japanese relations was tied to military-strategic contradictions. Throughout the postwar years, Tokyo regarded Moscow as its main adversary. "The Blue Book" of Japan's Foreign Ministry for 1989 for the first time recognized the validity of Gorbachev's "new thinking."[34] "The White Book" on Japan's defense for 1990 for the first time did not mention the existence of "the Soviet threat."[35] In turn, the Kremlin stopped by the late 1980s regarding Japan as an adversary and a threat to Soviet security.[36] It was recognized that Japan was not a strong military power and that it voluntarily limited its military build-up. This self-restraint was connected to the defense alliance with the United States. The question was raised: will termination of this alliance promote Soviet security interests? Will it not lead to intensification of Japan's own military build-up?[37]

At the 1991 summit the two sides pointed out that the cold war was over, stressed that the UN charter provision on "former enemy states" lost its meaning, and agreed to work together to promote global and regional detente further. Gorbachev repeatedly emphasized that Moscow did not want to inflict any harm upon Japanese–American relations or U.S. positions in the APR as a whole.[38] The Kremlin received signals that the United States was restraining Japan in discussions of security, but for Gorbachev this information did not matter much.

Economic interactions were also discussed at the summit. Soviet officials energetically advertised the USSR market, beckoning Japanese business circles to invest in it. The Japanese were not ready to respond positively due to the territorial issue and chaotic conditions in Soviet economic and political life. Gorbachev's leadership, desperate for foreign aid and support for the disintegrating Soviet economy, simply did not realize how unrealistic its economic proposals seemed to the Japanese. At that dramatic moment in the Soviet Union there were experts emphasizing the importance of Japan's economic model, but these voices were weak and without any practical consequences.

Before Gorbachev's assent to power Moscow tied its policy toward the entire Korean peninsula to Pyongyang. For decades it had limited itself solely to open and voracious support for Pyongyang's positions on Korean issues.[39] It was perceived as a strategic ally despite the fact that the Soviet leadership did not admire Kim Il-sung's cult of personality and his *juche* policy of extreme self-reliance.[40] The process of realistically assessing Soviet policy toward Korea finally began in 1987–88. Officials became acutely aware that the Korean problem posed a major obstacle to superpower cooperation in the region, establishment of an Asian security system, and Moscow's participation in international economic cooperation.

In 1987–88, policymakers began serious analysis of the South Korean position and its proposals, finding that they had quite a number of rational elements.[41] Changes also occurred in attitudes toward the U.S. military presence in South Korea. Some politicians even argued that U.S. troops played a deterrent role against a flare-up of an uncontrollable conflict between North and South while helping to limit Japanese military expenditures.[42] At first officials expressed a desire to expand political dialogue with the North, and intensify bilateral military cooperation, while increasing the scope of economic aid and contacts in the scientific, cultural, and sports fields.[43] In response to this approach, North Korea's leadership took reciprocal measures. Pyongyang cooperated with Moscow on its foreign policy initiatives and was receptive to a number of requests made by the Soviets in the military arena. As rapprochement progressed, some cooling occurred in North Korean–Chinese relations.[44] The PRC switched its tactics and position, however, because of steadily improving Sino-Soviet relations in 1987–88, a progressive reappraisal of the Far East strategic-military picture, and its own unwillingness to carry so much of the burden of aiding Pyongyang. All attempts to torpedo improving Soviet–North Korean ties ceased.[45]

By the time Gorbachev went to China in May 1989 to fully normalize relations, there were virtually no traces of competition between the

USSR and the PRC over North Korea. As Kim Il-sung contemplated adjustments in response to improved ties between Moscow and Beijing, new problems cropped up in Soviet–North Korean relations as a result of growing differences in the ideological, political, and economic spheres. In 1988 the Soviet Union reduced the level of military aid to the North and, after that, rejected all attempts by Pyongyang at reinforcing military cooperation. Additionally, the Kremlin pressured North Korea to accept international controls over its nuclear reactors.[46]

A Politburo document dated May 11, 1986 called for weakening the position of the United States in Korea and elevating the Soviet role in settling the Korean issue. This meant changes in Moscow's approach to South Korea, "which was becoming a factor of global, military-strategic balance."[47] Evolution of Soviet attitudes toward the ROK continued in 1988–89 under the influence of a number of factors, most notably the following:

1. Democratic elections were held in the South and a transfer of power took place based on their results to a lawful administration headed by Roh Tae-woo.
2. Seoul responded positively toward Soviet perestroika; Roh proclaimed a policy of rapprochement with the Soviet Union and other communist states.
3. Seoul persisted in pursuing a constructive approach in dialogue with the North and generated reasonable proposals within this framework.
4. South Korea began to articulate a distinct independent line from the United States, showing its resistance to Washington's attempts to block South Korean-Soviet contacts. Seoul now could withstand U.S. pressure in economic and other matters.
5. There was a manifestation of good feelings toward the Soviet Union on the part of the South Korean population, especially during the 1988 Olympic Games.
6. There was realization in the USSR of Seoul's outstanding achievements in economic development and a growing interest in studying South Korean ways and methods.
7. The Soviet Union was ever conscious of the unrealistic and unreasonable policies of the North and its inconsiderate and blatant pressure on the USSR concerning Seoul. Moscow was generally unhappy with Pyongyang and, as a result, there was diminishing readiness to heed Pyongyang's opinion.
8. Developments took place in Sino-Soviet relations, while cooperation between East European countries and South Korea began to flourish.

9. On a private business level, interesting and appealing propositions were made by the South Korean business community to the USSR.
10. Profound changes occurred in Soviet public opinion as a result of glasnost and democratization. There was an increasing rejection by the Soviet people of the ideological, political, and economic values of Stalinism and its clones abroad, North Korea being one of them. There was a surge of sympathy toward South Korea, no longer restrained by ideological and other stereotypes, thus resulting in pressure from below on Moscow to alter its previous policies in Korea. Large numbers of scholars, journalists, and public figures raised their voices in favor of normalizing relations with South Korea while condemning North Korea at the same time.

After the fall of the East European Stalinist regimes, the Soviet Union and North Korea were no longer considered to be ideologically close. At the same time, the economic situation severely deteriorated, and Moscow urgently needed and sought South Korean capital, technology, goods, and credits. Yet, the Soviet military opposed any drastic alterations in Moscow's strategy in the Far East. General V. Lobov, a top planner on the General Staff, wrote in the summer of 1988 of the continued and growing threat from the United States in the Pacific. He mentioned South Korea as one of the principal "springboards" for potential aggression against the "socialist commonwealth." North Korea was identified as "an important bastion," obstructing "Pentagon schemes."[48]

The principal arguments of those who pressed for rapid rapprochement with Seoul can be found in both government documents and public statements of the Soviet leaders. One of the most comprehensive explanations was given by Foreign Minister Eduard Shevardnadze right after official normalization of diplomatic ties between the USSR and ROK occurred. He listed six factors that finally prompted the Kremlin to act.

1. The essence of new thinking led the Soviet leadership to realize the necessity of official relations with the ROK. "We could not hope to achieve our goals in the Asia Pacific region (strengthening of peace and security, international cooperation, etc.) without recognizing reality there—the existence of two independent states on the Korean peninsula."
2. The growing political, economic, and military role of South Korea in the international arena made it a force which could no longer be ignored.

3. Economic interests of the Soviet Union would benefit.
4. There was mounting pressure from inside the USSR in favor of normalization.
5. The Soviet leadership came to the conviction that rapprochement with Seoul would promote relaxation of tensions between North and South Korea.
6. Normalization of relations with Seoul would positively influence progress in promoting normalization of relations between Pyongyang and both Washington and Tokyo.[49]

Gorbachev listened to the proponents of establishing diplomatic relations, and he agreed to meet Roh Tae-woo in San Francisco on June 3, 1990 following a visit to Washington. The summit was a complete success from Moscow's point of view.[50] Roh promised vast economic aid to the faltering Soviet economy, and Koreans urged the Soviet Union to declare official relations quickly as a prerequisite for extending the aid. On September 30 Shevardnadze met his South Korean counterpart in New York. After agreeing to establish official relations, he went out of his way to express good feelings toward Pyongyang. This, however, could not prevent a strong negative reaction there. Moscow, in turn, was angered with North Korea and virtually neglected its relations with this "ally."

Relations with South Korea immediately became a priority in the USSR's Asian-Pacific foreign policy. At a meeting with close associates, Gorbachev stressed that South Korea was the most promising partner in the East and opportunities there should not be lost.[51] Relevant to him was the fact that the Soviet Union and the ROK were both leaving behind totalitarian practices and trying to introduce democracy to their societies.[52]

Mongolia, up to perestroika, was a perfect Soviet satellite, which automatically followed Moscow's line and copied Soviet ways of life. Not surprisingly, the Mongolian leadership heartily welcomed Gorbachev's slogans. However, with the progress of perestroika and growing changes in Soviet society, Ulan Bator grew worried and irritated. Mongol leaders did not want any changes in their own country and began to take countermeasures against the "corrupting influence" emanating from "the big brother." They did not succeed. Encouraged by Gorbachev's words and actions, Mongolian society came alive. Anticommunist opposition took shape and openly challenged communist dictatorship. The Communist Party itself went through deep transformation. New leaders rejected Marxism–Leninism and opted for a market economy, democracy, and an open, multidirectional foreign policy. The special relationship with the

USSR ended and Soviet troops left the country. Anti-Soviet criticism became widespread. The Kremlin, busy with many other things, did not pay much attention to developments in Mongolia.[53]

Vietnam was a very important strategic ally of the USSR vis-à-vis both the United States and China. Moscow readily supported its intervention in Cambodia in 1978. As a result the Soviet Union found itself at odds with most East Asian nations. Upon coming to power Gorbachev set forward two contradictory goals: "strengthening solidarity" with Vietnam and normalizing relations with China. Moscow was stepping up its military presence in Vietnam and intensifying military supplies to the ally and at the same time was showing flexibility toward China in many fields. However, Beijing wanted concessions first and foremost in Indochina. It demanded that Moscow bring about Vietnamese withdrawal from Cambodia. Gorbachev could not allow himself to exert direct pressure on the proud and independently minded Vietnamese. Instead, the USSR set an example through its own flexibility in Afghanistan and in relations with the PRC. Finally, Vietnam agreed to withdraw its troops from Cambodia, made steps in the direction of reconciliation with China, and began to imitate Chinese reforms (which it earlier had denounced as anti-Marxist, pro-imperialist). Dissatisfaction with Soviet "new thinking" in Asia receded, but the importance of the Soviet ally for Hanoi also went down.[54] Similar trends were visible in Moscow's relations with *Laos*.

As for other Southeast Asian nations (members of ASEAN), the political settlement in Cambodia together with general changes in the USSR and its foreign policy gradually changed their perceptions of Moscow from quite negative to rather positive. *Indonesia* and *Malaysia*, fearing China and apprehensive of American domination, displayed a special interest in political ties with the USSR. Nevertheless, their economy was the prime preoccupation of ASEAN countries and in this respect the Soviet Union was still an outsider for them.[55]

Soviet relations with *the United States* in Asia had of course a special significance. These relations warmed up much later than most other aspects of the bilateral relationship. The dialogue of the two superpowers in that part of the world did not materialize until the spring of 1990. The reason for such a long delay was obvious: Soviet and American interests in the APR largely not only did not coincide, but directly collided.

As was mentioned above, Gorbachev right from the start set a course for the USSR of deep penetration into the political and economic life of the APR and turning it into an all-around power that could help to lead the region. This intention in itself was unacceptable to Washington.

Throughout the entire postwar period American strategy was aimed precisely against Soviet penetration into the Pacific basin. To achieve this goal Washington created a comprehensive system of military-political alliances and armed partners, pressing them to adhere to the tough, anti-Soviet policy. Most regional states were recruited into alliances with the United States. In the 1970s Washington managed to launch a strategic partnership with Beijing, elements of which continued up to the Soviet–Chinese normalization in 1989.

Washington was especially irritated with the methods employed by Gorbachev in his Asia–Pacific policy. Americans had become accustomed to considering the Pacific zone as their "internal lake." Suddenly the USSR intruded into this lake and demanded parity in armaments, strove to head the process of restructuring the system of regional security, and at the outset took pains to beef up regimes hostile to Washington in North Korea and Indochina. For the United States this line seemed threatening, bound to undermine American influence and positions, and to weaken its alliances. Consequently, Washington not only ignored Soviet initiatives but also tried to slow down improvement of Soviet relations with other states, starting with China and including South Korea.[56] As Gorbachev's perestroika advanced, however, American views began to change. Soviet activities in the APR looked less and less suspicious and increasingly reasonable. Washington welcomed Soviet–Chinese normalization, and it ceased objections to the rapprochement of Moscow with Seoul and Tokyo.

Regional Issues and Interactions

Gorbachev's leadership until the end of the 1980s continued to regard American military preparations in the APR as detrimental to peace and stability. Moscow also identified dangerous militarist tendencies in Japan, South Korea, and ASEAN states. On this basis, the Kremlin felt itself completely justified in pushing for arms control and disarmament measures in the region. However, if in the initial period Gorbachev's ideals and proposals rarely took into consideration interests, perceptions, and positions of regional states, with time the Kremlin began to adjust its policy in this field to realities. New realism was first manifested in Soviet decisions to take unilateral steps in arms control and disarmament: Moscow agreed to liquidate its intermediate-range missiles in Asia, to reduce its armed forces by 200,000 soldiers, to withdraw troops from Mongolia, to declassify certain data on its defense policies, to scale down utilization of military installations in Vietnam, and so on.[57]

In its proposals addressed to other regional states the Kremlin began to take into account their legitimate concerns, including their interest in preservation of the U.S. military presence in the Pacific. Strategic thinking was adjusted: understanding developed that the American presence indeed assured stability and limited ambitions of Japan and other regional states. Some Soviet proposals found a positive response. The most important result of Moscow's effort was launching in 1989 Soviet–Chinese negotiations on the reduction of armed forces and confidence-building measures in the border areas.[58] The United States also announced plans to reduce by 10 percent its military personnel in the APR. Regional conflicts were one area where Gorbachev's "new thinking" brought tangible results. Moscow terminated military intervention in Afghanistan and influenced Vietnam to withdraw troops from Cambodia. Thanks largely to the Soviet leader those two hot regional conflicts were largely overcome. The Soviet Union was also active in trying to achieve a settlement in Korea in concert with other interested parties (unfortunately, without results).

Gorbachev tried very hard to stir up productive forces in the Soviet Far East and to integrate it into the economic life of the surrounding region. Numerous programs, plans, and proposals were advanced, as hundreds of agreements were signed with regional states. However, growing chaos in the Soviet economy and society prevented any improvement in this regard. As for Gorbachev's ideas of building up a multilateral security system in Asia and the Pacific, they did not find a positive response. Some states (especially the United States) saw in these ideas Moscow's attempts to tip the balance of power in the region in its own favor. Others dismissed the proposals as a reflection of Soviet ambitions or pure propaganda efforts. An even more important obstacle to Gorbachev's ideas was a lack of objective and subjective preconditions in the region for such a collective system. Now, many years later, we witness the movement of regional states in this direction, very slowly and full of contradictions and obstacles.

Overall, summarizing Gorbachev's policy in Asia and the Pacific, I believe we can say that it was the most successful, effective and appreciated aspect of his perestroika. Even Gorbachev's bitterest opponents have nothing negative to say about the legacy of his eastern policy. Russia now enjoys good relations with a majority of states in the region. It is not involved in local conflicts there. Gorbachev's success in the APR was substantial and contrasted sharply (especially in the eyes of the opponents of "the new thinking") with his failures in the West. It is, of course, true that Russia's influence in the region is rather limited, but it is due to the well-known weaknesses of the Russian state, especially in the economic field.

Notes

1. See, for example, Evgeny Bazhanov, ed., *Russia within the Network of European Partnership and Cooperation. Proceedings of the International Symposium* (Moscow: Institute of Contemporary International Problems, 1995).
2. Politizdat', *The Twenty-Seventh Congress of the Communist Party of the Soviet Union. Proceedings* (Moscow, 1986), pp. 9–11.
3. Mikhail Gorbachev, "On Main Directions of Internal and Foreign Policy of the USSR." A Speech at the People's Deputies Congress on May 30, 1989 (Moscow), pp. 4–8.
4. All-Russian Center for Preservation of Contemporary Documents (ARCPCD), File 8, List 6, u. of s. 132, p. 24.
5. *Pravda*, February 26, 1986, p. 1.
6. "Developments in the Asia-Pacific Region and Countries of the Socialist Commonwealth," Analytical Papers, the International Department of the Central Committee of the CPSU (Moscow, January 1986), pp. 2–3.
7. *ARCPCD*, File 8, List 6, u. of s. 132, pp. 33–35.
8. *Pravda*, February 26, 1986, pp. 1–2.
9. "Current Tasks in the Asia-Pacific Region," The CPSU CC, Department for Relations with the Ruling Communist Parties of Socialist Countries (Moscow, September 10, 1985), pp. 2–3.
10. Evgeny Bazhanov, *The USSR and the Asia-Pacific Region* (Moscow: Znanie, 1991), p. 9.
11. "Current Tasks in the Asia-Pacific Region," pp. 7–8.
12. *ARCPCD*, File 8, List 6, u. of s. 165, pp. 11–12, 35.
13. Bazhanov, *The USSR and the Asia-Pacific Region*, p. 9.
14. *ARCPCD*, File 8, List 6, u. of s. 112, pp. 76–77.
15. *ARCPCD*, File 8, List 9, u. of s. 253, pp. 19–20.
16. "Concerning American Policy in Asia and the Pacific," An Analysis for the CPSU CC (Moscow: International Department, 1985), pp. 5–6.
17. *Pravda*, April 24, 1986, p. 1.
18. *Pravda*, July 29, 1986, p. 1.
19. *Unen*, July 10, 1987, p. 1.
20. *Pravda*, May 22, 1985, p. 1.
21. *Pravda*, April 21, 1986, p. 1.
22. *ARCPCD*, File 8, List 9, u. of d. 253, p. 68.
23. Bazhanov, *The USSR and the Asia-Pacific Region*, pp. 12–13.
24. Evgeny Bazhanov, *China and the World* (Moscow: Mezhdunarodnye otnosheniia, 1990), pp. 90–186.
25. Evgeny Bazhanov, "On the Run-up to the Summit," *New Times*, No. 19 (May 9–15, 1989): p. 34.
26. Evgeny Bazhanov, "Soviet-Chinese Relations: Lessons of the Past and Present Time," *Novaia i noveishaia istoria*, No. 2 (1989): 3–25; No. 3 (1989): 43–59.
27. *Renmin ribao*, June 6, 1989, p. 1.
28. See, for example, *Renmin ribao*, June 12, 1989, p. 1.

29. Evgeny Bazhanov, "The Substance of Change," *New Times*, No. 16 (1990): 20–22.
30. Bazhanov, *The USSR and the Asia-Pacific Region*, pp. 20–21.
31. Patoch Shodiev, *Iaponiia v sovremennom mire* (Moscow: Nauchnaia kniga, 2002), pp. 72–75.
32. *Izvestiia*, April 20, 1991, p. 1.
33. Bazhanov, *The USSR and the Asia-Pacific Region*, p. 28.
34. *Tokyo shimbun*, September 22, 1989, p. 5.
35. Shodiev, *Iaponiia v sovremennom mire*, pp. 82–83.
36. *ARCPCD*, File 8, List 11, u. of s. 124, pp. 45–47.
37. Personal archives, D. 12, pp. 32–33.
38. *Izvestiia*, April 20, 1991, p. 1.
39. *ARCPCD*, File 8, List 9, u. of s. 253, pp. 18–19.
40. *The USSR in Struggle for Peace, International Security, and Disarmament (1946–1977)* (Moscow: Znanie, 1978), pp. 226, 309, 352–53, 374.
41. *ARCPCD*, File 8, List 9, u. of s. 253, pp. 20–22.
42. *ARCPCD*, File 8, List 9, u. of s. 309, pp. 215.
43. V. Andreev and V. Osipov, "Friendship and Cooperation between Peoples of the USSR and the DPRK," *Problems of the Far East*, No. 4 (1986): 26–27.
44. O. Davidov and V. Mikheev, "Some Aspects of North Korean Foreign Policy in the Light of International Relations in the Far East," *Problems of the Far East*, No. 7 (1987): 18–19.
45. *Za rubezhom*, June 20, 1988, p. 9.
46. Natalia Bazhanova, *DPRK's Foreign Economic Ties*, (Mascow: Nauka, 1993), pp. 10–88.
47. *ARCPCD*, File 8, List 6, u. of s. 205, p. 162.
48. V. Lobov, "Who is Aspiring for Superiority?" *Krasnaia zvezda*, July 14, 1988, p. 4.
49. *ARCPCD*, File 8, List 6, u. of s. 109, pp. 17–18.
50. Ibid.
51. *Komsomol'skaia pravda*, April 28, 1991, p. 3.
52. *Trud*, April 20, 1991, p. 1.
53. Bazhanov, *The USSR and the Asia-Pacific Region*, pp. 33–35.
54. Bazhanov, *China and the World*, pp. 297–301.
55. Bazhanov, *The USSR and the Asia-Pacific Region*, pp. 37–39.
56. For details see Bazhanov, *China and the World*, pp. 218–32; Evgeny Bazhanov, "Equation with Many Unknown Quantities," *Pravda*, March 2, 1989, p. 3; Evgeny Bazhanov, "An Old Friend in China," *New Times*, No. 10 (1989): 15–17; Il Yung Chung, ed., *Korea and Russia. Toward the 21st Century* (Seoul: The Sejong Institute, 1992), pp. 61–112, 315–94.
57. *Security in the Asia-Pacific Region* (Moscow: Novosti, 1988), pp. 171–78.
58. *Ibid.*, pp. 168–69.

CHAPTER 3

Russia's Strategic Thought toward Asia: The Early Yeltsin Years (1991–95)

Alexei Bogaturov

Russian strategic thinking toward Asia under Yeltsin in the early years of his presidency was inconsistent, and tended to take a back seat to Moscow's preoccupation with the West. In the preceding years Asia had clearly been given a higher priority under Mikhail Gorbachev and the Soviet leadership. As indicated in the preceding chapter, the Sino–Soviet relationship, the Soviet role in the Cambodian conflict, the status of Soviet troops in Mongolia, and the war in Afghanistan were all major preoccupations of the Soviet leadership throughout the 1980s. Additionally, Gorbachev attempted to reawaken the dormant Soviet–Japanese relationship, and Tokyo was in fact the destination for his last official state visit as president of the USSR. Although relations with the United States and NATO were also of tremendous importance to the Soviet Union, it was recognized that many of the more pressing issues regarding Russia's foreign policy and Russian strategic thinking had to do with Asia.

With the collapse of the Soviet Union, and the sudden independence of the Soviet republics, the government of the Russian Federation was left to ponder the future of the new republic. Russian leaders were forced to prioritize their foreign policy strategies. Economic survival was the most pressing issue. Accordingly, the Russian government under Boris Yeltsin and Foreign Minister Andrei Kozyrev focused on developing relations with the Euro-Atlantic community. They framed their foreign policy strategy in terms of the common cultural identity between Russia and the West, and this may have been part of the rationale. However, it was clear that the potential for economic reconstruction and development based on the largesse of Europe and the United States was foremost on the minds of Russia's leaders. Had Asia been the region with the potential for massive funding of Russia's reconstruction, then the Pacific—not the Atlantic—may have been the focus of Moscow's diplomatic efforts in the first years of the Russian Federation.

This was not the case, and so Asia was less of a priority in the first couple of years of the first Yeltsin administration. To be sure, the newly formed Central Asian republics, because of their geographical location, and because of the existence of the large Russian diaspora in these nations, were necessarily higher on the hierarchy of Moscow's diplomatic strategy. Former partners in Asia, however, such as China, India, Mongolia, North Korea, and Vietnam, were relegated to the lower rungs of Moscow's strategic thinking in the early years of the Yeltsin presidency. Japan, because, of its dynamic economy and its accepted position among the West's rich, developed nations,[1] was accorded some attention in the early months of Boris Yeltsin's first term. In fact, in his memoirs Kozyrev wrote about Russia's relations with Japan in the section devoted to Russia's relations with Europe and the United States. Discussions of China and India were left in the chapter devoted to Asia.[2] Yeltsin and Kozyrev were preoccupied with developing a foreign policy devoted almost exclusively to the Euro-Atlantic community in the first year of the independent Russian Federation.

The rest of the Russian establishment, meanwhile, was engaged in an intense debate about the future of Russia's foreign policy, and indeed of the future of Russia itself, both as a governing entity and as a society. It took considerable time for large segments of the Russian leadership to understand that the epoch of bipolar stability—with all of its strong points and shortcomings—had come to an end, along with the institutionalized dialogue based on the strained, yet semi-normal Soviet–American relationship. The "de-institutionalization" of strategic thinking,[3] along with the slow and painful realization of Russia's reduced, largely regional, political role took the form of public disputes over with whom to make friends—Europe, the United States, or the former Soviet republics. These republics (along the fringes of Europe and Central Asia) were naturally Russia's closest neighbors, yet they were not necessarily the closest of allies to Russia. East Asia was hardly ever mentioned in Russian political debates, and few saw in the region either a preferential partner, or a developmental model worth imitating.

Debates between Russian *Atlanticists* and *Eurasianists*—well covered by Western and Russian political writings in the mid-1990s—hardly signified clashes between pro-Western and anti-Western orientations in international politics. Rather, these debates were between more *internationally* minded and more *nationally* minded scholars and politicians, the former favoring the adoption of American and West European models of political development, the latter advocating an inward-looking development of an "original Russian mode of democracy," which would be more organic and consistent with Russia's traditional cultural, economic, and political history. Asia rarely assumed a positive role in Russian political thinking; yet the "image of Asia" was occasionally used in politics as an instrument to balance what was viewed as unreasonably massive borrowing from Europe that may either harm the imaginary "core" of Russia's identity, or fail to function properly in the Russian domestic environment. Russian liberalism under Yeltsin contained very distinct and strong anti-Asian emotional components. Some would say that typical Russian "liberals" are almost automatically as much anti-Asian, as they are pro-European.

The whole period of 1991–95 may be subdivided into two stages. The first one covers the collapse of the USSR in December 1991 and extends to the first Duma election in December 1993. These were years of the dashed illusions of ordinary people and the unshakable romanticism of pro-Western elites. Almost everything Asian was neglected as presumably nondemocratic, and opposed to "Western" ideals. The second period includes the two years (1994–95) of Kozyrev's declining influence over Russia's foreign policy. A penchant for stressing Russia's European nature and the importance of the West for Russia's future development still dominated the thinking of the ruling elite, led by Yeltsin and his closest advisors. The ruling elite, however, found it necessary to take into account the nationalist sentiments of the Liberal Democratic Party and the Communist Party, especially after the former won a majority in the State Duma in December 1993. These "opposition" forces were skeptical about Kozyrev's *Atlanticism*, and they called for an independent international course. The left-leaning groups depicted China—and the Chinese reform experience—as a model for Russia. Later, in the first year of Yevgeny Primakov's leadership of the Foreign Ministry (from January 1996) Russia turned to Asia in a rather demonstrative manner,[4] and the concept of *multipolarity* was accepted by Russia, seemingly under China's influence.

Domestic Politics, Insecurity, and Threat Perception in Asia

The reduced global threat and the motive of reconciliation with NATO were a major part of Russia's official ideology in the days and months after the collapse of the Soviet Union, despite a programmed inertia that pushed popular thinking to identify "threats and enemies."[5] After decades of a systemic confrontation with the outside world it was highly unusual for an ordinary Russian to live without notions of external threats and enemies. Domestic political disorder, combined with the hardships associated with radical market reforms and the spread of separatist movements, constituted a rather volatile political atmosphere. The nation felt politically, socially, and economically insecure. The more liberal politicians talked about an "unthreatening international environment," the less persuasive they sounded to the public. By intuition people were looking for threats, and the state authorities needed to identify threats in order to calm down the people and to rebuild trust in the government, which had been seriously undermined by the drastic economic situation in the country in 1992–93.

The first official documents on Russian foreign policy and security (The Concept of Foreign Policy of the Russian Federation, 1992, and the Concept of National Security of the Russian Federation, 1997) cautiously, yet clearly, indicated potential threats that Russia was facing.[6] Firstly, they labeled as sources of threats the domestic economic crisis and Russia's inability to accomplish democratic reforms. Secondly, the documents stated that "third world" conflicts and waves of "instability from the south" may easily reach Russian territory and, therefore, should be viewed as potential sources of threat. By conflicts from the south, clearly, Russian policymakers at that point meant primarily the antigovernment war by the *Taliban* in Afghanistan. Indeed, in 1991–93 the radical *Pashto* Muslims supported by Pakistan, and previously sponsored by the American CIA, conquered Kabul and began to threaten Tajikistan, where Russian soldiers were still stationed. Furthermore, radical Islamic gangs invaded the Ferghana Valley, built bases there, and began to launch regular attacks into Uzbekistan and Kyrgyzstan. Russian military and intelligence sources warned that the "war from the south" could approach ever closer to Russia's frontier, which was by this time defenseless because it remained merely a symbolic administrative division line between integral parts of the former republics of the Soviet Union.

Add to this the internal conflict in the North Caucasus Russian province of Chechnya, which was also considered part of the general confrontation between Russia and "the hostile south." Chechen separatists were seen as the embodiment of this new threat, and were supported by money from Saudi Arabia, and "guided" strategically, tactically, and spiritually by the Afghan Taliban. Small wonder, consequently, that the image of a dangerous, hostile Islamic south was foremost in Russia's perceptions of Asia in the first years of the Yeltsin presidency. Popular opinion was haunted by the idea of Russia's weakness and fragility vis-à-vis Asia, as well as the unpreparedness of the Russian leadership to deter pressures and challenges from Asia. A natural reaction to such perceptions was a desire "to be stronger" or, at least, to put an end to "losing ground" everywhere, especially in Central Asia.

U.S. politics of "exporting democracy" in the early 1990s, combined with NATO's expansion, consolidated Russia's sense of defensiveness and heightened distrust of the external world. Moscow was unable to prevent what politicians and ordinary people saw as "pressures from Europe." The inability to "resist the West" bred determination, at least, to resist in the East, that is, to defend Russia's positions along its Asian borders. The deliberate conservatism of Moscow's course toward Asia "compensated" for the "imposed" weakness in the West.

The promises of Gorbachev's "new thinking" toward Asia were inherited by Yeltsin, although modified in important respects. Like his predecessor, Yeltsin also attempted to distance Russia from the leadership in Mongolia, to speed up cooperation with South Korea (at the expense of North Korea), to press for political dialogue on security matters with China, and to reinvigorate the Russo-Japanese dialogue. Japan, in turn, failed to take into account the complicated domestic situation in Russia in 1992, and chose to continue its demanding policy toward the territorial dispute. To many observers, complications in the dialogue with Tokyo contributed to the appearance that Russian foreign policy in the Far East remained unchanged since the cold war days.

Unlike the quasi-revisionist Soviet regime under Gorbachev in the 1980s, Russia in the 1990s was primarily a status-quo power in Asian affairs, with the exception of a relatively short two-year period between December 1991 and November 1993, when the influence of Foreign Minister Kozyrev was still fairly strong.[7] Meanwhile, many observers speculated that Russia and the West had tacitly negotiated an implied exchange: as long as Moscow agreed to major concessions in the West, politicians in Washington had enough prudence not to press Moscow too hard, and from all directions. While the West won many concessions in Europe, it acquiesced to Russia's unwillingness to give up what she could presumably preserve in her former postures in Asia.

Moscow's vision of Asian realities was increasingly influenced by the views of regional elites and the population of the Siberian and Far Eastern regions. In the early 1990s Russia's Far Eastern regions were left with almost no financial support from the federal government. Reduced assistance from Moscow was matched by reduced loyalty in the regions, which often resulted in attempts to gain economic "independence" that had the potential to develop into real separatism.[8] Russians in the non-European parts of the Russian Federation started to talk more aggressively about themselves as "Siberians" and "Far-Easterners."[9] However, they never saw themselves as "Asians." Local people preferred to see themselves as "Europeans who live in Asia," rather than regular Asians.

Perceptions of Asia in the Far Eastern provinces of Russia were more concrete and pragmatic than those of citizens in the European parts of Russia. Yet, their feelings toward Asia and Asian neighbors, too, were far from being friendly. Local people wanted transborder trade and freedom to cross national frontiers with little hassle, but they were anxious about rumors of the eventual transfer of the Kurile Islands to Japan, and early signs of a growing Chinese demographic presence on Russian soil. The population of the southwestern and southeastern Siberian regions (Barnaul, Tomsk, Omsk, and Irkutsk) was anxious about illegal or semi-legal immigration of Muslim groups (largely from the former Soviet republics of the USSR) to Russia.[10] Ethnically, the Russian population of the North Caucasus and Lower Volga regions of the Russian Federation was irritated by massive infiltration of non-Russian Asian immigrants from Azerbaijan (largely ethnic Armenians from Karabakh) and ethnic Chechens from the combat zones in Chechnya.[11] Everywhere in the border regions, Asia and Asian peoples were viewed with suspicion. But ironically, Asia also represented an opportunity to some for making money in trade, or in exploiting the Asian newcomers before they formed organized groups to defend themselves and corrupt local Russian authorities with bribes.

China Ties: "Non-Infliction of Damage" and the Balance of Forces

Although the Chinese reappeared in Russia in significant numbers in early 1993,[12] it was not until the mid-1990s that the Chinese "demographic expansion" and "peaceful colonization" of the Russian Far East was identified as a potential security threat. This idea was first expressed by the population and authorities in the Siberian and Far Eastern provinces,[13] and later by the federal government. This, however, did not result in the deterioration of Russo-Chinese relations. In fact, the bilateral relationship was improving in line with the normalization of Soviet–Chinese relations in 1989 when Gorbachev visited Beijing. Therefore, Russian perceptions toward China (if we speak of the bulk of the Russian population in which Far Eastern Russians are a clear "regional minority") in the first part of the 1990s were largely positive. Local Russians in the Far East were anxious about the Chinese "newcomers," while federal authorities stayed indifferent to local fears and demonstrated a growing interest in commercial and military-commercial deals with China. Leaders in Moscow seem to have overcome the fears and the deep distrust toward China that had marked Soviet thinking since the "Cultural Revolution" and the Soviet–Chinese border clashes in the late 1960s. In 1991 (under Gorbachev) a bilateral agreement on the eastern part of the Russo-Chinese border was concluded. Negotiations continued on the western part of the border until the signing of an agreement in 1994.

Boris Yeltsin was at first cautious toward Beijing. However, after the Russo-Chinese Joint Declaration was signed in December 1992 (during his visit to Beijing), Yeltsin recognized that China offered the potential for strategic balancing against the overwhelming economic, military, and political power of the United States and NATO in the West. Some Russian observers admitted that China's natural skepticism toward Gorbachev (who was seen in China as a weak leader, a poor political strategist, and a bad communist) provided common ground that facilitated Russo-Chinese dialogue under Yeltsin, who was well-known for his personal dislike of Gorbachev. The Kremlin's favorable impressions of potential for Russo-Chinese cooperation in Asia worked to neutralize the anti-Chinese sentiments of local people and the governors in the Russian Far East. The image of a security threat from China started to diminish—at least in federal media and in governmental circles, but alarmism toward China was quite intense in the Russian Far East, where governors cynically used anti-Chinese feelings to consolidate their electoral positions.

In fact, attitudes toward China were divisive around Russia. Beijing was working hard to persuade Moscow to upgrade China's place among its international priorities. Yeltsin was hardly ready to boost China ties as much as Beijing wanted, for Russia was too involved in the West in the early 1990s. Until 1994 China hardly appeared in Moscow to be a political alternative to cooperation with the United States and the EU. But several segments of the Russian elite were becoming more interested in China. Some were driven by economic pragmatism and wanted to benefit from trade with Beijing. Others were just "tired of the West," alarmed by the growing dependence on Washington, and prepared to balance the United States with China in Russia's priorities.

More Russians started to think about China in terms of profit and opportunity. Russian citizens in the Far East gained the right to visit neighboring Chinese cities on a preferential legal basis, becoming shuttle-traders and organizing small joint ventures with Chinese partners. Chinese food and consumer goods filled the shops and markets on the Russian side of the frontier. Negative images of the Chinese shaped by the criminal activities of the newcomers in Russia and their attempts to control local market places did not disappear, but a negative vision of China was balanced by pragmatic views by those who benefited or hoped to benefit from economic deals with Chinese.[14] Soon, illegal business dealings of Russian and Chinese working together, including regional administrations, gave added strength to Russo-Chinese ties at the local governmental level.

On a federal level, too, the idea of prospective benefits from dealing with China was winning more supporters in government offices. Beijing's image was now colored with upbeat calculations of how much China could pay for Russian arms, equipment, and advanced technologies. The Russian military, interested in arms exports, started to think about Beijing in a more favorable light. Memory of the historical rivalry with China and the possibility of renewed Russo-Chinese confrontation over Asia were opposed by the concept of friendship between Moscow and Beijing. Russia's arms sales to China began to cause concern in the United States, Taiwan, and some nations of Southeast Asia, including Vietnam. Such deals provoked a domestic discussion in Russia that involved largely academics and members of the media. Russian officials, nonetheless, had to respond somehow to this public debate, and they insisted that Russia was at least ten years ahead of Beijing in military technological prowess and, therefore, selling arms to a "friendly China" would never pose a threat to Russia's own security. The critics, however, referred to the troubled history of Soviet–Chinese relations with special emphasis on the border confrontations of the late 1960s. Moscow had invested a lot in modernizing and "nuclearizing" China in the 1950s, then the USSR had to work hard for at least two decades to neutralize the "China threat" in the 1960s and 1970s. Arguments against "special security arrangements" with Beijing sounded impressive, and advocates of Russo-China "strategic friendship" needed to reply conceptually.

A long-time critic of China, Mikhail Titarenko, articulated one of the most convincing statements for Russia's new policy in East Asia. Dealing with Beijing in the first part of the 1990s, he argued, stemmed from two basic principles: (1) non-infliction of damage to Russia's own security; and (2) preserving the then existing balance of forces in the Asia-Pacific area.[15] Despite his enthusiastic support for Russo-Chinese cooperation, even Titarenko found it possible to suggest that military/commercial cooperation with China, at least theoretically, could prove damaging to Russia's national security. Previously the Institute of the Far East, which he directed, looked like a sort of isolated island among relatively pro-Western research institutes. However, starting from the mid-1990s a cautious realignment indicated that support for closer ties with China was bringing much of the foreign policy elite together.

Russian experts were divided into competing groups.[16] A majority favored restoration of special Russo-Chinese relations, though even enthusiasts of cooperation with Beijing were prudent enough not to mention the possibility of anything similar to the former Soviet–Chinese alliance of the 1950s. Chinese were closely following changes in Russian attitudes, and soon started—beyond the efforts of any other Asian nation—to systematically build a high-level "China lobby" in Russia's power structures on the federal level, as well as on the regional level.

Beijing invested vast energy, money, and intellectual effort into constructing a positive image of a "supportive and inviting" China. Yet the leadership in Moscow was still cautious. Russian leaders had to consider America's possible reactions to a Moscow–Beijing rapprochement. The Kremlin was unwilling to harm relations with Washington by "going too far" in cooperation with China, whom the Americans started to see as a potential rival in Asia. Moscow was taking pains to provide a persuasive "justification" for every major case of Russo-Chinese cooperation that Americans might perceive as potentially damaging to their interests.

In April 1996, a multilateral agreement among Russia, China, Kazakhstan, Kyrgyzstan, and Tajikistan on military confidence-building measures along the border was signed. Moscow and Beijing immediately declared this as a sign of mutual trust, and a symbol of mutually beneficial cooperation. China suggested that the newly signed agreement would signal the start of long-term regional cooperation involving the smaller nations of Central Asia, alongside Russia and China. Not without hesitation, leaders in Moscow finally seemed to have found in China an acceptable, compatible partner; one that was not excessively provocative toward the United States. The newly emerged group (the future SCO) was clearly the first case of Asian multilateral regionalism in which Russia could participate on an equal basis. China was a power that helped Moscow to attain this goal, adding to its improving image in Russia.

The major source of Moscow's apprehension vis-à-vis Beijing was the perceived movement of Chinese nationals into Russia's Far Eastern regions.[17] Constant efforts on the part of the Chinese side to persuade Moscow of the gains it might achieve from cooperation provided

Russian leaders with an impetus to advance relations, prevent frictions, and to quell the dissatisfaction that existed at the regional level. By the mid-1990s a sort of fragile and dynamic equilibrium was reached between the positive and negative images of China. Liked or disliked, China had become a central element in Russia's strategic thinking toward Asia.

Losers and Losses: Japan and Korea

By contrast, Japan was losing Russia's attention. New initiatives sponsored by Gorbachev and his Foreign Minister Eduard Shevardnadze in the late 1980s produced a mini-"Japan boom" in the Soviet Union. Liberally minded Soviet scholars started to advocate reconsidering Soviet–Japanese relations, and to give attention to the proposition of transferring at least some of the disputed Kurile Islands to Japan after the signing of a Soviet–Japanese peace treaty. At that point not a few analysts in the USSR as well as Japan thought a compromise on the territorial issue was more realistic than at any time since 1956.[18] The expectations of a "breakthrough" in the territorial dispute were so strong in Moscow that unexpectedly there appeared a sort of competition between Gorbachev and Yeltsin around who has the "legal right" to state the conditions for a territorial settlement with Japan. Because of his recognized anti-Gorbachev sentiments, Yeltsin appeared firmer on the territorial issue. He insisted that no part of Russia's territory could be passed to any foreign state without the approval of the Russian Federation, of which he was president. However, some observers suggested that his stand was a tactical trick and could be changed after (and if) his personal fight with Gorbachev ended successfully. In 1991 Gorbachev gave up the idea of reconciliation with Japan at the price of the territories.

Objectively, the quarrel between the two presidents pushed the Russian public to think much more about Japan and the security of the Far Eastern frontiers of Russia. The theme of "the Japanese are coming" was revitalized, and it never has disappeared in Sakhalin Oblast, which administers the Kurile Islands. When members of Yeltsin's team in 1992 tried to introduce to Russian citizens in Moscow and in the Far Eastern regions the idea of a compromise that would stipulate the transfer of at least two of the four islands to Japan, they were severely criticized, both in the Supreme Soviet of the Russian Federation and in Sakhalin and nearby areas. Rumors of possible evacuation (and expected compensation for it from the Japanese side) spread among residents in the Far East, and were transmitted through deputies to the lobbies of the Supreme Soviet, where they inflamed passions each time Japanese affairs arose in discussions. Given the divisions in society and among policymakers, Yeltsin did not dare to "yield to Japan." His planned visit to Tokyo was twice postponed. When it finally took place in 1993, the two parties did not reach any agreement that could provide an impetus for new developments in bilateral relations. The Russian side did agree to the "Tokyo Declaration," which, in addition to recognizing in writing, as the Gorbachev and Kaifu declaration had done, that the issue at hand was *four* islands, accepted "law and justice" as the guiding principles of the negotiations. This was viewed as a victory in Tokyo, but resulted in nothing concrete.

Russia basically placed herself in the position of the USSR under Gorbachev: to recognize, in principle, the possibility of territorial concessions after signing a peace treaty, as it was defined in the Soviet–Japanese Joint Declaration of 1956, but without specifying the terms or the timing.[19] While Yeltsin apologized before the people of Japan for the cruel treatment of Japanese prisoners of war in the 1940s and 1950s in the Soviet Union, he could hardly control the nationalist sentiments that he himself had unleashed just a few years before to use against Gorbachev. The country was moving toward parliamentary elections in December 1993, which brought victory to right-wing nationalists. It was clear already in the fall of 1992 that the president had no support among the public or in the legislature to push for a territorial settlement. This became even clearer after the 1993 elections.[20] Both parties lost out. Russia, as before, had to dispense with large-scale economic cooperation from Japan. Tokyo's hard attitude toward Russia in the hope that Moscow would feel isolated in the region, and would have to take a more flexible stand on the territories, proved to be a miscalculation. As a result, in 1994 Russia started moving closer to China.

Militarily Japan was recognized as an American ally, as during the cold war. Therefore, from a security standpoint, Russia's relations with Japan were not considered more unfriendly or dangerous than relations with the United States, which were no longer seen as hostile. In these circumstances, Russians started to lose interest in Japan, while China was displacing it, initially for promising political—and later economic—reasons. As the situation unfolded in the mid-1990s, neither the Russian nor the Japanese leadership seemed to take the loss of the other as a special regional partner seriously, although preparations on both sides were under way to improve ties.

Japan was not the only "loss" for Russia's presence in Asia. North Korea and Vietnam were two other "losses." Japan was lost after Russian liberals had pressed hard for reconciliation, while North Korea and

Vietnam were lost after liberals had pressed for disruption in ties with them. The worsened relations between Moscow and Pyongyang were a reflection of improved relations between Moscow and Seoul. Gorbachev and the Soviet Union had sought conciliation toward and recognition of South Korea beginning in the late 1980s. After Gorbachev's 1990 meeting with Roh Tae-woo in San Francisco, Yeltsin carried on his predecessor's work and traveled to Seoul for a summit with the South Korean leader in November 1992 (despite the fact that he had cancelled the Japan leg of his trip to the Far East two months earlier). Yeltsin touted the Russian-South Korean relationship and called Seoul a "partner" for Moscow. President Kim Young-sam visited Moscow in 1994. Although Korean economic aid and investment was not as large as Moscow had hoped, Russia was able to repay some of the Soviet loans through the transfer of weapons to South Korea.

The "jealousy" and sense of betrayal that the North Korean leadership felt toward Russia's reconciliation with South Korea resulted in drastically reduced contacts between Moscow and Pyongyang. The North was considered to be poor, backward, stubborn, and even politically fragile. Russians saw little reason why they should struggle to sustain relations with the leadership in Pyongyang, with which it had proved increasingly difficult to deal. North Korea seemed especially irritated by the criticism leveled against it in the Russian media, as Russian experts started to analyze the Korean problem largely in terms of Russia's cooperation with the United States and South Korea. The most shocking thing was that Russian politicians tended to think that they could continue being influential in Korean affairs without preserving strong cooperative ties and a sympathetic dialogue with the North. After the 1992 Russia–South Korean treaty was concluded,[21] the North reacted emotionally. In 1994 Yeltsin let the public know that Russia was not going to extend the Russia–North Korean Treaty of Friendship, Cooperation and Mutual Assistance of 1961. The next year Moscow sent Pyongyang a draft of a new treaty, which was rejected. Russia was rapidly losing its influence over North Korea, to the point that in 1996 South Korea and the United States suggested four-party talks on Korea with no Russian participation.[22]

In Moscow, "liberal romanticist" views of the prospects for improving regional relations started to fade away. Most members of the foreign policy elite decided that Russia must move closer to more traditional realist policies. Korea was recognized as a sensitive place for Russian national security; therefore, by 1996 the Korean peninsula had become a symbol of the urgency of change in Russian foreign policy in order to restore Russian influence in Northeast Asia.

The divorce between Russia and Vietnam was less painful, and it was not necessarily Russia that was to be blamed for the deteriorating relationship.[23] Rather, the painful, zigzag process of reform in Vietnam aroused suspicions among liberal elements in the Russian government. Starting from 1991, Russia stopped all economic assistance to Vietnam as a consequence of the catastrophic economic situation in Russia. This unfavorable economic situation, combined with an ideological gap, led to a sharp downturn in bilateral interactions. Policymakers in Moscow failed to notice the growing economic success of Vietnam by the mid-1990s,[24] and the emerging prospects for restructuring and restoring cooperative ties with Hanoi. With no prospect of revitalizing its military presence in Southeast Asia to deter the maritime might of the United States, Moscow apparently could not understand why Vietnam might be useful. Yeltsin's team was apparently satisfied to know that Hanoi had no plans to harm Russia's interests.

Moscow's losses in Vietnam were partly compensated by improved relations with ASEAN as a whole. Russian leaders recognized ASEAN as a positive tool for regional economic cooperation. In 1991 Russia was invited to join the post-ministerial conferences of ASEAN, and in 1996 it was formally accepted as a new ASEAN "dialogue-partner." In 1994 when the ASEAN Regional Security Forum (ARF) was organized, Russia was invited to become a member. Some smaller nations (unexpectedly) considered Russian participation important for advancing toward regional security.[25] Encouraged, Moscow upgraded its economic and political contacts with Southeast Asian states, some of which (primarily Malaysia) even started to import Russian fighters and other armaments. Some people in Moscow calculated that the Asian smaller nations turned to Moscow in part due to growing distrust toward a "strong China."

South Asian Dimensions

The view of India as a preferential partner of Moscow hardly survived the collapse of the Soviet Union. In the early 1990s the thinking of Russian leaders was dominated by the view that in world politics they should deal primarily, if not exclusively, with rich, technologically advanced, and democratic nations. India was recognized as a democracy, but she did not have a reputation as a developing economic giant. Unlike during the Soviet era, Russian leaders were initially hesitant to advance military relations with Delhi. This was a time of Russia's "overall withdrawal" from Asia, Africa, and Latin America. India could not threaten

Russia, and Russia could not gain immediate benefits from relations with India. That was enough at this point for many Russian leaders to conclude that Moscow should pay less attention to South Asian affairs.

India itself was seriously reconsidering its international priorities. Troubled by Russia's withdrawal against the background of China's arrival in its new capacity of a stronger state, India needed to find someone to rely on. Therefore, New Delhi turned to Washington. U.S. leaders, however, were unsure about the continuation of the long-term relationship with Pakistan and only sketched vague prospects about filling Russia's former role in India's foreign policy. Soon, however, Washington was taking a firmly negative stand on the issue of Pakistan's nuclear program.[26] The more Pakistan's regime became responsive to the ideology and political practices of radical Islamic groups, the more apt Washington was to turn toward New Delhi.

Russo-Indian relations were still seen in Moscow as an instrument to oppose radical Islamic groups and press them from the South Asian "rear." In the early 1990s Pakistan was seen as a dangerously strong and aggressive player vis-à-vis the former Soviet republics of Central Asia, as well as a source of destabilizing tendencies affecting the arc of Russia's southeastern borders. In 1993, Boris Yeltsin visited New Delhi and signed a Treaty of Amity and Cooperation between Russia and India. Russia arms sales to India were reenergized and licenses for the production of advanced technologies were extended to India.

Independently from Russia and India, China herself was strongly disappointed with Pakistan's cooperation with radical Islam in Central Asia, as some of these groups maintained links with Turkic separatists in China's Xinjiang province. Moscow, however, was cautious to express antiseparatist solidarity with China, because Beijing's anti-Turkic and anti-Islamic sentiments did not match the visions of smaller Central Asian states that sympathized with Xinjiang Islamic minorities. Russian leaders viewed anti-Islamic slogans as counterproductive and inconsistent with Moscow's intention to strengthen relations with her neighbors in Central Asia. Only in the second half of the 1990s would Moscow and Beijing reach a mutual understanding about the threats from Islamic fundamentalist militant groups.

Islamic Asia: Between Ignorance and Concern

The fact that Russia is also an Islamic nation was formally recognized by the Russian government only after President Vladimir Putin came to power in 2000. Yeltsin's interest in religion seemed much less a priority.

After the October 1993 assault on the Duma, Yeltsin's relations with the Russian Orthodox Church soured somewhat. Meanwhile, his relations with Russian Muslims or Jews were never especially warm. The Euro-Atlantic democratic identity imposed on the nation by the Russian leadership left little room for the development of a Russian identity which could incorporate other ethnic groups. Domestically, Islam played a secondary role as a means for self-identification among Russian ethnic groups. But Islam came to play a major role as an instrument to develop a sense of belonging to a greater Islamic world among some groups. Russian domestic Muslim groups wanted to see themselves as parts of a much larger Islamic universe of which Russia was a part. Theirs was a view from inside Islam.

Meanwhile, in the early 1990s the Russian government tended to deal with Islamic nations in a most unreasonable way: they were viewed as lying outside Russia's "own universe" (presumably European and liberal democratic). No wonder, Moscow's relations both with Islamic groups inside the country and Muslim nations out of it deteriorated greatly under Yeltsin. Russian perceptions of Islamic Asia were colored with a mixture of fear, distrust, and scorn long before the events of September 11, 2001.

There were at least three types of dominant views in Russia of Islam in Asia in the early 1990s. The first one was that of Islamic revenge and *Pan Turkism* associated with Turkey's attempts to confront the "artificial" Russian/Soviet presence in the Caucasus and Central Asia. Turkey was viewed as rising state that would jealously use its chance to support anti-Russian sentiments of Islamic people in and outside Russia to weaken the Russian state. Negative visions of Turkey's foreign policy were combined, nonetheless, with a distinct and well-articulated interest to deepen cultural and economic ties with Turkey. Turkey had an image of a "rich, successful, economically attractive, but politically unreliable" country.

The second type of thinking can be marked as *cynical pragmatism*. Moscow was quite skeptical about countries like Iran, Iraq, and Saudi Arabia. They were seen as reactionary, but rich and strong enough to somehow trouble Russia in sensitive areas. In some cases Moscow hoped to extract economic and financial profits from dealing with these states. Russia also tried to keep stable relations with Muslim states, at least to minimize the damage it suffered from Islamic money that was used to inflame separatism and religious extremism in Russia's periphery.

The third version of thinking of Islamic Asia was that of a *mutually protective partnership*. Yeltsin personally had neither specific interest in the Islamic states of the former Soviet Union, nor the cultural sophistication to find a proper philosophical common ground for cooperation with them. However, merely by instinct he guessed that smaller nations, despite brave rhetoric, felt unprotected and defenseless. It was easy for Moscow to introduce Russia as a potential protector of smaller Islamic states, drawing on its Soviet record in the cold war arena. Soon politicians in Moscow started to understand that secular and moderately Islamic states protect Russia, too, by constituting a geopolitical barrier against militant Islam that was pressing from Pakistan, Afghanistan, Iran, and the oil-exporting Arab states of the Middle East.

Conclusion

Russia's strategic thought toward Asia in the early 1990s was hardly consolidated and homogeneous. Its major features were distrust, anxiety, and fear alongside economic pragmatism. Political cooperation toward selected partners could help to stabilize Russia's strategic environment. Russia's behavior was that of a typical inward-looking status quo power avoiding involvement in conflicts and reluctant to accept strategic commitments.

The notion of China's challenge, though already familiar to the Russian mind, was largely vague and not concrete. Economic isolation from the APR seemed more dangerous than the eventual peaceful Chinese colonization of the Russian Far East.

In the early 1990s the Islamic threat was not yet considered an acute problem. Separatism in the Caucasus was viewed though prisms of ethnicity rather than religion. The nature and the real mission and purpose of Islamic money coming to Russia from oil-exporting Arab countries were misunderstood and misinterpreted.

The period of 1992–95 was basically the first stage of Russia's general reaccommodation to her new status and diminished role in the world. Russian leaders saw no enemies in Asia, but they saw no allies either. Developing a strategy for a weaker Russia was problematic and full of hurdles. This inferiority complex was especially acute compared to the previous decades when the omnipotent Soviet Union could afford to undertake risky initiatives and make concessions. The new system of decision making made the Russian government more sensitive to public criticism, while the Russian public reacted quite painfully to Russia's new lower status. It is no wonder that the Russian leadership was increasingly prone to take a "patriotic" and defensive stand on many regional affairs. The closer Russia was moving to the climax of its weakness in 1998–99, the more conservative her world attitudes were becoming. The inertia of being a "great-power that makes concessions" thinned and faded away by the end of 1994 when the influence of Kozyrev was erased from major policymaking decisions. The period of the early 1990s was more the denouement of Soviet strategy in Asia, than the emergence of a new Russian strategy, which only started to reveal itself later on the basis of the comprehension in Moscow of the positive and negative experiences of 1992–95.

Overall, the first Yeltsin presidential term cannot be considered a success for Russia's Asian strategic thinking. The region was neglected. China policy emerged slowly. Japan policy did not work. Initial plans for the Korean peninsula left Russia with little influence. The retreat from South Asia and Southeast Asia only started to be reversed late in the period. Only faint outlines had emerged by 1995 of a new course that would gradually take root in Yeltsin's second term.

Notes

1. Japan was a member of the G-7 grouping.
2. Andrei Kozyrev, *Preobrazhenie* (Moscow: Mezhdunarodnye otnosheniia, 1995).
3. Etap za globalnym. *Natsional'nye interesy i vneshnepoliticheskoe soznanie rossiiskoi elity* (Moscow: Russian Science Foundation, 1993), p. 106.
4. Yevgeny Primakov, *Gody v bol'shoi politike* (Moscow: Sovershenno sekretno, 1999), pp. 207–16.
5. This institutionalized way of thinking about the need to identify "threats" still permeates parts of the leadership and the public in the United States, where the "China threat" now colors the perceptions of many strategic thinkers in the defense and intelligence communities.
6. Tatiana Shakleina, ed., *Vneshnaia politika i bezopasnost' sovremennoi Rossii, 1991–1998* (Moscow: MONF, 1999), pp. 18–20, 75–79.
7. The turning point in late 1993 was marked by the resignation of Georgy Kunadze, Russia's Deputy Minister of Foreign Affairs, who had sought to be the architect of a breakthrough in Russo-Japanese relations and became the target of criticism for being too conciliatory.
8. See for example, the autobiography of Sakhalin Governor Valentin Fedorov. Fedorov threatened to separate the Far East from Russia on more than one occasion. Fedorov's actual title was the Chairman of the Executive Committee of the Sakhalin Oblast Soviet. He began calling himself the "Governor of Sakhalin" and the self-styled moniker stuck. See, V. P. Fedorov, *Inostrantsy i my* (Moscow: MP Russkoe Pole, 1992).
9. Viktor Larin, *Kitai i Dal'nii Vostok Rossii v pervoi polovine 90-kh godov: Problemy regional'nogo vzaimodeistviia* (Vladivostok: Dal'nauka, 1998), pp. 51–54.

10. Sergei Golunov and Leonid Vardomsky, eds, *Prozrachnye granitsy: Bezopasnost' i transgranichnoe sotrudnichestvo v poiase novykh pogranichnykh territorii Rossii* (Moscow: NOFMO, 2002), pp. 406–88.

11. Galina Vitkovskaya and Sergei Panarin, eds, *Migratsiia i bezopasnost' v Rossii* (Moscow: Interdialekt, 2000), pp. 93–107.

12. Viktor Larin, "Kitaiskaia migratsiia na Dal'nem Vostoke," in Viktor Diatlov, ed., *Most cherez Amur: vneshnie migratsii i migranty v Sibiri i na Dal'nem Vostoke* (Irkutsk: Natalis, 2004), p. 111.

13. Boris Tkachenko, *Problemy effektivnosti vneshnei politiki Rossii na Dal'nem Vostoke* (Vladivostok: DVGU, 1996).

14. Viktor Diatlov, *Sovremennye torgovle menshinstva: faktor stabil'nosti ili konflikta?* (Irkutsk: Natalis, 2000), pp. 114–40.

15. Mikhail Titarenko, *Rossia: Bezopasnost' cherez sotrudnichestvo: Vostochnoaziatskii vektor* (Moscow: Pamiatniki istoricheskoi mysli, 1999), p. 258.

16. Alexei Bogaturov, *Velikiie derzhavy na Tikhom okeane: Istoriia i teoriia mezhdunarodnykh otnoshenii v Vostochnoi Azii posle Vtoroi Mirovoi Voiny. 1945–1995* (Moscow: Siuita, 1997), pp. 286–90.

17. Vilya Gel'bras, *Kitaiskaia real'nost' Rossii* (Moscow: Muravei, 2001), Ch. 2.

18. Vadim Ramzes, ed., *Znakom'tes–Iaponiia: K vizitu Yeltsyna* (Moscow: Vostochnaia literatura, 1992).

19. Mikhail Narinsky, ed., *Vneshnaia politika Rossiiskoi Federatsii, 1992–1999* (Moscow: Rosspen, 2000), p. 259.

20. Dmitrii Petrov, ed., *Iaponiia i mirovoe soobshchestvo: sotsial'no-psikhologicheskie aspekty internatsionalizatsii* (Moscow: Tsentr po izucheniiu Iaponii, 1994).

21. Anatolii Torkunov, ed., *Istoriia Korei: Novoe prochtenie* (Moscow: Rosspen, 2003), pp. 394–95.

22. Anatolii Torkunov, ed., *Sovremennye mezhdunarodnye otnosheniia* (Moscow: Rosspen, 2000), p. 373.

23. N. Bektemirova and V. Dol'nikova, eds, *Indokitai: politika, ekonomika 1990-e gody* (Moscow: Institut stran Azii i Afriki, 1999), pp. 64–74.

24. Ibid., p. 76.

25. Nikolai Maletin and Iurii Raikov, "ASEAN i problemy bezopasnosti v Aziatsko-Tikhookeanskom regione," in *Vostok i Zapad: regional'nye podsistemy i regional'nye problemy mezhdunarodnykh otnoshenii* (Moscow: Rosspen, 2002), p. 483.

26. Viacheslav Belokrinitskii, "Mezhdunarodnye otnosheniia v Iuzhnoi Azii," in Anatolii Torkunov, ed., *Sovremennye mezhdunarodnye otnosheniia i mirovaia politika* (Moscow: Prosveshchenie, 2004), p. 635.

CHAPTER 4

Russian Strategic Thinking toward Asia, 1996–99

Kazuhiko Togo

The period under analysis, the second Yeltsin presidency, lies between Yeltsin's first term in office and the rise of Putin. The first presidency was filled with a series of political explosions and economic turmoil, but in the four years from 1992 to 1995, President Yeltsin succeeded in establishing the major direction of Russian policy. Reform policies aiming to create a market-based economy and election-based political structure became the two pillars. Hyperinflation following the shock therapy in 1992 was gradually replaced by macroeconomic management of the economy. Still fragile and with a lot of flaws and confusion, Russia began to move toward a market-based economy. Yeltsin's victory in the 1996 presidential election confirmed the establishment of a nascent democracy, based on an electoral system. In the area of foreign relations, the initial policy to identify Russian interests with those of the West in 1992 was soon replaced by a new direction, emphasizing national interests and cooperation with the Commonwealth of Independent States (CIS). A shift from Atlanticism to Eurasianism began to take place. In this context, greater attention toward the East, particularly China emerged.

Through his second presidency, Yeltsin consolidated all of these directions. Reform policy survived the 1998 financial crisis, and the economy moved toward greater stability. Russian foreign policy became more articulate in pursuit of national interests. Foreign Minister Yevgeny Primakov's formulation of multipolarity, which may best represent Russian strategic thinking of this period, incorporated Russian national interests in dealing with both the West and the East, but on balance, moved Russia a little toward cooperation with the East. In retrospect, it may be viewed as inheriting and refocusing the Eurasianism that took shape during Yeltsin's first presidency. Russian East Asian policy toward China, Japan, Korea, and Southeast Asia developed in this context. In its entirety, Russia's position toward East Asia became better attuned to Russian national interests, better coordinated to the overall foreign policy and, thus, more strategic.

Before analysing the concrete aspects of Russian East Asian policy, some basic analysis is required to give greater clarity to the Russian position in terms of its geopolitics, politico-economic goals, and search for identity. In this context, I first analyze the following three issues: the eastward expansion of NATO from around 1995 through 1997, which became the fundamental turning point in geopolitics surrounding Russia; the implementation of economic policy, including the financial crisis in 1998 and Russia's relations with the IMF; and the notion of multipolarity developed under Primakov, probably the most important concept related to the issue of Russian identity. After the analysis of major aspects of Russian strategic thinking toward East Asia, that is, China, Japan, Korea, and Southeast Asia, a short conclusion provides a bridge between Yeltsin's presidency and the Putin era. In the analysis of each issue we examine the three factors—geopolitics, economic interests, and identity.

These three factors are construed as three pillars that form the contemporary theory of international relations: realism, liberalism, and constructivism. Thus, this chapter is an effort to develop an eclectic analysis of international relations on Russia, based on all three pillars of the field. It may, therefore, be viewed as a trial for writing a chapter on Russia, within the period of the second half of the 1990s, missing in recent volumes on security in East Asia.[1]

Three Fundamentals during Yeltsin's Second Presidency

NATO's Eastward Expansion

Russia had two fundamental security objectives on its agenda in the first years after its formation in 1991: how to reestablish a power balance with the United States, in particular, from the point of view of a nuclear superpower; and how to reestablish a power balance in Europe after the unification of Germany. The first agenda was initially solved by the unification of nuclear arsenals from the CIS to Russia and the START II agreement of 1993, but the second issue was left unresolved in Yeltsin's first term especially due to NATO's eastward expansion.

In the process of the unification of Germany, leaders of the West gave verbal indication, if not assurance, that NATO would not expand eastward.[2] However, after the demise of the Soviet Union, the ardent desire of East European countries to join NATO became apparent. This led to the proposal in January 1994 to conclude the Partnership for Peace (PFP) agreement with former Warsaw Pact countries, including Russia. Russia accepted the PFP, and concluded the framework agreement in June 1994 and the bilateral agreement in May 1995. But the reality of the expansion of NATO did not end there. In September 1995, NATO adopted its Basic Principle for accepting the East European countries as members.[3] This entire move took place while Russia was preoccupied with overcoming its internal economic and social difficulties. The inevitability of the eastward expansion of NATO, which was the symbol of the anti-Soviet military structure from the Cold War, deeply wounded the psychology of intellectuals and opinion leaders in Russia. In the autumn of 1995, those critical views against NATO's eastward expansion erupted throughout Russia. Media analysis and my own interviews at that time in Moscow strongly underlined that impression.[4]

Primakov's autobiography describes well the critical situation that the Russian leadership faced at the beginning of 1996, when he became the foreign minister. By then, NATO's determination to include at least some of the former East European countries became irrevocable. The issue began to be framed in terms of "how" and not "whether" it would occur. Russia had three options: "(1) to oppose the expansion of NATO and give up any relations with it; (2) to accept the expansion of NATO and make no attempt to influence it; and (3) to maintain [Russia's] opposition to the expansion of NATO and at the same time to focus on influencing the expansion process."[5] Russia chose the third one. Painful negotiations continued for another full year. After Yeltsin returned to the political leadership in the spring of 1997 following his illness, a Russo-U.S. agreement in March made a breakthrough and the Russia-NATO agreement was signed in Paris in May.[6] This paved the way to the Madrid NATO summit on July 8–9, which accepted Poland, Hungary, and the Czech Republic, as the first countries to become members of this organization.

If this had to be accepted as a "done deal," there was still no way of avoiding fundamental repercussions in Russian geopolitical thinking. First, this agreement put an end to the prospect of a geopolitical power balance, which Russians had seen emerging in the trans-Atlantic theater after the demise of the Soviet Union. A gradual path of NATO expansion toward the east under the conditions prescribed in the NATO-Russia May agreement closed the matter and stabilized the situation.

Second, this stabilization was not done to Russia's liking. Illusionary hopes of closing the issue based on the 1994 PFP agreement, or of creating a juridical framework for limiting military structures in the countries newly joining failed. Russia accepted the emerging reality with bitterness. Third, the short interval that emerged after the resolution of this issue and the upsurge in Russia's bitterness directed to the West left an opening for a psychological shift toward the East. As was already indicated in my interviews with Russian intellectuals in the fall of 1995 (see note 4), this shift from the West to the East became an underlying theme governing Russian foreign policy during Yeltsin's second presidency.

The stabilization of Russian security in its European context was greatly underpinned by the conclusion of the Contract on the Belarus and Russian Union in April and the settlement of Crimea and Sevastopol with Ukraine in May. Whereas the former was a step further toward the reunification of the two countries,[7] the latter was a difficult and bitter acquiescence to the reality that Crimea and Sevastopol belong to Ukraine, in exchange for withholding a substantial part of the command of the Black Sea fleet by Russia.

Russia's fear and anger against NATO's eastward expansion was further fueled by NATO's bombardment of Yugoslavia in the spring of 1999. But, as in the case of NATO's eastward expansion, Russian opposition did not prevent cooperation with NATO in order to bring about an early settlement.[8]

Economic Issues and the Impact of the Financial Crisis

Yeltsin's economic policy during his first term saw gradual success in curbing inflation, but it was very difficult to stabilize the budget by increasing tax revenues and restricting budgetary expenditures and to enhance production efficiency in concrete industrial sectors. In his second term, an unexpected financial crisis overwhelmed the Russian economy in the spring–summer of 1998. A worldwide decrease in energy demand due to the Asian financial crisis starting from 1997 lowered energy prices and threatened Russia's longstanding trade surplus. In May, overseas investors began to withdraw their investments, resulting in the triple crisis of currency, stocks, and securities. After the IMF, the World Bank and Japan agreed, in principle, to supply $22.6 billion of financial assistance by the end of 1999, in August, the second financial crisis erupted and on August 17 the ruble was substantially devaluated. The economic crisis provoked a political crisis;[9] Russia faced its most serious socioeconomic situation since the parliamentary revolt in October 1993. But in September, political forces across the spectrum coalesced in approving Primakov as the new prime minister. With political confidence regained, the economic crisis was also put under control, as a devalued ruble began to help Russian production, and rising oil prices, before long, brought a great sigh of relief.[10]

Through this process of overcoming one of the most serious crises in the 1990s, Russia learned several lessons. First, at the time of the crisis the IMF/World Bank played no small role in ensuring confidence through its $22.6 billion declared assistance. At the same time, the difficulty entailed in the conditionality negotiations that followed from September and the improving economic situation through rising oil prices gradually pulled Russia away from IMF/World Bank lending, and this tendency became more apparent in the next presidency. Second, from the perspective of sound industrial production, Foreign Direct Investment (FDI) counted in Russia, but all investors came from the West (see table 4.1). Thus, the West continued to be important for Russia, more so from the point of view of FDI than the loans from the IMF/World Bank or elsewhere.

Third, in this context, production of weapons from the traditional military-industrial complex added weight to maintain Russia's industrial capacity, while energy production had to remain as the most reliable source of dollar income, especially in the period of rising energy prices. These two export items had by nature something more than purely economic significance; they had strategic value for both the exporter and the importer.

Table 4.1 Cumulative Foreign Direct Investment to Russia (as of March 2002)[11]

Total	34,436	100 (%)
Germany	6,311	18.3
United States	5,306	15.4
Cyprus	4,544	13.2
United Kingdom	3,659	10.6
France	3,320	9.7
Netherlands	2,333	6.8
Italy	1,457	4.2
Switzerland	767	2.2
Japan	647	1.9
Austria	614	1.8
Others	5,478	15.9

Multipolar Diplomacy

The change from a policy friendly toward the West to one emphasizing national interests, the CIS, and the East involved a wide range of debates deeply rooted among Russian intellectuals and policymakers. It touched upon not only the concrete directions of external relations, but also the fundamental value of what Russia should be, that is the question of Russian identity. Sharing values with the West, sometimes called Atlanticism, was never a dominant school of Russian thought except for the short "period of euphoria" in 1992,[12] but it has always stayed an essential part of Russian thinking since then, either as one of many important factors to take into consideration among the moderate intellectuals, or as an object of strong criticism among staunchly conservative thinkers.

Leading political thinkers of *Yabloko* Party, such as Grigorii Yavlinsky,[13] Vladimir Lukin, or Aleksei Arbatov, all underlined Russian national interests while acknowledging the importance of cooperation with the West. Nationalist politicians, such as Ruslan Khasbulatov or Sergei Stankevich, from early 1992 became strong critics of Atlanticism, also emphasizing national interests and the relationship with the CIS countries. Gennadii Zyuganov and Lukyanov[14] became conservative opinion leaders who could be generally called Eurasianists, a way of thinking after the end of the cold war analyzed by James Billington.[15]

During the second presidency, Yeltsin kept his position as the banner bearer for democracy and a reform economy but also revealed himself as an autocratic leader bent on concentrating power in the hands of himself, his family, and surrounding oligarchs. In the constitutional structure of the new Russia, foreign policy was the prerogative of the president. The most active policy initiative by the Russian government during this period was, therefore, taken in a short period starting from the spring of 1997 until the summer of 1998, when Yeltsin's health was in relatively good shape. Nevertheless, taking the four years of Yeltsin's second term as a whole, it was probably Primakov's views of multipolarity that became the basis of consensus in garnering support for Russian foreign policy and bridging the gap with Russian internal debates on identity.

Soon after Primakov was appointed foreign minister, he emphasized "the necessity of improving relations with the CIS, while acknowledging the importance of improving relations with the West, and stressed that Russian foreign policy should become multi-directional."[16] In his autobiography, Primakov outlined his thinking that "an equal partnership with everyone" should be sought.[17] He further elaborated this thinking in an interview with the author in 2005: "Multipolarity is the description of a state of power. It starts with an objective analysis. It does not aim to create an alliance nor does it intend to split the world into blocs. Rather it aims to enhance cooperation among the multipolar actors. Cooperation is envisaged in a complex and divergent manner, but it is not meant to oppose a third party. Given the power which Russia and China possess, cooperation with China was sought as a natural development in the world of multipolarity, but a close Russia–China relationship was not aimed against a third party. By strengthening cooperation among Russia–China–India,[18] each country could enhance its position in the world, but that cooperation was not directed against any fourth party."[19]

Giving Russia a stable but unexaggerated position of "great power" (derzhava) or a "pole" in global politics underpinned Russia's policy to resolve contentious issues with Ukraine or to overcome the bitterness of the enlargement of NATO. It served as a basis for casting efforts to maintain reasonable relations with the West, while creating another basis for developing relations with the East. From the point of view of global geopolitics, given the fact that the United States was the singular unipolar power on all fronts of international relations and was prepared to enforce its will, with which Russia did not necessarily agree, the notion of multipolarity began to be interpreted as a basis for maintaining an autonomous and independent, if not antagonistic, position vis-à-vis the United States. But the notion of multipolarity also became Russia's response to the quest for its identity, a perpetual soul-searching by Russian intellectuals and opinion leaders. It responded reasonably well to "the disillusionment that many ordinary Russians feel about their unrequited love affair with the West."[20] Without becoming absorbed with a strand of geographic determinism that was assosiated with Eurasianism, the notion of multipolarity helped Russia to strengthen its relations with Asia and realize a distinct place in post-cold war international relations.[21]

Relations with China

The initial year of Atlanticism did not put China at the forefront of Yeltsin's East Asian policy, but after Japan lost its leading position in September 1992, Yeltsin reinstated China at the center. His visit to Beijing in December 1992 marked that change. The importance that

Russia attached to its China policy is shown in the five bilateral summit meetings which took place in the four years from 1996 to 1999.

Five Summits in Four Years

1. Yeltsin's visit to Beijing in April 1996. Yeltsin's visit was made two months before the election. There were certainly good reasons for him to make this visit a success, but two divergent and mutually contradictory factors created some ambivalence. On the one hand, solid relations with China would benefit the strengthening of Russia's external position, and for those internal political forces who favor an autonomous foreign policy vis-à-vis the West, this success was needed. Several factors stood out: eastward expansion of NATO inevitably drew Russia to seek a partnership in the East, and China was the most likely candidate; progress on border demarcation based on the 1991 eastern-border agreement and 1994 western-border agreement could enhance stability; tangible economic cooperation such as oil and gas cooperation or peaceful use of nuclear energy was always a welcoming factor.

On the other hand, a close rapprochement with China was not in Russia's interest. Yeltsin was trying to portray himself as an accepted member of the world leaders of the G-7, and just a week before his China trip, he hosted a G-8 Summit meeting in Moscow to discuss cooperation in the peaceful use of nuclear energy. Distancing himself sharply from the West was not in his interest; in the election process, Yeltsin was fighting fiercely against Russian communists, whereas China was governed by none other than the Communist Party of China. Closeness with China could arouse confusion in Yeltsin's election campaign. Handling of the border was also tricky: If Russia were perceived to be too concessionary to China, public opinion could be antagonized.

Yeltsin and Primakov carefully orchestrated the visit to meet these two possibly contradictory requirements. First, the key conceptualization which emerged from this visit was "the strategic partnership of mutual coordination of equality, trust and orientation towards the 21st century" promulgated in the "China–Russia Joint Statement." On the way to Beijing, when Primakov briefed the president about the state of preparation of the visit, Yeltsin requested that some politically powerful message be added, and, thus, the expression "the strategic partnership towards the 21st century," which subsequently symbolized the relationship, was proposed by Primakov, accepted by the president, and then by the Chinese side.[22] Second, the notion of multipolarity was clearly included in the Joint Statement with the statement "the tendency in the world toward multi-polarization is heightened"[23] but as a narrative of the international situation rather than as a normative criterion toward which they were striving.

Third, Russian anxiety toward NATO's expansion was expressed only in indirect wording of concern about "bloc politics."[24] Yeltsin had to be satisfied with Jiang Zemin's statement at the joint press conference that Jiang "understands and supports President Yeltsin's position to oppose the eastward expansion of NATO, and the expansion of blocs does not meet the trend of the contemporary world."[25] Fourth, in getting China's support for opposing NATO's eastward expansion, Yeltsin did not spare his support not only to China's Taiwan policy but also to Tibetan policy.[26] China was in dire need of having Russian support of its Taiwan's policy after the Taiwan Straits crisis and the election victory of Lee Teng-hui in Taiwan in March 1996.

Fifth, as for the territorial demarcation, progress was not announced in this visit. It may well be that the progress on demarcation was still too slow to achieve concrete results,[27] but no announcement also well served Yeltsin's pre-election situation. Instead, a visible step was made for four (Russia, Kazakhstan, Kyrgyzstan, and Tajikistan, all of which border China) plus one (China) to meet in Shanghai just after the bilateral summit and agree on a statement about "Confidence-Building in the Military Field in Border Areas." Sixth, fourteen agreements were signed, including on government-to-government cooperation in the energy field, on the peaceful use of nuclear energy, and on the protection of intellectual property. The energy cooperation included an agreement on China's participation in the exploitation of a gas field in Irkutsk.[28] Yeltsin proudly stated in the press conference that the two countries intend to bring the amount of trade to $20 billion by 2000 from $5.5 billion in 1995.[29]

2. Jiang Zemin's visit to Moscow in April 1997. From the Russian perspective, Jiang Zemin's return visit in April 1997 was indeed made in a timely manner. Yeltsin had just recovered from a lingering illness after his reelection in July 1996. He had just finished the Helsinki meeting with President Clinton to settle the NATO expansion that left a bitter aftertaste. Negotiations on Crimea with Ukraine were also moving ahead with bitterness. Yeltsin was in a position to embrace a strategic partner in the East, more so than a year ago, without the inhibitions of pre-election constraints. Another factor that encouraged Russia–China relations was the impact of rising tensions between China and Taiwan over the previous year. This could have made Russian arms sales more attractive to China. Against that background, the two leaders adopted a "Joint

Statement between the PRC and the Russian Federation on Multi-Polarization of the World and Establishment of a New International Order."

First, on the conceptual level, the strategic partnership between the two countries was elevated a step higher: on NATO's eastward expansion, though indirect, a more straightforward expression was included in the joint statement: "the two countries express their concern on the enlargement and strengthening of military blocs. Such a tendency creates a threat to the security of certain countries and may result in heightening regional and global tension."[30] On multipolarity, not only was it emphasized in the title of the joint statement but it was expressed with a normative expression: "the two countries will enhance multi-polarization and a new international order of the world, based on the spirit of partnership."[31]

Second, cooperation among the Shanghai Five developed further by reaching an agreement to withdraw forces which exceed 13,400 within 100 km of their respective borders.[32] Third, after the Cross-Strait tensions in March 1996, Russia succeeded in agreeing with China to sell two missile-launching destroyers of a new type, four kilo-class submarines, and a missile defense system. During Jiang Zemin's visit, the ministers of defense of the two countries held talks, as a result of which further arms sale agreements were reportedly reached.[33] Vladimir Kumachev, deputy director of the Institute of International Security and Strategic Research, argues that "Russia is clearly benefiting from the revitalization of its military-industrial complex, which is the key factor for the restoration of production capacity. Since the standard of China's military capabilities is not that advanced, Russian weapons exports centered on defense capabilities would not harm Russian national interests in the coming decades."[34] Despite certain worries among long-term thinkers about the impact of a rising China, economic necessity must have dictated Russia's arms exports to China.

3. Yeltsin's visit to Beijing in November 1997. Only a half year later, Yeltsin's return visit in November was conducted in a very different international environment than April, and it had consequences on the outcome of the visit. Major decisions on the eastward expansion of NATO were already made. Prime Minister Hashimoto became conspicuously active in improving relations with Russia in his Krasnoyarsk meeting with Yeltsin. Jiang Zemin had just finished his first visit to the United States.

First, in this situation, the "China–Russia Joint Statement" had different language than the two previous ones. Multipolarity was reconfirmed, but more so in emphasizing the positive results achieved from this concept: "Active deeds by Russia and China toward the construction of a multipolarized world are gaining support by the international community."[35] This statement was underpinned by a unique judgment that "the two countries are satisfied with the positive role played by China, Russia, the United States and Japan through recent contacts of their leaders."[36] Cooperation among the four countries, where the United States is not playing a unipolar role, probably looked like a manifestation of the multipolar world that had been advocated already for nearly two years by the two countries.

Second, another factor incorporated in the joint statement was a "solemn declaration" that all demarcation related to the eastern border was achieved. Given the difficulty involved in this demarcation process based on the May 1991 agreement,[37] particularly in the three areas around Lake Khanka, Ussuriisk, and Lake Khasan, the two leaders had good reasons to be more confident on the achievement made in their bilateral relations.[38]

Third, in economic cooperation, the joint statement included a clear reference that military-technology cooperation is an important area for bilateral cooperation and that this cooperation is not directed against a third country.[39] A Memorandum on the Natural Gas Pipeline from the Eastern Siberia Area to China was concluded. Although many substantial decisions would be needed before actual implementation,[40] it was another concrete step for energy cooperation between the two countries.

4. Jiang Zemin's visit to Moscow in November 1998. The international situation affecting Russia a year later could be characterized by the financial crisis during the year 1998, Primakov's appointment as prime minister to overcome the political and economic crisis, and Yeltsin's considerably weakened health at the time of the visit of Jiang.[41] Thus, the agreed joint statement "China–Russia Relations at the Turn of the Century" reconfirmed only that "the development of international relations toward multipolarization is helping the creation of a new world order." Another statement declared that the demarcation of the 54 km Russia–China western border was completed.[42]

5. Yeltsin's visit to Beijing in December 1999. The impact of events in 1999 from the Russian point of view was profound. There were at least three factors that brought Russian interests colliding with those of the United States and NATO. In all of these factors, Russia found an ideal partner in China. First, expansion of NATO was now substantiated by NATO bombardment of Kosovo and an open attack against Yugoslavia under the name of "humanitarian intervention." China, to whom

NATO had been a relatively remote issue, came to agree wholeheartedly with the Russian position after the U.S. bombardment of the Chinese embassy. Second, the new U.S. initiative on missile defense and the possibility of backing away from the ABM treaty created strategic anxiety in Russia. The possibility of extending the Theatre Missile Defense (TMD) to Taiwan infuriated China, which became a determined ally in opposing the MD initiatives put forward by the outgoing Clinton administration. Third, new tension, which emerged in and around Chechnya from the fall of 1999, became the most important domestic issue for Yeltsin and his new Prime Minister Putin. Strong criticism from the West based on "human rights" angered and isolated the Russian leadership. China, which shared a common concern in the Xinjiang Muslim separatism, was the first country to support Russia on the basis that this issue was an "internal matter," and in return, China was keen to welcome Russian support for its position on Taiwan as an "internal matter."

Yeltsin's health was not at its best, and retrospectively, he had only three weeks before announcing his resignation. Nevertheless, Yeltsin made his last visit to Beijing on December 9–10, and the joint statement adopted was unambiguous in emphasizing the convergence of interests between the two countries in opposing the way the United States was trying to shape the world.[43] The harshness of the language of the joint statement leaves us to wonder who the real initiator was on the Russian side in taking this direction. Some sense of balance seen in Primakov's approach seems to be lacking. Was it really instigated by the president? Usually the wording of these statements is not prepared at the presidential level. Was it Prime Minister Putin's suggestion? It is unlikely that he would lead in a foreign policy matter that, in principle, did not belong to his jurisdiction. Was it Foreign Minister Ivanov and others in the Ministry of Foreign Affairs? It is hard to tell.

At any rate, out of the ten points put forward, seven were a reconfirmation of the convergence of interests against the U.S. position, although not addressed directly by name: first, a call for all nations to set up a multipolar world; second, an urgent plea to maintain the ABM treaty and Russian support of China's position of not including Taiwan in any TMD system; third, an indirect accusation against NATO activities in the name of "reinforcing and expanding military blocs—using the concepts of human rights and humanitarian intervention"; fourth, a plea to safeguard the authoritative role of the United Nations; ninth on the list, a plea to fully respect the sovereignty and territorial integrity of Yugoslavia and the lawful rights of all nations in the Kosovo region; tenth, Russia's reaffirmation of its support for China's Taiwan policy and

China's reaffirmation that Chechnya is an internal matter, acknowledged by mutual satisfaction"; and sixth on the list, a common fight against "international terrorism, religious extremism, ethnic separatism, and trans-national criminal activities."[44] Other points included in the statement were resolution of the Iraqi issue in accordance with UN resolutions (eighth); a self-congratulating appraisal on the Shanghai Five development process (seventh); and the importance of WTO accession both for China and Russia (fifth).[45] The joint statement concluded with the usual announcement that "Such coordination between the two countries in international affairs is not targeted at any third nation." As if to symbolize the closeness of bilateral relations, two protocols to finalize the demarcation on the eastern and western borders as well as an agreement on joint economic use of border islands were signed.[46]

Russian Strategic Thinking toward China

1. Geopolitics. Russian policy toward China seems to be primarily guided by the short-to-medium term geopolitical interests during this period. It was a continuation of the policy that had already been established during Yeltsin's first term, but it took much clearer shape during this term. Such hard factors as NATO's eastward expansion, NATO's bombardment of Kosovo based on the concept of "humanitarian intervention," and a fear of nuclear vulnerability caused by U.S. missile defense initiatives alienated Russia and led it to seek a partner in the East, and China was there fully meeting Russian interests. The commonality of democratic values as a leading ideology did not last anyway more than a year after the demise of the Soviet Union, and it was again severely challenged when Chechnya became a focus of international attention at the end of the 1990s. As was shown in the sharp contrast between the Russian approaches to the 1998 and 1999 summits, in all these moves, it was a realist instinct and calculation of the power balance that played a leading role in determining Russian policy.

The same realist thinking brought constraint not to let Russia drift excessively toward the East. The United States was a real unipolar power and, whether you agree or not, it was not a country with which to fight at all cost. Europe was becoming a more proactive pole in international politics, and Russia had no reason not to capitalize on it. In the long-term perspective, Russia, at least some opinion leaders and policymakers, remained cautious in resorting exclusively to the strategic partnership with China whenever its relations with the West were strained. Li Jingjie (see note 21) explains Chinese thinking about why this cautious attitude remains influential among Russian intellectuals: "(1) a fundamental fear in facing the rise of China, which contrasts to the decline of Russia; (2) ever expanding Chinese population in contrast to the declining Russian population and the resulting demographic imbalance; (3) abundant energy resources, which in turn create a fear that Russia might just turn into an energy supplier; (4) a long-term fear that China might turn North after the resolution of the Taiwan issue."

2. The role of economics. Economic relations in the purest sense of the word, that is, trade and investment, in reality did not figure much in Russia–China relations in this period. Notwithstanding Yeltsin's plea to bring the total amount of trade to $20 billion, trade figures in the four years did not change much (see table 4.2). An impressive amount of negotiations from prime ministers to officials and down to the level of companies took place, but they produced few real changes in economic relations.[47] Gilbert Rozman describes how historic Russian anxieties and bureaucratic mentality nurtured in the Soviet system prevented flourishing border trade and close economic ties with China in the Far East. At the same time, lack of competitiveness prevented Russia from emerging victorious in competition for the Chinese market, for example, selling Russian turbines for the Three Gorges hydroelectric project or civilian aircraft.[48] However, two areas were different: arms transfers and energy supplies. They were the two areas where China needed stable sources to consolidate its strategic position, something more than just fulfilling market-based economic necessities.

"During the 1990's, China has officially purchased roughly $1 billion of Russian weaponry and military technology per year."[50] The purchase of the first two "Type 956E" *Sovremennyi*-class destroyers in 1997 together with its weapons packages of the SS-N-22 *Sunburn* and SS-N-26 *Yakurt* anti-ship missiles was considered to be of particular importance. So was the purchase of four Kilo-class diesel-electric submarines during the 1990s.[51] Why was Russia selling these to China? The majority view is that economic necessity for the military-industrial complex prevailed above everything. "The bedrock reality is that Russian defense firms

Table 4.2 Russia–China Trade $billion (Russian Statistics)[49]

	1996	1997	1998	1999
Total	5.7	5.3	4.4	4.4
%	4.3	3.8	3.8	4.3
Exports	4.7	4.0	3.2	5.2
Imports	1.0	1.3	1.2	0.9

needed Chinese business in order to survive."[52] Rozman explains that the reason why Nazdratenko, the governor of Primorskii krai, abruptly softened his tone criticizing the border agreement with China completed at the end of 1997 could be largely associated with the production of helicopters in his krai to be exported to China, starting in 1999.[53] Strategically, selling weapons has contradictory implications: from a short-to-medium term perspective, the transfer of weapons certainly brings much closer security and business ties with one's counterpart. But from a long-term perspective, a militarily strengthened China may become a threatening factor for Russia. In the latter half of the 1990s, economic necessity along with the short-to-medium term strategic perspective took the lead in Russian policymaking.

The huge potential of Russian energy sources, in particular gas and oil, is a truism, so is the rapidly growing energy needs in China with its rising economy. From the Russian perspective, the need to attract massive investment to exploit and then to sell its energy resources comes from dire economic necessity, but once direct energy cooperation is established, it can result not only in geoeconomic but also in geopolitical consequences. Whatever the immediate motive, proposals examined include: Kovykta gas near Irkutsk, highlighted in 1996 and 1998 Russia–China summits, and in February 1999 in Zhu Rongji's visit to Moscow,[54] with an annual production of 20 billion m^3 requiring an estimated $10 billion in investment for exploration and pipeline construction;[55] an East-West gas pipeline from Western Siberia through Xinjiang to Shanghai; a direct oil pipeline from Angarsk in eastern Siberia to Daqing; hydroelectric stations in Siberia which may supply China with 15–18 billion kW of electricity annually; and construction of six nuclear reactors, helped by Russia, which may generate up to 1.5 trillion kW.[56]

3. *Finding a common basis in the concept of multipolarity.* The concepts of multipolarity and strategic partnership governed the five Russo-Chinese summits from 1996 and 1999. In underpinning the commonality of geopolitical interests and neutralizing differences between the two countries, these concepts worked well. Russia found a stronger partnership with China, and succeeded in having a more stable place in dealing with all international issues. But did it solve the question of identity? No, it did not. As Li Jingjie stated "Russia will stay Russia, neither the West nor the East" (see note 21). But then, if neither the West nor the East, what is Russia, where does Russia belong? It is often said to be a "pole," but what kind of a pole? The answer is not clear. The concept of multipolarity fulfilled an important role in the foreign policy arena, giving Russia a stable position to bridge from Yeltsin's first term to the rise

of Putin. But the fundamental question of Russian identity was not answered and Russia continues to tread a painful path in search of itself.

Relations with Japan

In the short-lived months after the demise of the Soviet Union in 1992, when Russian foreign policy was directed primarily toward the West, Japan occupied the conductor seat in Russian policy toward the East. But after the failure in reaching a breakthrough that resulted in Yeltsin's cancellation of his September 1992 visit, relations stagnated for four years.[57] During his second term, when Yeltsin was at the height of his leadership in the autumn of 1997, he displayed initiative in his policy toward Japan that animated the relationship with an unforeseen momentum until the spring of 1998. The period ends with declining momentum, but enough to be rekindled in the first year of Putin's presidency.

Four Years in Transition

1. Before the Krasnoyarsk summit (January 1996–November 1997). For the Russian leadership the first half of 1996 before the election was a preparatory period for future relations with Japan. Yeltsin met for the first time with Hashimoto, a newly elected prime minister in January 1996, at the Nuclear summit in April. Hashimoto's chemistry was a good match for the president. Primakov, who was also appointed as foreign minister in January 1996, made a small overture in his early press conference to defer the territorial issue to future generations, but Japanese leaders immediately indicated that it was not in Japan's interest. The first round of the government-to-government committee on trade and economics was held between Foreign Minister Ikeda and First-deputy Prime Minister Soskovets in March. Japan's decisions to send the head of the Defence Agency in April (for the first time in history) and a Maritime Self-Defense escort vessel *Kurama* to Vladivostok in July (after an interval of seventy-one years) were warmly welcomed by Russia.

Foreign Minister Primakov visited Japan in November 1996 when Yeltsin was still on leave to recover from his heart operation. The visit was conducted very much at Primakov's pace. In line with his view of multipolarity, he emphasized the importance of enhancing relations with Japan. He explicitly withdrew his suggestion to defer the territorial issue to the next generation, and he agreed on the political importance of concluding a fishery agreement around the four islands without harming the legal position of the two sides.[58] He also proposed consideration of further economic cooperation on the disputed four islands without harming the legal position of the two sides. It was an approach based on realism and step-by-step progress in bilateral relations. The Japanese side reacted positively.

Yeltsin came back to the commanding position in the Russian government in March 1997. While preoccupied with other vital issues, in particular NATO's eastward expansion, relations with Japan began to acquire certain momentum. The Russian minister of defense's visit to Japan, as well as the ministerial talks on trade and economics, proceeded smoothly. The Russian side appreciated Hashimoto's basic consent to include Russia as a member of G-8. The bilateral meeting between the two leaders at the fringe of the Denver G-8 summit confirmed the warm personal relations between the two leaders. New cooperation to expand Japanese investment to Russia was highlighted by Hashimoto. Hashimoto's proposal to hold an informal summit in the Far East to strengthen confidence building, later called a no-necktie meeting, was warmly received by Yeltsin.

Prime Minister Hashimoto's speech on July 24, 1997 at a meeting of Japanese businessmen, the Japan Association of Corporate Executives Keizai Doyukai, included messages which Russian opinion leaders have long awaited: a geopolitical vision that Japan was prepared to move to a "Eurasian policy from the Pacific Ocean" after the conclusion of "the Eurasian policy from the Atlantic Ocean" by the formation of an expanded NATO; acknowledgement that the weakest link which needs to be strengthened among the four countries (Japan, Russia, China, and the United States) was Japan–Russia; warm appreciation of Russia's reform efforts and Hashimoto's personal message of friendship toward Yeltsin; readiness to expand the relationship, including energy cooperation; and resolution of the territorial issue based on the principles of trust, mutual interest, and a long-term perspective.

The dynamic worldview and the nondogmatic approach to the territorial issue were heartening to many Russian policymakers and opinion leaders.[59] G.B. Karasin, deputy foreign minister for Asia, told Tamba, deputy foreign minister for political affairs that "what Hashimoto said in the speech was so important that it compares to the Tokyo Declaration of 1993; it is an excellent speech with foresight toward the future. Russia must send a signal too." In fact, on July 29, Russia proposed to hold a no-necktie meeting at Lake Baikal, and in August Krasnoyarsk was proposed instead.[60] Wada Haruki cites Kistanov's article in *Nezavisimaia gazeta* on October 30, 1997 in explaining how Russian intellectuals became fascinated with Hashimoto's turn toward Asia: "Hashimoto's

July thesis has a historic character and signifies Japan's turn to Russia. But the underlying implication of this policy change is that it is a variation of Japan's policy to 're-enter Asia' even at the expense of keeping some distance with the United States."[61]

2. *From the Krasnoyarsk summit to the Kawana summit (November 1997–April 1998).* When the two leaders met on the afternoon of November 1, 1997 in a boat along the River Yenisei at Krasnoyarsk, Yeltsin concentrated on the territorial issue and emphasized that he was fully aware of the nature of the Kurile issue, knew the Tokyo Declaration almost by heart, and proposed a time limit, namely the year 2000, to be set for the resolution of this issue. It was a stunning proposal that no one in the Japanese delegation expected to hear, neither Hashimoto nor Tamba.[62] Why did Yeltsin make this proposal? By all accounts, Yeltsin's personal style of running politics played an important role. The proposal was made without any consultation with his supporting staff. It was meant to display a historic initiative, to make a breakthrough on an issue that had been left unresolved for more than a half century. But personality alone does not explain this. Objective conditions have to be taken into account as well: First, Russian geopolitics were shifting from the West to the East. The geopolitical vacuum created after NATO's eastward expansion left room not only for China but also for Japan. Second, Japan's economic power, although it was facing real difficulty in the 1990s after the end of the bubble economy, still had allure. Its emphasis on investment and energy must have appealed to the Russian leadership. In fact, in Krasnoyarsk Yeltsin asked Hashimoto to consider financial assistance of $3–4 billion.[63] Third, Russian military officers were noticeably relaxed on Japan's security danger. In his May visit to Japan, Defense Minister I.N. Rodionov, at a briefing on Japan–U.S. defense guidelines, stated that "Russia is not concerned about close US–Japan relations and instead welcomes them."[64] And fourth, Russia must have felt that all policy initiatives displayed by Hashimoto and his team, symbolized in the July speech, presented a new approach and an opportunity for Russia to open a qualitatively new relationship with Japan.

In fact, Krasnoyarsk did not disillusion Yeltsin. Hashimoto presented a new proposal to enhance economic cooperation called the Hashimoto–Yeltsin plan.[65] Just as Yeltsin's proposal to resolve the territorial issue was a surprise for the Japanese leadership, the Hashimoto–Yeltsin plan was a surprise for Russia. But it was a pleasant surprise, and afterwards the Russian side began accentuating the achievement at Krasnoyarsk in the economic arena.[66]

After Krasnoyarsk, initiatives to advance the relationship across a broad spectrum were taken almost exclusively by the Japanese side. Three examples should suffice: first, Hashimoto and Tamba made an unprecedented effort to invite Russia as a member of APEC at the Vancouver APEC summit and Russia successfully became a member from the Kuala Lumpur summit in 1998[67]; second, in answering Yeltsin's request, Japan decided in February 1998 to make available $1.5 billion of financial assistance jointly with the World Bank, the first and the last "un-tied" financial assistance made by Japan[68]; third, Japan gave careful consideration and made the first conciliatory proposal on the territorial issue on the basis of which it thought to conclude a peace treaty within the designated time frame.

In contrast, after the Krasnoyarsk proposal to conclude the peace treaty by 2000, Russia basically stuck to its position. Primakov was fast to visit Japan in November to assure that the Russian Ministry of Foreign Affairs was in line with the president, but no one from the Russian side ventured to propose a solution on the islands at Kawana on April 18–19, 1998, where the second no-necktie meeting took place. In fact, the proposal made was an extension of Primakov's idea of economic cooperation: to build a joint marine-product processing factory on the disputed islands.[69] Nevertheless, Yeltsin's response to the proposal made by Hashimoto on the morning of April 19 at Kawana merits analysis. All accounts about that meeting indicate that Yeltsin was impressed, almost to the point of accepting it, and then was stopped by Yastrzhemski, Yeltsin's press officer, and asked Hashimoto to allow some time for consideration.[70] At the afternoon press conference, Yeltsin suddenly disclosed that "Ryuu (Hashimoto's abbreviated first name) made an additional interesting proposal, and we need to study it. I cannot answer it now, but I remain optimistic."[71] Not only the press corps, but everyone in both delegations was shocked by this disclosure of a proposal, which naturally required utmost confidentiality. It is hard to speculate on the reasons for this disclosure. For Japanese observers, Yeltsin certainly looked sympathetic to this proposal. Tamba reiterated in his memoir that at least by the Birmingham summit on May 15, 1998 Yeltsin was sympathetic to it.[72] But then, why did he make this disclosure? He probably wanted to show the world how enthusiastic he was for finding a breakthrough, while also eager to gauge the reaction from the Russian political elite and public opinion.

In reality, Yeltsin's disclosure led to an avalanche of media reports on the content of the proposal. The majority of the reports indicated that the proposal was a combination of drawing a border line between Urup and Etorofu (assigning sovereignty over the four islands to Japan) but leaving the current status of the islands for some time to come (with all administrative rights to Russia). The Russian administration and media soon united to oppose it. By the autumn of 1998, the Kawana proposal was discarded by an overwhelming majority of government and opinion leaders, even before the two sides entered into serious negotiations on it.[73] Did Russia lose an historic opportunity to overcome differences with Japan, because of President Yeltsin's unexpected disclosure? Or, was the disclosure an instinctively thought out measure to correctly gauge Russian public opinion and eventually make a balanced decision? Whichever, Russia and Japan lost a strategic opportunity to substantially narrow the differences between the two sides.

3. *From the Kawana summit onwards (April 1998–December 1999)*. The political and economic situation for the Russian leadership rapidly deteriorated after the Kawana meeting. The economic crisis in May and August was followed by a political crisis, which led to Primakov being chosen as prime minister. On the Japanese side, failure of Hashimoto's economic policy caused a substantial defeat in parliamentary elections in July 1998, which resulted in Hashimoto's resignation. But $1.5 billion of Japan's financial assistance committed in February became an integral part of the IMF/World Bank package of $22.6 billion as the sole bilateral assistance from the West. Both administrations tried to keep the momentum. Obuchi, Hashimoto's foreign minister and successor, visited Moscow in November 1998.

Yeltsin's health was at one of its lowest points. The meeting was conducted in the Kremlin, but he was heavily supported by his aides. The Russian counterproposal was made in the form of a three-page paper, and the Russian side insisted that the Japanese side give it careful consideration after the meeting. Was it worth such consideration? In fact, the Russian proposal included some genuine concessionary ideas. Alexander Panov, then Russian ambassador to Japan, in his autobiography published in Japanese gives a careful account of this proposal: (1) it consisted of concluding two consecutive treaties, one to legally agree that the frontier was not demarcated and the second to agree on the actual demarcation; (2) the first treaty should also specify a transitory regime, including a "special legal regime" to be approved by the two governments. Panov emphasized that the "Russian side was prepared to adopt an unthinkable measure: a 'special legal regime' to be prepared by the two governments to ensure joint economic and other activities on the islands. A country was giving this special status to another country.

There seemed to be no precedence in international relations."[74] Despite Panov's efforts, the Japanese side reacted cautiously.

In 1999, territorial negotiations reached a stalemate, the two governments each adhering to its own (Kawana or Moscow) proposal. $1.5 billion of Japanese financial assistance was in the process of implementation, but its conditionality in conjunction with the World Bank soon brought negotiations into some difficulty. Investment programs in the Hashimoto–Yeltsin plan took time to materialize. Defense exchanges continued but soon lost their initial flamboyance to affect the fundamentals of the relationship. Rather, parliamentary debate on the Japan–U.S. defense guideline in the spring of 1999 and China's open criticism that the "surrounding situation" in which the guidelines may be evoked might cover Taiwan ignited some fear on the Russian side that the newly introduced notion may be directed against Russia. Rather than seeing a strategic opportunity to improve its relations with Japan after NATO's eastward expansion, Russia now began to fear that the new Japan–U.S. guidelines were an eastern version of the "expansion of military blocs" (an expression used in the third point of the Russia–China statement of December 1999). Japan's efforts to explain that in reality, Russia was not a target of the guidelines succeeded in suppressing the ill feelings, but Yeltsin was in no mood to visit Japan again to discuss the territorial issue. If cordial relations continued, by the end of 1999, Japan was clearly not in the driver's seat in Russia's East Asian policy.

Geopolitics, Economics, and Identity

Again, geopolitics looking east after NATO's eastward expansion seem to have been the first consideration for Russia to renew its interest toward Japan. But the economic factor was no less important. The Hashimoto–Yeltsin plan and $1.5 billion assistance proposed by Japan without anticipating the coming financial crisis created a psychological basis for development of the relationship. Geopolitics, economics, and a strong element of Yeltsin's personal leadership played essential roles in opening a short-lived window of opportunity between the two countries from the autumn of 1997 to the spring of 1998. It was well sustained and reciprocated by the strategic calculations and the personality of Hashimoto.

Multipolarity and treating Japan as a possible pole also permeated Russian policy toward Japan. This approach envisaged a step-by-step development of relations. It carried the imprint of Primakov's thinking, and his views are well reflected in Russian proposals related to the four islands: (1) to support the fishery negotiations (November 1996); (2) to propose joint economic activities (November 1996); (3) to propose a joint marine-product processing factory (April 1998); and (4) to establish a "special legal regime" to bridge the gap between the first treaty and the second treaty (November 1999). It is no secret that Panov, who is said to be the author of the Moscow proposal, has deep respect for Primakov's pragmatism and that Primakov was the most influential policymaker as prime minister when Yeltsin's health was deteriorating in 1998–99. As for identity, although historically and culturally Russia and Japan have an important similarity of being torn between the West and the East, as was pointed out by Lukyanov (see note 14), the two countries were far too apart to contemplate any historical and philosophical commonality and deduce from it practical policy implications.

Relations with Korea

Russian policy from Gorbachev to early Yeltsin brought an abrupt shift from North Korea to South Korea. This resulted in exacerbation of relations with the North and creation of cordial but not dynamic relations with the South. Yeltsin's second term was a time of trying to overcome this failure and to regain for Russia a more central role in the Korean peninsula. It brought some success, but in relations to both the North and the South, more dynamic and strategic thinking had to await the next presidency.

Relations with North Korea

Russia's humiliation probably reached its peak when the four-party talks were proposed by the United States and South Korea in the spring of 1996 to discuss peace on the Korean peninsula to the exclusion of Russia. Viktor Pavliatenko's view that this format was "politically improper and legally groundless" well represented the sense of indignation that Russia was left out from the most important format that might decide the peace and security of the Korean peninsula. Being excluded from the nuclear-related 1994 framework agreement and the KEDO was one humiliation, but being excluded from the fundamental issue of unresolved peace from the Korean War, where the Soviet Union was a vital, if not an up front, player was another matter.[75]

Russia tried to improve relations, but, as Gilbert Rozman writes, Russia was simply not able to entice the North through regional cooperation such as the Tumen River area project.[76] Instead, it offered in 1995 a proposal to conclude a new Treaty of Friendship and Good Neighborly Cooperation to replace the old Treaty of Friendship, Cooperation and Mutual Assistance signed in 1961. North Korea did not ignore this approach and the new treaty was initialed in March 1999, but the signing did not take place until Putin took over the leader's role in Russia.[77] Another informal sounding, which was disclosed in 1998, was to transfer a kilo-class submarine,[78] which would benefit the Russian economy and animate Russia–DPRK trade figures that had been sharply in decline,[79] and would no doubt help to improve political ties with the North. But all such efforts did not prevent North Korea from vehemently criticizing Russia before President Kim Dae-jung's visit to Moscow in May 1999.[80] A more decisive step had to await the next president coming to power in Russia.

Relations with South Korea

Russia's main interest in South Korea was associated with the potential for huge investment and financial assistance to be directed to Russia's reform. As the second leading capitalist economy in the region, the South does not have the historical difficulty with which Japan is fixated. On the contrary, the Korean population within the Soviet Union in the Far East and Central Asia might act as a catalyst for improved relations. South Korea's initial reaction of providing $3 billion in loans and its determination to stay in the Russian market longer than others seemed to justify Russian expectations. But as Russia showed its inability to redeem the loan, and as South Korea became disillusioned by Russia's lack of influence on the North, South Korea's interest in Russia shrunk. During his second term, however, Yeltsin and his government did not consider it in their interest to let South Korea drift away. But rather than creating an effective economic mechanism to induce South Korean investment into the Far East,[81] political steps to boost the relationship and selling weapons became the two directions taken by Moscow.

1. Seeking political momentum. Things did not proceed smoothly. In October 1996, a mysterious killing of a member of the South Korean Consul Generate in Vladivostok clouded the relationship for a while. But then, it was reported that he was engaged in information gathering on North Korea and that he might have fallen victim to an operation from the North.[82] Primakov's visit to Seoul in July 1997 was probably the first important political gesture made by the Russian side to create political momentum. The joint statement included positive messages such as that Russia welcomed all measures taken for the enhancement of peace in the peninsula and hoped for the success of the four-party talks and welcomed the works done by KEDO. An agreement was reached to set up a hotline between the two presidential offices.[83]

The relationship seemed to become warmer when Kim Dae-jung was elected president in December 1997 and began repeating that he intended to improve relations with all four countries (United States, China, Russia, and Japan) for the peace and stability of the peninsula.[84] Kirienko, Minister of Fuel and Energy, emphasized in March 1998 that the Kovykta gas field was open for joint ventures not only with China and Japan but also with South Korea and Mongolia.[85] Nevertheless, the relationship was clouded again in July 1998, this time with much greater impact, when Russia expelled a South Korean embassy official and arrested a Russian Foreign Ministry official on a spy case. South Korea retaliated immediately by expelling a Russian diplomat from Seoul, and it took two solid meetings between the two foreign ministers at the fringe of an ARF meeting in Manila at the end of July to rectify *pro forma* the situation.

Kim Dae-jung's visit to Moscow in May 1999 finally dispersed the cloud over relations left by the spy incident. Russia was forthcoming to grasp this opportunity, and at the summit meeting Yeltsin expressed his support for the sunshine policy. In return, Kim expressed his understanding of the value of the six-party talks that Russia favored.[86] Thus, toward South Korea, greatly helped by the sunshine policy initiative, Russia consolidated its position, in a manner that could be renewed by a new president.

2. Arms trade and defense cooperation. Geopolitical rapprochement, as seen above, was heavy going. South Korean investment and economic ties did not develop as expected. But as in the case of China, arms sales and enhancement of defense cooperation became probably the steadiest development seen in this period. From the Russian point of view, selling arms, or using arms to redeem its debt, was primarily motivated by economics. But it naturally had security implications. When North–South relations were tense, they added more fuel to the tension between Russia and North Korea (see note 80). The situation would change as North–South relations changed in the first half of 2000.

1. On September 17, 1996, the Korean Ministry of Defense announced that, as a part of a redemption of the previously supplied loan, about thirty BMP-3 combat armored vehicles would be delivered from Russia.[87]

2. On December 12, 1996, the Korean Defense Ministry announced that the second delivery of BMP-3 armored vehicles and other weapons would be made by the end of the year.[88]

3. On November 20, 1997, Russia and Korea signed their first agreement on military technology cooperation. Itar Tass reported that the major purpose of the agreement was to redeem Russian debt through arms deliveries.[89]

4. On April 20, 1999, the Korean Defense Ministry announced that the first military good will missions would be exchanged in June from Korea and in August from Russia respectively.[90]

5. Many speculative reports appeared during the preparatory stage of Kim Dae-jung's visit to Moscow that Russia was trying to sell its *kilo* submarine, already sold to China, to redeem its debt totaling around $1.7 billion, but the Korean side was not attracted.[91]

6. On December 2, 1999, the Russian defense minister visited Seoul in a second visit since 1995. Both sides agreed to enhance military exchanges and cooperate in the prevention of a North Korean missile launching.[92]

Geopolitics, Economics, and Identity

Unlike China or, even, temporarily, Japan, Korea was not considered to occupy a driver's position in Russia's East Asia policy during this period. The Russian geopolitical objective was to regain a more central role in the Korean peninsula with regard to those issues that concerned peace and security there. This meant to fill the vacuum created by earlier policy with North Korea, while consolidating political ties (restoring political momentum) and economic-security relations (selling arms) with South Korea. Since tensions continued between the North and the South, the results of Russian policy could not be even. Despite some zigzagging, Russia gained more with South Korea than the North. Identity was of little consideration.

Southeast Asia

Alexander Panov recounts in his autobiography that during his tenure as the deputy foreign minister in charge of the APR for two and a half years from January 1994, he and his staff took the first steps to rebuild Russian relations with Southeast Asia, where "no sufficient attention had been given"[93] after the new Russia replaced the Soviet Union. The beginning of dialogue with ASEAN, Russia's participation in ARF, the first sell of Mig-29s to Malaysia, Russia's application to join APEC, high-level visits to Australia and New Zealand, are examples of the achievements made in this period.[94]

Russian policy toward Southeast Asia in the second half of the 1990s developed precisely on the basis that had been achieved during Panov's period. Primakov was well suited to strengthen this direction, as he was known as "the man of the Asia-Pacific region" under Gorbachev.[95] He sought to strengthen multilateral ties with Southeast Asia as an indispensable component of a multilateral structure in the APR, an idea dating back to Brezhnev's proposal of "Asian Collective Security Initiatives" in 1969 and Gorbachev's proposal of a CSCE type "All Asia Security Conference" made in his Vladivostok speech in July 1986, which was hardly realized by Russian participation in Pacific Economic Cooperation Conference (PECC) in September 1992, when the major regional structure had already moved to APEC. During the cold war, multilateral structures proposed by the Soviet Union were aimed at power politics considerations to drive a wedge among the opposing powers in the region, such as China as seen in Brezhnev's first Asian Collective Security proposal or the United States as seen in other proposals related to naval force reductions. But at the same time, they were related to the deep-rooted Russian desire for identity and recognition as a legitimate member of the Asian–Pacific community.

In the Russian Federation, a leadership role in Southeast Asia was not sought any more. But to be left out from major regional organizations was not acceptable both from the point of view of regional power relations and the search for Russian identity. Primakov invited ASEAN Secretary General Ajit Singh to Moscow in June 1996 and requested that Russia's position be elevated to a "dialogue partner" with ASEAN. ASEAN was not that enthusiastic, and it was a last-minute decision that Russia gained that position together with India and China in the July 1996 ASEAN and its "dialogue partners" meeting in Jakarta.[96] Russia's major success in the latter half of the 1990s was the decision taken by APEC in Vancouver in November 1997 to accept Russia as its member, as described in the above-mentioned section on Japan. Yeltsin's efforts to improve Russo-Japanese relations resulted, through Japan's support, in this acknowledgement of Russia as a member of the APR. Russia's actual participation, however, did not produce tangible results, partly because of continuing Russian economic difficulties, including its financial crisis in 1998, and partly because of Yeltsin's ailing health, which meant that newly elected prime ministers attended instead: Primakov at the Kuala Lumpur APEC summit in November 1998 and Putin at the Auckland summit in September 1999.

The second direction for policy toward Southeast Asia was to strengthen bilateral relations, but concrete results were meager. Panov told Japanese reporters in July 1996 that in addition to Malaysia, contracts of arms sales were sought with Indonesia, Thailand, and the Philippines,[97] but the Asian financial crisis prevented smooth development of such sales.[98] Yeltsin's widely anticipated visit to Indonesia in April 1998 did not take place because of the president's ailing health.[99]

Conclusion

In the second half of the 1990s, the core strategic thinking of Russia toward East Asia was geopolitics. Russia was seeking a partner, or partners, with which to coordinate its foreign policy, which affects its national interests and its position in the global politics. The East was juxtaposed to the West, but Russia was not seeking in the East an ally, or allies, to counter the West.

The West was too powerful and important for Russia to discard or to stand against. The power of the United States was too great. Whether Russia liked it or not, and whether Russia acknowledged it verbally or not, the majority of Russian intellectuals and policymakers were aware of that. Europe was forming another unity within the broad spectrum of the West or trans-Atlantic structure, and Russia had no reasons to antagonize or stand against it. But in the foreign policy put forward by the West, be it NATO's eastward expansion, bombardment of Kosovo, or newly formulating missile defense system, there were things Russia could not accept. To counter these moves, which did not meet Russian national interests, Russia looked for a partner, or partners, in the East. The concept of multipolarity fit Russian thinking well. Without geographic determinism, it helped to consolidate Russia's position in global politics and to counter pressures emerging from the West, in particular from the United States.

China, with its rising economic and political power in the Asia–Pacific region, became Russia's leading partner in East Asia. In long-term geopolitical considerations, cooperating with China could have several divergent repercussions. But in the short-to-medium term, Russia saw much to gain and little to lose by way of strengthening its strategic partnership. For a while, Japan had promise as an attractive co-partner, but the bilateral difficulty did not allow Japan to keep that position for long.

Economic factors played an important role as well. The West cannot be disregarded given the importance shown by the IMF/World Bank's involvement at the time of the financial crisis or in cumulative Foreign Direct Investment. In fact, Japan, and South Korea as well, was viewed in this context as an important member of the West, which might assist Russia. Economic interests with the East could be considered only in balance with Russia's economic interest with the West.

Given the reality of the Russian economy, what attracted Russian policymakers most in their economic deals with the East were arms sale and energy. But in addition to economic necessity, arms sale and energy cooperation had security implications. They could have contradictory short-to-medium-term and long-term interests. Overall, Russian policymakers in this period were very much forthcoming in expanding Russia's activities in the two areas. Arms sales to China, South Korea, and possibly North Korea, and joint energy exploitation with China, Japan, and South Korea all became an important part of Russian strategic thinking.

The search for identity is almost a perpetual question for Russia. At the demise of the Soviet Union and creation of a new Russia, this issue naturally was bound to rise to the surface of Russian intellectual debates. The embrace of multipolarity gave Russia a more stable position in world politics. It matched well recognition that "Russia will stay Russia, neither the West nor the East," but many more years of soul searching would be needed to give an answer to the question: "what is Russia, if not West nor East?"

Overall, Russian strategic thinking in the latter part of the 1990s helped Russia to gain a more secure and stable position in world politics, including in East Asia. Some recognized problems, such as border issues with China, decades' long relations of distrust with Japan, confused relations oscillating between short-term economic objectives and long-term desirability of gaining the trust of both Koreas, were partially resolved or improved. Although to varying degrees, Russia succeeded in winning greater trust without resorting to excessive dependency in relations with China, Japan, Korea, and Southeast Asia. At the center of this strategic thinking lies geopolitical thinking based on a balance of power, and the notion of multipolarity served well to formulate it from the perspective of identity. This thinking proved to be sustainable to bridge the confusion during Yeltsin's first presidency and the new direction to be taken under Putin's presidency. Russian East Asian policy was not always met with acclamation by the West, but that policy was reasonably prioritized and coordinated to sustain Russian relations with the West and the East in sound balance. Russian policy objectives vis-à-vis China, Japan, Korea, and Southeast Asia were also on the whole sufficiently prioritized and coordinated not to create undue confusion or misunderstanding.

Naturally, Yeltsin's second term cannot be acclaimed with successes only. Russia's inability to resolve some of the crucial security matters in relation to NATO's eastward expansion, Yugoslavia, and Chechnya led to the impression of overdependence on its relations with China by the end of 1999; indecisiveness in handling the territorial issue with Japan might have led Russia to miss a window of opportunity at a time when Japan behaved with genuine strategic thinking and flexibility; and little was done in reality to overcome hurdles in Russia's relations with South Korea. In particular, despite Primakov's creative role, Russian foreign policy was only in its full swing when Yeltsin's health was reasonably sustainable from the spring of 1997 to the summer of 1998. An impression of indecisiveness and inactivity, far from any strategic thinking, cannot be denied in the rest of the period.

Notes

1. Katzenstein and Sil write: "we could view constructivism, liberalism, and realism as three sides of a triangle that takes for granted the centrality of some core assumptions of international life, for example, in their respective focus on identity, efficiency, and power." Peter J. Katzenstein and Rudra Sil, "Rethinking Asian Security: A Case for Analytical Eclecticism," in J. J. Suh, Peter Katzenstein, and Allen Carlson, eds, *Rethinking Security in East Asia, Identity, Power, and Efficiency* (Stanford: Stanford University Press, 2004), p. 8. In their "Introduction" Ikenberry and Mastanduno also state that the analyses in this book "draw on the full diversity of theoretical approaches in contemporary international relations scholarship to illuminate interactions among the three critical players: China, Japan and the United States." At the same time, the theoretical analysis in the "Introduction" converges into the three basic trends: realism (balance of power and styles of hegemony), constructivism (history and memory), and liberalism (institutions and economic interdependence). G. John Ikenberry and Michael Mastanduno, eds, *International Relations Theory and the Asia-Pacific* (New York: Columbia University Press, 2003), pp. 1–21.
2. Primakov's autobiography cites many quotations from Western leaders to this effect from that period. Yevgeny Primakov, *Russian Crossroads, Toward the New Millennium* (New Haven: Yale University Press, 2004), pp. 129–30.
3. Ozawa Haruko, *Roshia no taigai seisaku to Ajia Taiheiyo* (Tokyo: Yushindo, 2000), p. 126.
4. Ibid., pp. 127–28. My interviews: Bessmertnykh, September 26, 1995: "The major reason for the increased sense of isolation in Russia comes from NATO's expansion. Enforcing its expansion eastward at this juncture has a serious danger, which might turn Russian strategic interest to the east, notably to China"; Karaganov, October 4, 1995: "NATO's expansion to the

east may change Russia from a status-quo power to a revisionist power. For the moment it is limited only in the psychological arena, but weakening of Western relations is also calling for the revival of the alliance with China"; Migranyan, October 3, 1995: "NATO's recent move, including its eastward expansion means a new containment policy of Russia. Russia is bound to react to it. Greater attention to the CIS and such countries as China or Iran is bound to take place."

5. Primakov, *Russian Crossroads*, p. 136.

6. On the key question of nuclear weapons deployment, Russia basically had to agree to NATO's three "NO's," that NATO had no "intention, plan nor reason to deploy the nuclear weapons among the enlarged members."

7. The first agreement between Belarus and Russia was concluded on April 2, 1996 in the form of the Contract on the Creation of a Belarusian and Russian Community.

8. For Primakov's reaction on NATO's bombardment of Kosovo, see "U-turn over the Atlantic" in Primakov, *Russian Crossroads*, pp. 263–78.

9. On August 21, the State Duma adopted a non-binding resolution asking for Yeltsin's resignation with 245 "Yes" and 32 "No" votes. Primakov, after being appointed prime minister, stated that "The direct result of the crisis was not the devaluation of the ruble or the decrease of government expenditure but a complete crisis of confidence." See Shimotomai Nobuo, ed., *Roshia hendo no kozu* (Tokyo: Hoseidaigaku, 2001), p. 80.

10. Shimotomai ed., *Roshia hendo no kozu*, p. 45.

11. http://www.gks.ru. Current figures also reflect the same tendency that investment comes from the West. See Kasai Tatsuhiko, "Roshia no taigai kankei o torimaku kankyo no henka to keisai gaiko," in Matsui Hiroaki, ed., *9.11 Jiken igo no Roshia gaiko no tenkai* (Tokyo: JIIA, 2003), p. 77.

12. Probably the turning point was Yeltsin's "urge" to implement foreign policy based on national interest revealed at the MOFA conference in October 1992. See Ozawa, *Roshia no taigai seisaku*, p. 96.

13. Grigorii Yavlinsky's role in advocating the Grand Bargain is well known. He also emphasized his vision to create "a new structure of international relations in the Asia-Pacific region where Russia, China, Japan the U.S. and ASEAN would create cooperative relations without harming the interest of each other, in which Japan and Russia can play an effective framework for cooperation" (July 1, 1994, author's interview).

14. Lukyanov's view can be seen as one of the most traditional *Slavophile-Euraianist*: "The Russian people have a deep rooted fierce anger against the rapid Americanization and Europeanization. Civilizational protest is emerging from Russian collectivism (*sobornost'*) and spiritualism (*dukhovnost'*) against western individualism and materialism. Protection of the weak, state-control of the key industries, industrial policy in running the economy are all essential. Parliamentary elections and freedom of speech must be maintained and pluralism rather than autocracy should govern the political

system. Russia should regain its pride through the notion of 'great state community.' Japan, with its spiritualism, state-led planning economy, and companies-led welfare society has a lot of commonality with Russia. While stretched between the East (tradition) and the West (Americanization), Japan succeeded in preserving a unique Japaneseness. This is what Russia has in common with Japan, and what Russia can learn from Japan" (April 25, 1995, Moscow, author's interview).

15. James Billington, *Russia in Search of Itself* (Washington, DC: Woodrow Wilson Center Press, 2004), p. 84.

16. Ozawa, *Roshia no taigai seisaku*, p. 116.

17. "When I took office at the Foreign Ministry I was confident that Russia could and should actively seek an equal partnership with everyone, look for and find areas of common interest, and work them with the others. And when interests don't coincide (and experience teaches us they won't always), we should try to find solutions that will neither sacrifice Russia's vital interests nor lead to confrontation. Clearly that is the dialectics of Russia's post-Cold War foreign policy. If areas of common interest are ignored, the result may at best be another Cold War. The alternative is partnership" (Primakov, *Russian Crossroads*, pp. 126–27).

18. Primakov's remarks on the "Indo-China-Russia strategic triangle sparked a debate" following his visit to India as prime minister in December 1998. See Shams-Ud-din and Bhaswati Sakar, "Indo-Russian Relations: An Overview," in Shams-Ud-din, ed., *India and Russia Towards Strategic Partnership* (New Delhi: Lancer's books, 2001), p. 8.

19. From an interview by the author on March 15, 2005 in Moscow.

20. Billington, *Russia in Search of Itself*, p. 80.

21. The immediate reaction of Li Jingjie, a leading Chinese scholar on Russia–China relations, to the author's query about "multipolarity" was "identity." "Before Primakov, Russia was wavering between the West and the East. It was a natural phenomenon which may occur after the demise of an empire that happened in the transition from the Roman Empire to Italy; from the Ottoman Turkish Empire to Turkey; and from the Soviet Union to the Russian Federation. In Primakov's thinking, Russia realized that Russia will stay Russia, neither the West nor the East." (June 28, 2005, Beijing).

22. Author's interview with Primakov on March 15, 2005 in Moscow.

23. China–Russia Joint Statement signed on April 25, 1996. See *Yomiuri shimbun*, April 26, 1996.

24. *Yomiuri shimbun*, April 26, 1996.

25. *Kyodo News Service*, April 25, 1996.

26. "Russia re-confirms that the PRC is the sole legitimate government representing China and that Taiwan is an inseparable part of Chinese territory. Russia does not possess official relations or contacts with Taiwan. Russia confirms that Tibet is an inseparable part of China." *Yomiuri shimbun*, April 26, 1996.

27. The fact that Jiang Zemin's visit to Moscow in April 1997 did not produce concrete results on the border demarcation shows that an agreement was not that easy.
28. *Asahi shimbun*, April 26, 1996.
29. *Kyodo News Service*, April 25, 1996.
30. *Kyodo News Service*, April 23, 1997.
31. Ibid.
32. On the agreement of April 26, 1997, see *Sankei shimbun*, April 27, 1997.
33. *Asahi shimbun*, April 26, 1997.
34. *Sankei shimbun*, April 27, 1997.
35. *Sankei shimbun*, November 11, 1997.
36. Ibid.
37. Iwashita Akihiro, *Churo kokkyo 4000 kiro* (Tokyo: Kadokawa, 2003), p. 28.
38. Iwashita Akihiro, *Churo kokkyo 4000 kiro*, pp. 29, 31, 34, 40. See also Kazuhiko Togo, "Russian Security Policy in East Asia," *Militaire Spectator*, Jaargang 173, October 2004, pp. 518–19.
39. *Sankei shimbun*, November 11, 1997.
40. Ibid.
41. The Yeltsin–Jiang meeting took place only for half an hour at a hospital in Moscow due to Yeltsin's pneumonia.
42. *Asahi shimbun*, November 24, 1998.
43. http://www.discerningtoday.org/members/jiang-yeltsin_jnt_st.htm
44. The sixth point against international terrorism may be understood as expressing solidarity with the United States after 9/11, but before then, this clause was to express more Russia's fight against separatist fundamentalists in Chechnya, which was causing particular anxieties among the West due to Russia's disregard for "human rights."
45. Even this clause which sounded innocuous from the U.S. point of view had such bite as the necessity of maintaining "the balance of rights and obligations and take into consideration differing levels of socio-economic development."
46. *Asahi shimbun*, December 10, 1999. (Naturally the issue of three remaining islands was left unresolved. See note 45).
47. See for instance "Putin's visit to China," *People's Daily*. http://english.people.com.cn/200007/18/sino-russia.html
48. Gilbert Rozman, *Northeast Asia's Stunted Regionalism, Bilateral Distrust in the Shadow of Globalization* (Cambridge: Cambridge University Press, 2004), pp. 210–17.
49. Kasai Tatsuhiko, *Roshia no taigai kankei*, p. 74.
50. U.S. Defense Department, "Annual Report on the Military Power of the People's Republic of China," Report to Congress, 2002, quoted in American Defense Council, *Policy Papers: The Sino-Russia Strategic Partnership*, p. 20. http://americandefensecouncil.com/China_Russia,asp
51. American Defense Council, *Policy Papers*, pp. 24–25, 27.
52. Ibid., p. 19.

53. Rozman, *Northeast Asia's Stunted Regionalism*, p. 213.

54. *Sankei shimbun*, February 26, 1999.

55. Iwashita Akihiro, "9/11 igo no Churo kankei," in Matsui Hiroaki, ed., *9/11 Jiken-igo no Roshia gaiko no tenkai*, pp. 221–22.

56. American Defense Council, *Policy Papers*, pp. 47–50.

57. Yeltsin visited Tokyo in October 1993 and issued the Tokyo Declaration. This brought back the relationship to the level it was a year earlier, and the Declaration thence became an agreed basis for the territorial negotiations. But after the communist-nationalist victory in Duma elections, the momentum did not last long.

58. The agreement found its breakthrough in the summer of 1997 and was signed in February 1998. The political impetus given by Primakov and then by Yeltsin became an important driving force for this success. See Togo Kazuhiko, "Eritsin daitoryo no honichi no seika to Nichiro kankei no zento," *Sekai keizai hyoron*, July 1998, p. 15.

59. For the full text of the speech: http://www.kantei.go.jp/foreign/0731douyukai.html. On the following day after the speech, a Russian foreign ministry spokesman made a statement "wholeheartedly welcoming it." Primakov, who was on a visit to Korea, immediately echoed this. *Nezavisimaia gazeta* carried the full text of the speech in August. See Sato Kazuo and Komaki Yoshiaki, *Nichiro shuno kosho* (Tokyo: Iwanami shoten, 2003), pp. 101–03.

60. Tamba Minoru, *Nichiro gaiko hiwa* (Tokyo: Chuo koron, 2004), pp. 17–18.

61. Wada Haruki, *Hoppo ryodo mondai*, (Tokyo: Asahi shimbunsha, 1999) pp. 367–68.

62. A vivid description of that meeting on November 1 is given in Tamba's autobiography, *Nichiro gaiko hiwa*, pp. 11–14.

63. Tamba, *Nichiro gaiko hiwa*, p. 30.

64. Sato and Komaki, *Nichiro shuno kosho*, p. 64.

65. http://www.mofa.go.jp/mofaj/kaidan/kiroku/s_hashi/arc_97/russia97/hyoka.html. The plan outlines six pillars for cooperation: (1) investment cooperation; (2) Russia's participation in a multilateral international economy; (3) enhanced assistance to Russia's reform; (4) cooperation in a managers' training program; (5) energy dialogue and cooperation; and (6) cooperation on the peaceful use of nuclear energy.

66. Yeltsin stated at the press conference that the two sides have discussed forty-three items. The Japanese side did not have a clue what these forty-three items meant, but, most likely, all items in the Hashimoto–Yeltsin plan were included.

67. Tamba has left a detailed account how Hashimoto and he prepared the groundwork with Bill Clinton, for a decision to accept Russia as a member of APEC in Vancouver. See Tamba, *Nichiro gaiko hiwa*, pp. 20–23.

68. Sato and Komaki, *Nichiro shuno kosho*, pp. 133–36.

69. Ibid., p. 180.

70. Ibid., p. 185.

71. Tamba, *Nichiro gaiko hiwa*, p. 60.

72. Ibid., p. 66.

73. The Japanese government disclosed only in September 2000 that the proposal contained: (1) a border demarcation between Urup and Etorofu and; (2) maximum concessions were to be made by the Japanese side. In January 2005, Yachi Shotaro, vice-minister for foreign affairs, gave a press conference stating that the content of maximum concessions is to "acknowledge for some time to come Russian administrative rights." See *Asahi shimbun*, January 5, 2005.

74. Alexander Panov, *Kaminari nochi hare* (Tokyo: NHK, 2004), pp. 107–109.

75. Viktor Pavliatenko, "Russian Security in the Asian-Pacific Region: The Dangers of Isolation," in Gilbert Rozman, Mikhail Nosov, and Koji Watanabe, eds., *Russia and East Asia: The 21 Century Security Environment* (New York: M.E. Sharpe, 1999), p. 35.

76. Gilbert Rozman, "Russian Foreign Policy in Northeast Asia," in Samuel S. Kim, ed., *The International Relations of Northeast Asia* (Lanham, MD: Rowman & Littlefield Publishers, 2004), p. 212.

77. The new treaty was signed in February 2000. See Koizumi Naomi, "Roshia no taiiran, Iraku, Kitachosen seisaku," in Matsui Hiroaki, ed., *9/11 Jiken-igo no Roshia gaiko no tenkai* (Tokyo: JIIA, 2003), p. 110.

78. *Sankei shimbun* reported on June 23, 1998 that, according to Alexander Matsegora, a research officer of the Committee of Geopolitics in the Duma, informal talks were being held between Russia and North Korea to sell a *kilo* 636 class submarine, the same type of submarine which Russia constructed for China, the first of which was sold in October 1998 and the second to be sold by the end of 1999. Interfax reported that one *kilo* 636 costs $300 million.

79. The Russia–North Korea trade turnover decreased from $311 million in 1992 to $85 million in 1997. See Viktor B. Supian and Mikhail G. Nosov, "Reintegration of an Abandoned Fortress: Economic Security of the Russian Far East," in Rozman, Nosov, and Watanabe, eds., *Russia and East Asia*, p. 93.

80. The Korea News Service as of May 26, 1999 criticized the sunshine policy of President Kim Dae-jung and warned Russia, without naming it, that "anyone who supports such criminal activities of South Korea will be labelled as taking an anti-KNDR policy." It also stated that "A certain country in the area wants to gain a small amount of money by selling submarines and other military equipment." See *Kyodo News Service*, May 26, 1999.

81. Some examples of unanswered South Korean efforts, such as the Nakhodka industrial park, are cited in Rozman, *Northeast Asia's Stunted Regionalism*, p. 213.

82. *Asahi shimbun*, December 6, 1996.

83. *Asahi shimbun*, June 26, 1997.

84. For Kim Dae-jung's statement on December 19, 1997, see *Asahi shimbun*, December 19, 1997.

85. *Asahi shimbun*, March 4, 1998.

86. *Sankei shimbun*, May 29, 1999. The joint statement issued on May 28 included Russian support for the sunshine policy and the basic recognition that the six-party talks can be held in parallel with the four-party talks. See *Kyodo News Service*, May 28, 1998.

87. North Korea so far has been supplied only with less qualified BMP-1 or BMP-2 armored vehicles. See *Kyodo News Service*, September 17, 1996.

88. *Asahi shimbun*, December 12, 1996.

89. *Asahi shimbun*, November 21, 1997.

90. *Asahi shimbun*, April 23, 1999.

91. *Asahi shimbun*, May 18, 1999; *Sankei shimbun*, May 27, 1999.

92. *Asahi shimbun*, September 3, 1999.

93. Panov, *Kaminari nochi hare*, p. 11.

94. Ibid., pp. 12–13.

95. Primakov became the chairman of the Soviet Pacific Economic Cooperation Conference (PECC) Committee in March 1988 and represented the Soviet Union as a guest participant in the Osaka PECC plenary meeting in May 1988.

96. *Daily Yomiuri*, July 3, 1996; *Sankei shimbun*, July 27, 1996.

97. *Kyodo tsushin*, July 21, 1996.

98. *Yomiuri shimbun*, March 1, 1998.

99. *Sankei shimbun*, January 21, 1998.

CHAPTER 5

Russia's Asia Policy under Vladimir Putin, 2000–5

Dmitri Trenin

Though Asia traditionally was, for Russia, a "secondary" geopolitical direction by and large, its importance has been steadily rising since the 1990s. By the mid-2000s, this rise has acquired a new quality: Russia increasingly acts as a Euro-Pacific nation.[1] This has been the result of several factors. Top among them are the opening of Russia in the wake of the fall of communism and the dismantlement of the Soviet Union, and the rise of China. Russia's biggest problem at the beginning of the twenty-first century is the lack of a functioning model for regional development in East Siberia and the Far East, the sparsely populated but resource-rich part of the country. Unless Russia develops such a model, it is likely to see its eastern provinces become a raw materials appendage of China's growing economy. If, at the same time, Russia's western regions continue to perform a similar function for the European Union, the prospect of the country, which once was co-terminus with Eurasia, turning itself into something that can be described as "Euro-China," a weak land torn apart by the rival forces of attraction, might become a reality. Thus, averting such a scenario is Russia's premier national interest. Moreover, the dynamism of China and India, especially in contrast to Europe's sluggishness, makes them, as well as Japan and Korea, highly attractive for Russian business executives. Looming across the Pacific is an alternative point of entry into the United States, as well as opportunities in Canada to the north and Latin America and Australia to the south. The combined power of the Pacific Rim economies is such that Russia can no longer afford an Asia–Pacific policy that is second-best to its Euro-Atlantic dimension. Moreover, to be successful and competitive, Russia needs to reverse the traditional approach to foreign policy. Instead of looking at it in terms of projection (of power, influence, etc.), it needs to see it as a means to attract external resources for the benefit of an essentially domestic agenda.

Such an approach is only beginning to take shape, still mostly at the declaratory level. This chapter analyzes the policies of the Putin administration toward the Asia–Pacific,[2] and its underlying principles. The thrust of these policies is still on bilateral relations with the individual Asian nations, but a more general approach to the region is slowly emerging. However, the more traditionalist view, which tends to see foreign policy as a self-contained "field," has not wholly disappeared. This prevents Moscow from fully using the opportunities that exist and from effectively managing the resources that Russia possesses. Following the pattern of Russia's still compartmentalized Asian policy, the chapter examines the drivers that shape its bilateral relations with the key players in the region one by one, focusing on the principal challenges, responses, and opportunities. We then proceed to assess the contribution of the "Putin period" for the evolution of Russian strategic thinking about Asia, weighing the "pros" and "cons." The chapter concludes with an outline for a more enlightened Russian Asia–Pacific strategy, which would seek to maximize the opportunities existing in and reduce the risks coming from the region.

China: Learning to Live with the Rising Dragon

Putin was the first Russian leader to publicly acknowledge the central challenge that a rising China poses for Russia. Ever since Russia and China entered into regular diplomatic relations, which occurred in the mid-nineteenth century, and essentially until the late twentieth century, China was regarded by Russians as a backward and incoherent giant, famously incapable of getting its act together. Whether as an object of colonial expansion under the czars or the Soviet Union's junior communist ally-turned-rival, it was treated accordingly, that is, as an object of Russian policy, never an equal partner. Even in the immediate post-Soviet period, still-arrogant Russians sometimes viewed China as a tool in their futile attempt to counterbalance the American world hegemony, which they found impossible to stomach in the aftermath of the cold war. Whether the Chinese were likely to subscribe to that idea bothered these people little.

Putin, on the contrary, immediately broke away with the hollow rhetoric of multipolarity, replacing *Primakovism* with pragmatism.[3] He also stunned his audience in Blagoveshchensk, Amur region, in July 2000 when he publicly mused about which language will be the lingua franca in twenty-first century Siberia, Chinese, Korean, or Japanese. Even though he would occasionally use the multipolar phraseology, Putin clearly disabused himself of the illusion that Russia could be the leading element in the Moscow–Beijing "duo."

Putin was thus reacting to the new realities, which so many others had failed to face up to. While most Russians, reeling from the collapse of the Soviet Union and the dramatic diminishment of their country's international standing, were focusing on America's rise to the position of the world's unique superpower, Putin paid attention to an even more stunning, but strangely overlooked change that occurred simultaneously. In 1990, the Soviet Union and China were still rated roughly even, in terms of their GDP. Ten years later, China was ahead by a factor of three. Moreover, its per-capita level, measured in the more advanced coastal provinces, was approaching, and even surpassing that of Russia.

This was a change that few Russians could take calmly. Having been accustomed to their own relative backwardness and poverty vis-à-vis the West, that is, Europe, America, and more recently Japan, they felt "natural" economic, technological, and military superiority vis-à-vis the East, above all, China and India. Historically, when the going got tough for Russia in the West, it usually had the option of turning East to compensate itself through new territorial acquisitions or new junior allies. Now, Russia was flanked in *both* West and East by countries that were economically more powerful, technologically advanced, and militarily (at least in conventional terms) stronger than Russia itself. This was wholly new, utterly unpalatable, and abhorring. Whereas Boris Yeltsin looked the other way and the policy elite turned plainly schizophrenic, simultaneously trying to recruit Beijing for its anti-American posse and to exploit the "yellow peril" sentiments among ordinary Russians, Putin had to come up with a policy that made some sense.

To begin with, he continued with the policy of strategic partnership enunciated by Russia's first president in 1996. The end of the "parallel Cold War" which the Soviet Union waged in the East from the early 1960s through the late 1980s remains a precious achievement of Mikhail Gorbachev's foreign policy, which no Kremlin leader would want to undermine, whatever else they may think of their predecessor's policies. Any alternative to friendship with China would be a disaster for Russia, in the beginning of the twenty-first century even more than at the close of the twentieth.

Thus, following in Yeltsin's footsteps, which themselves were building on Gorbachev's initial opening to China, Putin signed, in 2001, a friendship treaty with Beijing, the first one in fifty years. In contrast to the treaty concluded between Stalin and Mao, the present document lays the foundation not for some new alliance, but for a good-neighborly "relationship of equals"—a milestone for China. The treaty reaffirmed the goal first set in the Yeltsin–Jiang declaration of 1996, of building a Sino-Russian strategic partnership in the twenty-first century. The meaning of partnership is still loosely defined in terms of good-neighborly relations, nonparticipation in arrangements with third parties that may be seen as hostile by the other partner, and long-term collaboration, especially in such areas as energy and military technology.

Putin also saw the wisdom of completing the settlement of the Russo-Chinese border. Again, the first step there was made by Gorbachev in 1991 and the second one by Yeltsin in 1994. The decision of principle to renounce Stalin's unilateral move to draw the border along the Chinese bank of the border rivers was again made by Gorbachev, and implemented under Yeltsin. It fell to Putin, however, to fully recognize its consequences and follow up in 2004 with the painful "fifty-fifty" solution to the outstanding issues, including the disputed river island territory in the vicinity of Khabarovsk, Russia's main stronghold in the Far East. Thus, Putin decided to finalize the border settlement in its entirety rather than leaving small "holes" in it that would, in theory at least, leave Beijing an option of withdrawing from the "incomplete" agreement and making the case again for the return of territories ceded by the Qing dynasty under "unequal treaties" with the Russian empire. After the return of Hong Kong in 1997, Macau in 1998, and the setting of the 2020 deadline for the reunification of Taiwan with the mainland,[4] some Russian observers, Andrei Piontkovsky and Alexander Sharavin among others, saw the Russian Far East as the next station in Beijing's drive to do away with the vestiges of historical humiliation and restore China to its "natural" position as the dominant power in East Asia. Putin must have heeded them: Better to act now than gamble with the future.

Also, rather than insisting on Moscow's traditional senior position in relations with Beijing, Putin focused his efforts on codifying the essential equality of the two states. Since time is probably not on Russia's side, such a move appeared wise. Again, acting on Yeltsin's legacy, Putin agreed in 2001 to transform the loose five-nation arrangement that accompanied the settlement of the former Sino-Soviet border into a permanent body, the Shanghai Cooperation Organization (SCO). Within the SCO, ever since its foundation, Russia and China were both formally and informally the two co-leaders, with the post-Soviet states of Central Asia placed between (and beneath) them. Still, the SCO actually legitimizes China's involvement in Central Asia, that is within the former boundaries of the Soviet/Russian empire, which Moscow still regards as its prime sphere of interest.[5] Russian acquiescence is a testimony to the Kremlin's awareness of its own limitations, China's ambitions, and the new states' formal independence. Under these circumstances, the SCO, though a Chinese idea, could function as a means of managing a difficult situation and avoiding conflicts and misunderstandings with Beijing. As a de facto "veto-wielding" co-leader of the organization, Moscow has been trying to steer the SCO into such channels that give it an advantage (such as security building), rather than those (like economic development assistance) which favor its friend-cum-rival.

In 2005, the SCO took a major step by demanding a U.S. military withdrawal from Central Asia. This served as a reminder to Washington that Beijing and Moscow regard the region as their backyard, not America's. At the same time, the organization expanded to include several observers—India, Pakistan, Iran, and Mongolia. Despite obvious American interest, the United States was not invited to sit in on SCO meetings. At the time of the SCO prime ministers' meeting in Moscow in October 2005, Putin emphasized the organization's importance by mentioning the combined population of the member-states and observers, about 3 billion people. What he did not mention but could hardly ignore was that of that number, however, only 5 percent are Russian citizens.

Under Putin, Moscow has also been trying to use the Commonwealth of Independent States and other post-Soviet bodies (such as the Single Economic Space, the Eurasian Economic Community, and the Collective Security Treaty Organization) as instruments for binding Central Asia closer to Russia. In a characteristic move, Putin saw fit, in 2004, to make a stopover in Dushanbe, Tajikistan, after a visit to China, and meet there with all SCO heads of state, minus the Chinese, of course. At the same time, Russia joined the Central Asian Cooperation Organization, the only country outside the region to be able to do so. In 2005, the organization merged into the Russia-dominated Eurasian Economic Community.

While Chinese commentators routinely lament the U.S. post-9/11 military presence in Central Asia, and urge Russia to "stand up" to American efforts to ease it out of the region, the Russians initially (and privately) counted on the U.S. presence there as a useful temporary place-holder, keeping the region outside of the sphere of much more permanent Chinese domination, until such time when Russia regains its strength and can fend for its own interests more actively and effectively. By the mid-2000s, however, Moscow felt Washington had overstayed its welcome, and was giving no signs it planned to move out of Central Asia. In addition, the Kremlin was both shocked and humiliated by the "orange revolution" in Ukraine (2004), and the toppling of regimes in Georgia (2003) and Kyrgyzstan (2005), all of which were ascribed to U.S. machinations. Thus, the Russian leadership was only pleased to watch the Uzbek President Karimov, in the wake of the controversy over the brutal suppression of the armed revolt in Andijan, terminating the American military presence in his country and realigning Uzbekistan with Russia, including a treaty of alliance signed in November 2005. While trying to dislodge Americans from Central Asia, the Russians, however, were anxious not to let the Chinese exploit the opening. A mere discussion in the spring of 2005 of establishing an "SCO military base" in Kyrgyzstan (and thus, indirectly, giving the Chinese military access to the region) provoked a barrage of official denials and hostile comment.

In Russia's policies, geopolitics is closely followed by economics. In the post-Soviet era, the Far East and Siberia's economic link to China is not only beneficial, it has become vital. Putin has inherited two principal areas of economic exchange with China: cross-border trade and what is officially referred to as "military-technological cooperation," which stands for Russian arms and military technology exports to China. In his own tenure Putin added a third one, energy exports.

Border trade with China keeps eastern Russia afloat. So far, it has added little to the region's development, but cheap Chinese goods are vital to the survival of the generally poor Russian population, and trade as a means of part-time employment eases the region's social problems. Like Yeltsin, Putin has been trying to expand Sino-Russian trade beyond the relatively narrow base of $5–6 billion, and was able to advance toward the goal set in 1996 for the start of the new millennium, that is $20 billion, leading to another objective set by the two governments in 2005 of $60 billion in turnover by 2010. The current level is, of course, still many times less than China's exchanges with Japan, the United States, and South Korea.

One significant element of Sino-Russian trade, however, is missing from China's economic relations with the more advanced nations, namely, weapons and military technologies. Again, Putin has been continuing the policy course set in earlier times. Since 1992, Russia's defense exports to China have averaged $1 billion annually. To the defense manufacturers involved, these sales have been what the border trade was to the ordinary Far Easterners: a means of survival. Putin, much more closely involved in managing and expanding defense exports than Yeltsin, has been very supportive of the China connection. This support is based on the conviction that, in the foreseeable future, China's military will be looking east (Taiwan) or southeast (the South China Sea) rather than north. Also, the Russians feel certain that, should they abstain from arming their next-door neighbor, other countries (Ukraine, Israel) would step in. The eventual lifting of the European Union's arms embargo on China is already viewed as a medium-term threat to Russian exports. As long as they last, however, these exports are credited with bringing in proceeds that Russia can use to revive its own moribund arms industry.

As time goes by, however, China has become more demanding, insisting on receiving ever-more advanced systems and technologies rather than off-the-shelf purchases. While the arms manufacturers have been pressing for easing the remaining restrictions on arms and technology transfers, the Russian government sought to promote exports by preparing to stage the first-ever joint Sino-Russian military exercise in 2005. Basically, the current arms-trade trends favor the customer, and Russia is likely to be selling more advanced technologies to its neighbor.

The August 2005 military exercise held in Shandong peninsula and the Yellow Sea is illustrative of the new realities in Sino-Russian relations. Moscow's idea of the exercise was that of a dynamic arms exhibition, a moving show to impress the Chinese buyers. Beijing, however, planned a show of force to impress Taipei, Tokyo, and ultimately Washington. The actual result suited the Chinese agenda perfectly. On the military side properly speaking, the exercise demonstrated that the two national contingents—1,500 Russians and 8,500 Chinese—barely interacted. Their interoperability level, as expected, is extremely low.

As discussed above, Putin's main contribution to the Russo-Chinese economic agenda has been in the energy field. China's energy demand is rising along with Russia's emergence as an energy superpower. Yet, the supposedly complementary relationship between the two has not started smoothly. The China oil export connection was first seized upon by Mikhail Khodorkovsky, then CEO and the principal owner of the YUKOS oil company. Khodorkovsky not only sought to strengthen the oil companies' independence from the state, but worked to do away with the government's monopoly on pipelines. Khodorkovsky's clear political ambitions led in 2003 to his downfall at the hands of the Kremlin, and to the destruction of his giant company, which was partly nationalized.

The Chinese were initially slow to understand the intricacies of the YUKOS saga, but they were quick to note the abrupt cancellation of a highly important oil project. In the second half of 2003, their confidence in Russia as a partner plunged to an absolute post-Soviet low. The December 2004 decision by the Russian government in favor of building a pipeline to the port of Nakhodka (later changed to Perevoznaia 300 km away) on the Sea of Japan, rather than to the Chinese inland oil center of Daqing, led Beijing to believe that Japan had outbid China in Moscow. Russia's subsequent overture to China in the form of a promise of long-term oil delivery guarantees, in exchange for a major loan, and a potential option of buying into Russian oil companies, previously denied to China, helped to soothe Beijing's anger at the beginning of 2005.

Finally, the highly contentious area of Chinese migration into Russia has seen little change during the Putin years.[6] The authorities have done little to legalize Chinese migrant labor, or to improve the corrupt practices of the police when dealing with the immigrants. At the same time, the government failed to provide reliable assessment of the number of Chinese visitors and residents in Russia, thus allowing the wild "estimates" to run unopposed and stir anti-Chinese sentiments. One cannot but conclude that, for all his preoccupation with the migration issue, which first surfaced in the remarks made in Blagoveshchensk in 2000, Putin has not been able to find a solution to this highly important, and potentially explosive, issue.

In sum, on Putin's watch, relations with China continued to improve and deepen, and the principal reason for that has been the Kremlin's realization that the increasingly powerful China had to be treated with utmost consideration. The apparent consistency of many of the Kremlin's policies under successive leaderships owes much to Beijing's long-term strategy toward Russia, which set the basic framework for the relationship.

While the hope of a strategic partnership with the United States in the wake of 9/11 and the expectation of a progressive integration *with* the European Union around the same time held out the prospect of a westward-oriented Russia, the subsequent cooling of relations between Russia and both America and Europe led Moscow to move closer to Beijing.[7] In contrast to historical precedents, the current West-East vacillation of Russian foreign policy is a movement between two poles of attraction, each of which is more powerful than Russia. When Moscow, having sustained a setback in the West, turns East, she has to expect adapting to a different "senior partner," rather than getting any form of "compensation," as in the past.

Within Putin's omnidirectional, but still too loosely coordinated array of policies in Asia, China undoubtedly remains the principal element. By comparison, Japan comes as a rather distant second, closely followed by India, with Korea closing the list of Moscow's principal Asian partners. Clearly, the Kremlin needs to use the potential offered by close ties to Japan, India, and Korea both to increase economic benefits to Russia and to avoid falling within China's sway. Putin has made several important steps in that direction, but much more has to be done. The sections that follow examine each bilateral relationship in its own terms, and add some general observations with regard to the rest of Asia, such as ASEAN countries, Mongolia, and the international institutions.

Japan: Which Way Out of the Impasse

Putin inherited from Yeltsin the ill-advised commitment, made in Krasnoyarsk during the meeting with Prime Minister Hashimoto Ryutaro in 1997, to achieve a settlement of the border dispute and a peace treaty by 2000. His first task, therefore, was to put the deadline to one side, while not causing new damage to the relationship. Essentially, Putin managed to do this in his own Siberian summit, at Irkutsk, with Prime Minister Mori in 2001. Privately, the Russian president offered a deal to Japan that would transfer to it two of the disputed islands and provide for large-scale economic collaboration both in the Kurile Islands area and in the Russian Far East as a whole. This, however, never worked. The Japanese let the 2000 deadline pass without much acrimony, because Putin's accession to the Kremlin had raised new hopes that a settlement was now within reach, but they refused to compromise on their demands and expunged those who would.

This seemed to put the border issue back in a deep freeze, much to Tokyo's chagrin, but the emergence in Japan of an ambitious and highly atypical leader, Prime Minister Koizumi, not only brought the old process to a halt but also, for a time, injected new life into the relationship. The Putin–Koizumi meeting in Moscow in January 2003 resulted in an "action plan" to develop Russo-Japanese cooperation in a number of areas, with an emphasis on economics and trade, but also bringing in culture and people-to-people exchanges. Not ready to resume serious negotiations on the border issue, the two leaders, as a face-saving measure, decided to appoint several well-respected and well-connected people on both sides to form a Committee of Wise Men (and Women) to develop a long-term strategy for the relationship, to include the eventual resolution of the border dispute. After eighteen months of deliberations, the committee came back with some useful guidance in a number of areas, but no real breakthrough. The border issue, the top Russian member said, had to be saved for future generations. This episode showed, predictably, the limited value of Russo-Japanese agreements, which left the border issue unresolved.

Faced with the need to address that sticking point well ahead of his long-planned visit to Japan, Putin made a preemptive move in late 2004 by stating that the Kremlin was ready to finally solve the territorial issue on the basis of the 1956 Moscow declaration, signed and ratified by both countries, but annulled by the Soviet Union four years later. Coming soon after the complete finalization of the Russo-Chinese border, the Putin offer of giving up two (smaller) islands, while keeping the two other (much bigger) ones was considered in Japan unacceptable, although some argued the need to consider Putin's wish for a compromise solution. The Japanese were in no mood to compromise. Moreover, a few individuals, in order to bolster their negotiating position, started making claims that, apart from the "Northern Territories," Sakhalin's status was also unregulated, legally speaking. This hardly surprised Putin, or made him worry too much. He had been able to clear the air before his visit, which finally came in November 2005, dampening Japanese expectations and avoiding a diplomatic failure. The Kremlin made it clear it did not expect a solution to the border problem for at least a decade.

The islands' issue clearly impacts on the Japanese, and, to some extent, the Russian thinking about the other country, but there is much more to the bilateral relationship than that. It is not only the unresolved border that prevents more active trade and investment by Japanese business groups in Russia, including the Far East and Siberia. As long as the business climate in Russia, and especially in the Far East and Siberia, remains rough and inhospitable, as long as crime and corruption are unchecked, and infrastructure undeveloped, no amount of political good will can make Russia an attractive partner, not to speak of a land of opportunity for Japanese business interests.

Something important has changed, however. From the late 1980s through 2000, Moscow experienced an acute shortage of financial resources. Under Gorbachev, plans were being hatched to transfer the South Kuriles for $28 billion in Japanese loans. Since the early 2000s, by contrast, the Russian government is awash with oil and gas money. It is not investment funds that Russia needs, but rather advanced technology and expertise. Japan could be important in that regard.

The overall Russo-Japanese relationship has markedly improved since 1990. As with Germany and other EU countries, this relationship is basically demilitarized. After a century of wars, military conflicts, and decades-long confrontation, a new armed collision between Russia and Japan has become virtually unthinkable. In recent years, there has been a modest amount of security cooperation. It is also striking that in all of Northeast Asia the Russians are the most (and perhaps the only ones) well-disposed toward Japan and the Japanese.

At the beginning of Putin's second term as president, the Kremlin's authority over the regional governors has grown. Following the terrorist attack at Beslan in September 2004 the Kremlin abolished direct popular elections of regional governors, who are now being nominated by the president and serve at his pleasure. In contrast to the situation a decade previously, no governor stepped out of line when Putin decided to close the border issue with China. There was only moderate criticism in the local newspapers, not taken up by the Moscow-based media. The governors of the Far Eastern regions, however, lobbied hard in favor of a pipeline route that would pass through their territories, which meant Nakhodka and the region, rather than Daqing.

Putin's decision in December 2004 in favor of the Nakhodka (now Perevoznaia) route for the main oil pipeline from Eastern Siberia, based on the idea of "strategic development" of the Far Eastern territories, meets Japan's hopes. The Kremlin now expects Japan to invest in the project as Koizumi said it would. Having moved toward China on the islands and toward Japan on energy, Putin may think he has squared the circle. And he may be right—for now. Yet, this is still short of a long-term strategy. Moreover, the pipeline is to be built in two stages, with the first stage to reach the Chinese border in a few years and make possible an extension to Daqing while no date is set for the second stage and some question the adequacy of supply. It may be that China will win on energy after all, especially if Japan keeps delaying.

In the twenty-first century, Russo-Japanese relations need to be addressed through the prism of each country's core interests, rather than from the usual perspective of international relations and power balances. For Russia, Japan is a major external resource for its internal development, especially in the country's east. It is a resource that Moscow has to find a way to utilize. For Japan, Russia could be a major source of energy and potentially a rare genuine friend on the continent of Asia. An eventual solution could only come as a compromise. This compromise could extend well beyond the territorial issue and include political aspects, such as Russia's active support for Japan's UN Security Council membership, special economic and administrative provisions covering the territory that will not be transferred to Japan, and security collaboration.[8]

Korea: From the North's Nukes to the
South-driven Reunification

When Putin had just become Russia's second president, a joke started making the rounds in Moscow intellectual circles. The new leader, it went, had decided in favor of a Korean model for Russia. What he had not decided was, *which* Korean model to follow. Despite its brief popularity, the joke was both unfair to Putin and too undemanding of him. The second Russian president was by no means a secret admirer of Kim Il-sung's *juche* doctrine. As for South Korea, *chaebolization* has been seen as an option by some of Russia's influential circles, but this hardly pleased the liberal intelligentsia. In reality, of course, neither Korean model was implemented in Russia.

Putin's first major foray into Korean affairs was his 2000 attempt to mediate between Pyongyang and Washington. For years, this had been the hope of those in Moscow who argued that Russia's comparative advantage in world affairs was its knowledge of, relations with, and leverage over those states that America viewed as rogues. North Korea, alongside Iraq, Iran, Serbia, and Cuba, was a case in point. Putin invited Kim Jong-il to Russia and made a first-ever (and the only one to date) visit to Pyongyang by any Russian/Soviet head of state. However, this attempt at domesticating the North Koreans and scoring points for Moscow in Washington ended in failure when Kim Jong-il publicly disavowed the promises that he had privately made to Putin. A subsequent Russian attempt at follow-up with Kim was equally unsuccessful. Moscow had to leave the heavy lifting to Beijing, and was content with receiving an invitation, after initial hesitancy in Washington, to the six-party talks on the North Korean nuclear program.

Russia's hopes of playing a significant role in an eventual settlement, for example, as a co-guarantor of North Korean security, alongside the United States and China, suffered a blow at the hands of Pyongyang, which refused to consider anything but a grand deal at the nuclear talks. Russia had no serious leverage with North Korea, and it feared alienating it by taking a hard-line position on its nuclear program. The Russian government assumes that while Pyongyang has a nuclear weapons program, it is unlikely to have usable nuclear weapons. Even if North Korea had one or two such weapons, the argument goes, it is highly unlikely that it would start a war. Pyongyang's strategy is to achieve survival of the regime by means of blackmail and brinkmanship. Not only a war—even a nuclear weapons test—seems unlikely, according to this thinking. Similarly, the Russian government does not believe there is a likelihood of a preemptive U.S. strike at North Korea, given the North's conventional strength, Seoul's proximity to the DMZ, and the like.

Thus, at the talks, Russia has had to keep a fairly low profile, occasionally criticizing American inflexibility, and only mildly regretting North Korean provocations. Privately, of course, the Russians were much irritated with the North Korean behavior, which undercut Moscow's hopes. From 2003, Russia's passivity is to be explained by Moscow's realization that an eventual solution would be for Washington and Pyongyang to make, with Beijing's political facilitation and South Korea and Japan's financial and economic support. Under the circumstances, the most Russia could do was to insist on being "in," a party to the process, for both the Korean nuclear issue at hand, and the apparently emerging regional security arrangement for Northeast Asia. Within two or three years, Putin's early ambitions of managing the nuclear issue through a revived special relationship with Pyongyang have been replaced by de facto passivity. Moscow did not mind Beijing taking the lead as Washington's principal partner in bringing Pyongyang to a negotiated settlement.

Russia also hoped that a solution to the nuclear issue would allow the implementation of a transcontinental railroad project. The project, first proposed in the 1990s, calls for radical upgrading of the much-dilapidated North Korean rail line, its linkup to the South Korea system, and modernization of the Trans-Siberian railway. Should this be done, overland container traffic would become competitive with shipping goods by sea between Japan and Europe. It is not clear, however, that in that case containers would necessarily have to make a detour across the Russian Far East rather than taking a straight line across China's Manchuria. In any event, the railroad project remains a pipedream until there is a resolution to the Korean nuclear issue and a general rapprochement on the Korean peninsula, which is a long way off.[9]

Russia's more realistic business interest is to build a gas pipeline to South Korea, more likely across China and the Yellow Sea than through North Korea. If the project of delivering Russian pipeline gas to China and South Korea is implemented, Russia's economic, but also political, role as a major energy supplier to the region will grow substantially. This requires close interaction between the energy companies, such as Gazprom and TNK-BP, and the Russian government.

In the 1990s, many Russians viewed South Korea as a scaled-down, but also unproblematic alternative to Japan as a trading partner and technology supplier to Russia. However, the nonpolitical problems that plague Russo-Japanese economic relations are equally present with regard to Korea. No amount of foreign policy goodwill can substitute for the lack of pro-reform, anticorruption drive within one's own borders.

Russia understands that in the long term the Pyongyang regime is not viable, and that Korea will eventually be reunited under Seoul's auspices. There is a concern, however, that a reunited Korea might be too closely allied with the United States, and that its energies and resources will be mobilized for the sake of reintegrating the North. Thus, the consensus in Moscow is in favor of the continuation of the status quo. This view, however, misses a number of interesting possibilities. One is that a united and rather nationalistic Korea, wedged between China and Japan, might be well disposed toward Russia, its only other neighbor. Second, the process of reintegration could offer some opportunities for Korean labor imports to Russia, and for Russian business activities in northern Korea. Third, the view of South Korea as America's cold war satellite and, thus, Moscow's nominal adversary, is, mildly speaking, outdated.

India: Trying to Widen the Base of Strategic Partnership

Of all major powers in the world, not merely in Asia, India is, from Moscow's perspective, the least problematic. India's acquisition of a nuclear weapons capability did not lead even to brief tensions in its relations with Russia. Moscow trusts New Delhi and sees its enhanced stature as helping balance the situation on the continent of Asia, and in the entire world. Moscow supports India's bid for permanent membership in the UN Security Council. Even the substantial warming of Indo-U.S. relations did not raise concerns in Moscow: Russia considers India to be "sovereign enough" to avoid becoming America's "pawn." The problem of Russo-Indian partnership is how to expand the genuinely friendly relationship beyond the narrow confines of general political declarations and arms and military technology sales. The arms relationship has been thriving under both Yeltsin and Putin, with India receiving more sophisticated Russian weaponry than China.

Putin has reached out to his Indian counterparts by instituting annual summit meetings to review the whole gamut of relations, not just their weapons component. The war on terror came as a useful *chapeau* for that. In practical terms, the Kremlin sought to find ways of cooperation in the energy sector and in software development. As a result, there has been an increase in India's investment in the Russian oil industry (around $1 billion each in the Sakhalin-1 and Sakhalin-3 projects) and in various exchanges. However, no breakthrough has been achieved so far.

Since the publication in 2003 of the Goldman-Sachs report on "BRICs" (Brazil, Russia, India, and China) as the rising economic powers of the twenty-first century, Russian business executives have been increasingly interested in doing business with India. Alongside China, India is regarded as a land of the future, which absolutely needs to be engaged in a serious and big way. The problem is lack of specific business interest *now*, and the habit of waiting for the governments to move first. The Indo-Soviet trade used to be conducted on a government-to-government level, and this pattern has not yet been broken. Domestic economic structural obstacles on both sides, and the still unresolved issue of the Indian rupee-denominated debt (which the Russians put at $2 billion) work as major impediments to giving the relationship a solid economic foundation.

Even before 9/11, Russia and India had been cooperating to fight Islamist radicalism in Afghanistan. By tradition, Moscow de facto supports Delhi's position on Kashmir, and as a quid pro quo hears virtually no criticism from India of its own anti-terror activities in Chechnya. Russia would welcome in principle India's rising interest in Central Asian stability, which could help redress somewhat the balance among the major powers in the region. In 2005, India, alongside Pakistan, was admitted to the SCO as an observer. Although this somewhat challenges the current status of the SCO as the bihegemonic structure guaranteeing Sino-Russian geopolitical parity in a key region, this may be a sign that Russia is looking for India's involvement as a means to manage the growing influence of China in Asia. In October 2005, Russia and India held a small military exercise in the Indian Rajasthan desert, two months after much bigger Sino-Russian war games on the Yellow Sea coast.

There has been some formal follow-up during the Putin presidency to Yevgeny Primakov's famous statement in late 1998 about an Asian "trio" to include Russia, China, and India. Foreign ministers have been meeting occasionally in the three-way format, although the idea of a joint Russo-Sino-Indian military exercise is still considered premature. In the 2000s, the bilateral relations among the three countries have further improved and solidified. Moscow believes that an amicable relationship with both emerging giants is a must. India and China have mended their fences and are willing to engage with each other. Russia, of course, will not do anything that would seriously alienate China. At the same time, its leaders understand that a strong, friendly India is good for Asia's stability and Russia's security.

Russia and the Rest of Asia

Russia's interest in other Asian countries is of a smaller order of magnitude than in the nations discussed above. In December 2005, Russia held its first-ever summit meeting with ASEAN states. It also seeks to promote contacts between ASEAN and the SCO. With regard to the individual ASEAN countries, Moscow has been primarily active as arms supplier, trying to expand its presence in the region beyond Malaysia and Vietnam. The 2004 tsunami has resulted in a temporary setback for these efforts in Indonesia due to shifting budget priorities, but Russian arms dealers, supported by the Kremlin, are likely to press on. Russia has also been trying to exploit old Soviet-era ties to Vietnam to expand energy cooperation.

In Putin's years, Moscow also "rediscovered" Mongolia, which had been all but forgotten in the wake of the Soviet breakup and the Moscow-Beijing rapprochement. However, Russia's new ties to Mongolia are very different from the time when that country was popularly regarded as an extension of the Soviet Union and its formal independence was a sign of Moscow's need for a friendly buffer state between the USSR and China. Ulan Batar, for its part, has no desire to recreate the special relationship to Moscow. In the present circumstances, it looks more to the United States for political backing (George Bush rewarded it for sending a small contingent to Iraq with a presidential visit in November 2005) and to Japan for financial support.

Putin became the first Russian leader to participate in APEC summits, which Russia joined in 1999. However, Russian officials have been able at best to enhance their understanding of the processes and problems of the vast region. These summits have often been used by Moscow for holding on their margins informal bilateral discussions with Asian and American leaders. The ARF (ASEAN Regional Forum) meetings also allow Russia to make its political presence known. It is more worrisome that Russia, also under Putin, has been largely inactive with regard to integrationist trends in Northeast Asia. A new economic community embracing China, Japan, and Korea is emerging in the region, with Russia as a clear outsider. This is likely to have long-term negative consequences. Having sensed that, Moscow sought admission to the East Asian Summit, inaugurated in December 2005, but Japan, Singapore, and other nations blackballed the idea.

Overall Assessment of Strategic Thinking toward Asia in the Putin Years

In terms of Russian strategic thinking as a whole, the Putin years mark a return to Russia's traditional role of a lone power. Long gone is the urge to join the Western institutions, whether European, such as the EU, or Euro-Atlantic, such as NATO. The Russian ruling elite has roundly rejected the notion of Russia becoming a junior partner of the United States. Joining the "queue" outside NATO's door is totally unacceptable. While Putin and his associates consider Russia a European country, they are wary of the EU's "normative empire" which seeks to "Europeanize," that is, assimilate its neighbors. The Kremlin's ideal of a Greater Europe is a pact between Moscow and Brussels as two co-equal partners.

By the mid-2000s, the Russian ruling elite has finally regained confidence it lost at the time of the breakup of the Soviet Union. This confidence rests, above anything else, on the new financial strength resulting from the oil and gas proceeds. The current situation is the reverse of Russia's predicament of the 1990s, when it constantly had to beg the Western financial institutions for new loans to keep going. Now Russia is repaying the past loans ahead of time. But it is more than just the abundance of money that distinguishes the new situation.

Amid all the trials and tribulations of the 1990s, the Russian rulers have kept the notion of Russia as a great power intact. However, this was mostly due to the post-Soviet inertia and the stubborn hope that Russia "will be great again." Meanwhile, inertia was gradually losing its drive and the hope was slowly wearing thin. Nuclear weapons as the only demonstrable proof of Russia's greatness, was losing its appeal as a credible argument in the twenty-first century. The gap between the elite's self-image and the reality was growing wider.

Then, soon after 9/11, came the rescue: the Russian leadership rediscovered the country's international status as an energy power, indispensable to the world economy. The notion of strategic stability built on the balance of terror was succeeded by the concept of energy security based on the reliability of energy supply. As a country that did not interrupt oil and gas shipments even as its communist system was collapsing, Russia earned the distinction of a reliable provider of energy to the international markets. In the thinking of the Russian leadership, the old maxim ascribed to Tsar Alexander III, which postulated that Russia had only two true friends in the world, the army and the navy, was modified. Now, the two friends' new names were oil and gas.

The born-again great-power mentality manifested itself in the concept of sovereign democracy, which started gaining currency at the start of Putin's second term. Never mind democracy: in reality, post-Soviet Russia has a tsarist political system.[10] Sovereignty, however, needs to be taken seriously. The sovereign in the formula is the ruling elite, which dominates the government bureaucracy. The state, that is, the government bureaucracy, is back as the principal and hegemonic player.

The ruling elite wants the world to see Russia as a serious country, no joke (as in Yeltsin's times), and refuses to listen to lectures or litanies from outsiders. The Russians (i.e., those who speak for Russia) should be masters in their own home: Russia is for the Russians, it is no one else's business.

This has important practical implications. The energy sector, which has acquired strategic importance of the highest order, has witnessed a rapid expansion of state ownership and government control. The party of power, previously a loose confederacy of loyalist bureaucrats to serve as an election machine, is becoming a full-fledged bureaucratic party, permanently marginalizing the opposition. Outside interference in Russian politics has been barred, and foreign influence in policy-related areas limited. In a way, domestic sovereignty is a companion to the international great-power status. It is believed to be a rare and precious quality. In the Kremlin administration's view, only a handful of countries really enjoy it: the United States, China, India, and now Russia. Sovereignty is independence. While Gorbachev and Yeltsin ceded the country's independence, Putin and his team have regained it. Such is the Kremlin mood.

In this scheme of things, Russia's independence is, first of all, independence of the West. New financial strength and the status of an energy power have allowed Moscow to rethink Russia's relations with both America and Europe. Russia no longer needs their benevolence to survive. Begging for money, taking advice, and accepting oversight are all history. At last, Russia is on its own, and it is ready to compete with its former mentors. Anyway, international relations are primarily about competition. Cooperation is secondary, and its terms are set by the partners' relative weights. Unlike in the days of the cold war, nonmilitary aspects of power rivalry are coming to the fore. Thus, Russia needs to make full use of its assets, which are its vast natural resources of energy, fresh water, clean air, and its very position on the globe as the ultimate central power. Indeed, its direct neighbors are the European Union, China, Japan, and the United States. Others, such as India, Iran, and the Persian Gulf states, are close by.

This has led to the emergence of what might be called new Eurasianism. This is more of a practical policy than an academic concept. Russia's "European choice" is not to be seen as a desire to join the EU, no matter in how distant a future. Rather, this is to be interpreted as a wish to be institutionally on par with the EU, to build a "Europe away from Europe." As discussed, the Kremlin sees Russia and the EU as co-equals.

Since Russia is in the process of integrating itself into the world rather than into Europe, it pursues a foreign policy *tous azimuths*. In the

Russian foreign policymaking, the importance of Asia is rising, even as the former fixation on the United States and the traditional preoccupation with Europe are receding. Like everyone else,[11] the Russian leaders are taking account of the growing role of China and India in the world economy and world affairs in general. By contrast, the traditional West (the United States, the EU, and Japan), while still dominant, are seen as grudgingly ceding ground to the emerging powers. What Russia needs in this dynamic environment is freedom of maneuver. Being Eurasian is no longer inferior to being European; it is being able to get the best of both worlds. Thus, something like an Asia policy is gradually emerging in Moscow, with the Russo–Chinese–Indian trio at its core.

An Asia policy is important in its own right, but it can also help strike a better balance in relations with the United States and the EU. In other words, to get ahead in the West, turn East. The sudden upgrade of the SCO has impressed a number of observers outside of Asia. Putin underlined the weight of the new alignment by saying that half the world's population lived in the region covered by the SCO and its observer states.[12] And neither the United States nor the EU has been invited, even as observers. As Moscow tilts toward the East, Westerners are kept in the cold.

Ironically, Moscow is as eager to join Eastern groupings today as it was eager to join Western organizations in the 1990s. The difference is that, while it often failed in its endeavors under Yeltsin, it is scoring points under Putin. Of course, the organizations themselves are very different, too. Top of the list is the SCO, where Russia is a co-leader. Then comes APEC, with its high-profile regional summitry. In 2005, Russia inaugurated its own forum with ASEAN, and applied, but so far failed to join, the newly established but vague East Asia Summit. Moscow, however, succeeded in becoming an observer in the Organization of the Islamic Conference—a major achievement in the light of the controversy over Chechnya.

The mid-2000s have become a watershed in Russia's policies toward the post-Soviet region. Rather than preaching integration within the CIS, but essentially ignoring the former Soviet republics, Moscow has adopted a policy of active bilateralism. The CIS, which includes Central Asia, is now de facto the principal truly "active zone" of Russian foreign policy. Having suffered major setbacks, some of them, as in Ukraine, very humiliating, it has had to shed the remaining imperial illusions, along with the system of imperial preferences. Moscow is betting on a long game, hoping to sit out the rivals. It has mounted a counter-offensive, and claims a first victory achieved, in Uzbekistan. The goal is no longer to recreate a post-Soviet community around Russia, but for Russia to become the de facto and de jure premier power in the former Soviet space.

The new conceptual underpinning of Moscow's foreign policy looks sufficiently coherent, based on a long tradition, and backed with a fair amount of resources. The general policy approach, however, has a few problems. The weakest point of the policy is exactly its linchpin, energy reliance. The current high level of oil and gas prices may last long, but energy prices are notoriously unstable. A collapse of these prices, or a premature exhaustion of Russia's resources, can lead to a major national crisis. Russia's political system, moreover, pushes the country toward becoming a petro-state. Already, the level of corruption is unprecedented in Russia's history. The custodians of the state are literally eating it out. The economy's capacity for innovation is not growing and may be falling. With so much emphasis on international competitiveness, domestic competition, both political and economic, is strictly limited. Sovereignty, unless it is checked, may lead to isolationism. The prospect of the sovereign bureaucratic regime falling under its own weight is not a fantasy and may become a reality within a decade or so.

The current estrangement from the United States and EU may become a chronic problem. "Defense of sovereignty against a hostile West" may become a mantra, and a mandate for anti-Western policies. Honest doubting and occasional concerns in the West about the path Russia has taken may gradually lead to permanent suspicions regarding the former adversary. The West would stop treating Russia as a potential friend and ally, and start seeing it as a problem at best, and a potential adversary at worst.

The new Eurasianism may degenerate into a primitive swinging game, in which Russia would join rapidly shifting coalitions, none of which it could lead. The balance of power would be back, but Russia, though unentangled by permanent alliances, would not be free to act. As a relatively minor addition, a makeweight, it would have to look up to its partners. Having lost Europe, it will not have discovered Asia, but rather remain caught in between.

Tough tactics in the former Soviet space may result in unforeseen consequences. Ukraine could eventually weather the energy crisis and become independent from Russia. Uzbekistan, though now in Russian hands, threatens to explode, with no one knowing how to prevent it or what to do when the next crisis strikes. Belarus, led by its maverick president on whom Moscow does not have a handle, remains a long-term problem. The Asian connection, it is true, may create a feeling of compensation for the rebuffs received in the West, but where does Russia turn when it encounters problems in Asia? It is not only the West that can challenge Russia's sovereignty. What happens when China's influence will grow to the point where the Russians will find it unmanageable? Other problems relate to the implementation of correct policies. The Far East and Siberia have been emphasized in the Putin administration's rhetoric, but a new model for their development has still not been defined. Resource extraction alone, even if it is intensified, will not make eastern Russia a developed region.

Conclusion: The Way Forward

Popular political mythology talks about Russia as a double-headed eagle, as in its state emblem, with one head facing West, while the other one is eyeing East. In reality, Russia has been giving the East and the West very different, and most unequal, treatment. St. Petersburg and later Moscow have been *facing* Europe and America; Asia, by contrast, has always been a backyard, a backwater, and an afterthought. At the beginning of the twenty-first century, such an attitude is no longer sustainable. There are several compelling reasons, some in the form of challenges, others as opportunities.

The principal domestic reason is the situation of eastern Russia, especially East Siberia and the Russian Far East. Since the collapse of the Soviet Union, the territories have been going through a deep crisis. The former model of their development is inapplicable; a new model is yet to be devised and implemented. Meanwhile, the vast region has been going through depopulation, de-industrialization, and general degradation. Russia's territorial integrity and national unity in the twenty-first century will not be decided by Chechnya. Rather, it will depend on whether Moscow will find a way to perform the feat of dual integration of the Far East and Siberia, that is, with the rest of Russia and with its Northeast Asia neighborhood. Eastern Russia is vulnerable. The quality of Moscow's statesmanship will be tested by whether it can rise up to the challenge in the East.

The principal external challenge is the rise of China. Most Russians are fixated on the Unites States, whose fortunes shot up after the end of the cold war, even as Russia's own plunged. In fact, the change of fortunes between Russia and China is even more dramatic. In 1990, the two countries had a rough parity as far as their GDP was concerned. In 2005, China's GDP dwarfs Russia's by 4:1. The gap is likely to continue to widen. As China steadily rises to become Asia's premier power, and a global player, Russia has to give her as much attention as it does to the United States.

The main lesson of the 1990s is that Russia cannot be institutionally integrated into such Western institutions as NATO and the EU. It can only earn its place in the world as a freestanding great power through deep domestic transformation and a sophisticated and forward-looking foreign policy that seeks to attract external resources for the task of domestic modernization. In order for Russia to be treated as a co-equal by Europe and the United States, it has to work hard to exploit the economic potential that exists east of the Urals. To use a Chinese stratagem, to get closer to the West, Russia needs to move East.

Russia has important assets that can come in handy in that part of the world. Top among them is its energy resources. On oil, a decision was made to lay the pipeline to the Nakhodka area, thus meeting the expectations of the Japanese. The Chinese can expect to benefit from a spur that would go to Daqing. The Indians are welcome with their investments, as are the Chinese. These are decisions of paramount importance. On natural gas, momentous decisions are yet to be made. There exists a window of opportunity for a major gas-supply deal with China and South Korea, which may close in 2006 if the Chinese opt for liquefied natural gas (LNG) from the Persian Gulf and Indonesia rather than Russian pipeline-transported gas.

Energy diplomacy is rightly the centerpiece of Russia's Asia strategy. Yet, in order to be effective, assorted decisions need to be built into a national strategy. The strategy has to meet two principal criteria: (1) it needs to be integrated, including all relevant policy areas, from energy and security to cross-border migration and technological innovation; and (2) it needs to be long-term, looking at least twenty years ahead. Such intellectual and policy coherence will give Russia a major advantage.

The principal elements of the new strategy would include:

- an energy strategy seeking to turn Russia into a major oil and gas supplier to the countries of Northeast Asia, China, Japan, and Korea and, by the same token, attracting significant Asian investments to help develop the Russian Far East and Siberia (RFES);
- a proactive immigration policy designed to attract labor resources to the RFES of such quantity, quality, and ethnic diversity as would meet Russia's needs, while not endangering domestic stability; effective border controls, a system of quotas, and mechanisms of naturalization, would be at the center of the new approach;

- a security doctrine aimed at constructing a regional security arrangement for Northeast Asia, perhaps on the basis of the current six-nation talks on Korea, and a system of bilateral security relationships between Russia and its neighbors, China, Japan, and South Korea;
- a political strategy seeking a stable and friendly relationship with China that would benefit Russia, yet not make it Beijing's vassal; clearing logjams with Japan, thus helping turn it into Russia's principal partner in technological modernization of RFES; outreach to Korea helping to bring about a soft landing for the Pyongyang regime, and eventually the reunification of the country which might then become even closer to Russia;
- a technological innovation strategy whose objective would be to fully exploit Russia's scientific and educational potential and turn its research centers and universities, from Novosibirsk to Vladivostok, into locomotives of regional economic transformation;
- a new regional development policy for RFES, based on energy and infrastructure development, and scientific and technological advancement, and aimed at integrating the region more fully with the rest of Russia, as well as with its Asia–Pacific neighborhood.

In sum, this strategy calls for elevating Russia's Asia policy to the level of relations with America and Europe; openness toward the outside world, rather than neo-isolation, and integration of policy goals, ways, and means in different spheres. It is really striking how closely interrelated and interdependent the various elements of the proposed strategy are. If Russia plays its cards wisely, it stands to gain enormously, thanks to the multiplication effect. It can also lose heavily if its actions remain incoherent and lacking vision. For the proposed strategy to take hold and produce results, it is vital that it is provided with an effective implementation mechanism.

To ensure maximum effectiveness, the mechanism has to be headed by a presidential envoy enjoying the powers of a federal coordinator of Russia's Asia policy in Moscow *and* a viceroy (*namestnik*) in the region; easy and constant access to the president of Russia; and a high status in the Kremlin administration. Dual-based in Moscow as well as in the region (e.g., Khabarovsk), this official would need a relatively small but highly qualified staff composed of diplomats with a keen understanding of Asian politics; economists competent in Asian economics and finance; migration specialists; country experts; military and security aides, and so on. Since Russia's principal assets are in the energy sector, the presidential envoy would be best served by a permanent advisory council of senior representatives of the companies, both Russian and foreign, active in the sector.* Present-day Russia is de facto run by one person, its tsar-like president. This may make many things look simpler, but contains vast potential for failure translated all the way down the line. The above idea would provide the president with good professional advice and competent policy implementation. The strategy, however, would continue to be the Kremlin's responsibility.

* In late 2005, Putin replaced retired general Konstantin Pulikovsky with Kamil Iskhakov, the former mayor of Tatarstan capital Kazan, as the presidential representative in the Far Eastern federal district. However, the envoy's responsibilities have remained unchanged.

Notes

1. Since I first used the description in a 2003 article in the journal, *Russia in Global Affairs*, the term has gained some currency in the Moscow expert community.
2. The paper constantly refers to President Vladimir Putin, and far less to other policy actors, whether institutional or individual. This reflects the author's conclusion that on matters of more than routine nature it is the president who is the ultimate, and often sole, foreign policy decision maker. For a fuller expose of this argument, see Dmitri Trenin and Bobo Lo, *The Landscape of Russian Foreign Policy Decision-Making* (Moscow: Carnegie Moscow Center, 2005).
3. This is not an accepted term, of course. Yevgeny Primakov's name is usually associated with the idea of multipolarity, which in practice meant looking for ways to counterbalance U.S. dominance in international affairs following the end of the Cold War. Multipolarity advocates sought to use geopolitical alignments as their chief instruments.
4. This deadline, and the goal itself, were made more credible by the passing in 2005 in the People's Republic of an anti-secession law.
5. To the Chinese historians, of course, Central Asia lies within the boundaries of eighteenth century China's sphere of influence. From their much longer time perspective, Russian rule in the region was a relatively brief phenomenon.
6. The officially estimated number of Chinese residents in Russia is a mere 300,000, of which some 50,000 live in Moscow. There is, of course, a major potential for growth. See V. G. Gelbras, *Rossiia v usloviiakh global'noi Kitaiskoi migratsii* (Moscow: Muravei, 2004).
7. This was a result of the YUKOS affair, the Beslan hostage tragedy, the tightening of the Russian political regime and the intense competition between Russia, on the one hand, and the United States and EU, on the other, in the former Soviet space, from Ukraine to Uzbekistan.

8. Dmitri Trenin and Vasily Mikheev, *Russia and Japan as Reciprocal Development Resources: A Report by a Carnegie Moscow Center Working Group* (Moscow: www.carnegie.ru, April 2005).

9. The idea of using the overland route to link Western Europe and Northeast Asia remains popular in Russian business, academic and government circles. There are also plans to revive, for container traffic, the China Eastern railroad, built by the Russians in the early 1900s. Thus, cargo from *Vladivostok* would go to Chita via Harbin, i.e., across Northeast China, rather than making a detour via Khabarovsk.

10. Dmitri Trenin, *Reading Russia Right* [Washington: Carnegie Endowment for International Peace, *Policy Brief 42* (special issue), October 2005].

11. See the Goldman Sachs so-called BRICs report (2003) and the U.S. National Intelligence Council's 2005 report, *Mapping the Future.*

12. See Putin's remarks to the prime ministers of the SCO states in Moscow, October 26, 2005, www.president.kremlin.ru

PART 2

Geography

CHAPTER 6

The Russian Approach to China under Gorbachev, Yeltsin, and Putin

Alexander Lukin

Russia inherited from the USSR good working relations with China. The last Soviet leader Mikhail Gorbachev, who had viewed the normalization of relations between Moscow and the West as the priority of Russian foreign policy, simultaneously started from the notion that ending the outdated conflict with the most powerful socialist state after the Soviet Union would serve the interest of world socialism. The process of normalization of relations with China began already at the start of the 1980s; however before Gorbachev, the inclination of Soviet leaders to normalization was based on strategic and ideological conceptions, a desire to find a common language with a "socialist" neighbor and to strengthen the position of the Soviet Union with respect to the United States. Such an approach fit firmly within the limits of the dominant strategic conception of the time, the "triangle" of relations among the great powers. From the time Gorbachev came to power and pronounced his "new thinking" in foreign affairs, previously commonly shared strategic conceptions began to give way. In their place came the idea of the primacy of "universal human values" and broad international cooperation. Corresponding to these new political ideas, strategic thinking in the Soviet approach to China was, to a significant degree, strengthened by the idea of the necessity of economic and political reforms inside the country. This reflected the determination of

Gorbachev for regularization. The anti-Chinese lobby, the leaders of which had made their career in the period of escalation of tensions and flowering of myths about the China threat, although not completely destroyed, in the mid-1980s lost control over the decisions of the government and the Central Committee of the Communist Party, and the new Soviet leadership moved toward the establishment of normal and even friendly relations with its eastern neighbor.

One of the principal goals of the new foreign policy of the USSR under Gorbachev was the establishment of favorable external conditions for conducting internal reforms. Its realization largely depended on reconciliation with Beijing. Improvement of relations with China was necessary for the success of Gorbachev's policies. A sharp reduction in armed forces and military expenses, rapid development of Siberia and the Soviet Far East linked to the expansion of border trade, regularization of the Soviet role in Afghanistan and Cambodia, and participation of the USSR in regional economic cooperation in the Asia–Pacific Region (APR)—all of these and a variety of other foreign and domestic policies of Gorbachev were directly connected to the state of Soviet–Chinese relations. The struggle for control with various groups in the party, the KGB, the army, and the Ministry of Foreign Affairs, which received dividends from the confrontation and therefore were interested in its prolongation, was severe but necessary for supporting the course of reconciliation with Beijing, which became one of the cornerstones of Gorbachev's foreign policy.

The new Soviet leader turned with interest to Chinese economic reforms, which in the opinion of some of his advisors and experts could be claimed as a possible example for the USSR.[1] Moreover, with his policies Gorbachev liquidated the so-called three big obstacles, which, in the view of Beijing, stood in the way of the normalization of relations. Removal of Soviet forces from Afghanistan and Mongolia, the end of Soviet support for the pro-Vietnamese regime in Cambodia, and the reduction in troop buildups along the Chinese border were less concessions of Moscow to Beijing than organic parts of the general strategy of the Gorbachev leadership. The course for improving relations with the PRC was important for Gorbachev also because from the point of view of domestic politics it was safe and could be presented as an important achievement of the policy of "new thinking." In contrast to Gorbachev's line to the West, which many saw as leading to the abandonment of positions and one-sided concessions, practically all forces inside the country supported restoration of relations with Beijing. As a result, the process of restoration of bilateral relations, which had began in the first half of the 1980s, was practically completed by 1990. The normalization was formally consolidated by the exchange of visits of the leaders of the two countries. In May 1989, the Soviet leader was in Beijing, where he was received by the informal leader of the PRC, Deng Xiaoping, and the following year Premier Li Peng visited the USSR.

The Image of China in Russia in the Post-Soviet Period

The collapse of the Soviet Union naturally overturned many Russian perceptions of their country and the outside world, affecting as well the image of China. At the beginning the relationship with China in Russian border regions was very positive. Both local elites and the local population reacted with enthusiasm to the possibility of border trade and direct economic contacts; however, this economic interest soon began to change to skepticism. Rising dissatisfaction with the quality of goods and the conduct of Chinese traders was to a certain degree a natural phenomenon connected to the broadened horizons of public opinion in border regions. Besides, the local press, having become freer, in search of sensations constantly published various criminal stories linked to Chinese traders-gangsters, poachers, Russian traders seized and held hostage in China, contraband, the destruction of poor-quality Chinese goods, the arrest of Chinese illegally in Russia, and so on.[2] Nevertheless, dissatisfaction in this period reached an excessive level. One of the most important consequences of this rapid growth of economic ties in the period when visas were not required was an increased Chinese presence in the border regions, which brought to life old fears in the local population. Local papers and even scientific journals were filled with articles about the fact that China under the guise of economic cooperation was consciously carrying out a policy of resettlement of the surplus population of its Northeast provinces into the Russian Far East and Siberia in order to resolve the economic and social problems of these provinces and, as a result, to claim the Russian territory, which earlier had been part of its sphere of influence. According to one survey, 64 percent of the population of the southern part of the Far East expressed fear over the threat from Chinese demographic expansion.[3]

Opinion toward China in border regions may not have been very positive, but it can only partially explain the experience of relations in recent years. It is taken for granted that leaving its imprint on this public opinion, despite the growing popularity among the Moscow elite of the idea of the "Asian nature" of Russia, is the fact that the population even in these far away eastern regions, by tradition, is oriented to the capitalist West and expects basic support for the economic development of Russia to come from there. The very fact that the biggest interest in friendship with China is found among persons older than sixty and supporters of the Communist Party at the same time as younger people prefer South Korea, the United States, Japan, and Germany,[4] indicates that China still cannot convince the most dynamic and active part of the Russian population that it represents an effective, dynamic market economy, independent of ideology, cooperation with which can bring real benefits.

Views of China at the center significantly differed from those in the border regions, in terms of greater diversity and a much broader approach. A complication in distinguishing different positions is that the boundaries separating groups holding similar positions on China do not correspond with other boundaries in domestic politics. Groups with a similar outlook on China could even be in antagonistic political camps. One of the principal groups which on most questions is located in the "pro-China" camp consists of supporters of the patriotic socialism of the Communist Party of the Russian Federation (CPRF) and traditional Soviet socialism. The collapse of socialism in the Soviet Union and Eastern Europe forced many of them to reconsider their prior criticism of Chinese reforms. Not changing their partiality to traditional socialism, they adjusted their position in regard to Deng Xiaoping and his policies. The very people who several years earlier had criticized the supporters of Deng for dismantling socialism and switching to the side of imperialism today see in China the example of a socialist state, which has resolved the problems of establishing a powerful state, successfully opposing the United States and the West on the international arena and in the process raising the living standards of the population, and simultaneously preserving the authority of the communist party, that is, realizing the aims that the USSR could not. The views of those known as patriotic supporters of a strong state are close to those of the supporters of the CPRF, expressing support for an anti-Western alliance with China not for ideological, but for geopolitical reasons.

Supporters of Chinese reforms and close ties with China are by no means all supporters of the program of the CPRF and anti-Western geopolitics. Belonging to this category are also many of those who speak in favor of a market economy and normal relations with the West; however they consider Russian economic reforms unreliable and failing, and the Chinese path to transition to the market more successful. Often speaking out in favor of China's economic experience are some economists and political figures, for example A. Shatalin and A. Vol'skii, and a variety of specialists on East Asia who in Soviet times took unorthodox positions. Another group of researchers and politicians who more often than not positively evaluate Chinese reforms in foreign policy have spoken in support of Russia adopting a balanced course, cooperating both with the West and with China, extracting advantage from its intermediate position.

The anti-Chinese position in post-Soviet Russia is also held by people who support various, often contradictory, positions on other questions. In this case, the contrast is sharpest since concern about relations with China occurs mainly in two groups found at opposite ends of the political spectrum: radical pro-Western advocates, who are striving to turn Russia into part of the Western world and to liquidate any Eastern influence; and the extreme nationalists, for whom an alliance with China, even in the struggle with the West, is dangerous since it can relegate Russia to a subordinate position and deprive it of its distinctiveness. Former Prime Minister E. Gaidar, for example, described in detail the necessity for Russia to break away from its "Eastern" past, equated to the "Asiatic mode of Production," and to enter into the civilized Western world. Starting from this strategy, he declared, "It is necessary to strengthen the military alliance with the West and to forestall our potential to be held back by the Far East. Traditionally, we always concentrated there substantial military resources. And it will be necessary to support that at an appropriate level, however heavy the burden."[5]

The most antagonistic sentiments toward China are held by the extreme nationalist groups. As indicated above, a significant part of the nationalists approve the anti-Western policies of China and call for an alliance with it. However, for another part of even more radical nationalists China is too Westernized and, besides, represents an eternal geopolitical threat to Russia. Characteristic of this is the opinion expressed by V. Zhirinovsky, declaring that "Today Russia has two main opponents— the USA and China—, which want to destroy it."[6]

The Evolution of Russia's Approach to China under Yeltsin

After the fall of the USSR, Russian foreign policy firmly concentrated on relations with the West as a result of which its eastern vector was left in a secondary role. Although from the Russian side (with some exceptions) one did not speak of the "insignificance" of China for Russia, the adjustment of relations with the West and the desire to make Russia an equal member of the Western community became the clear priorities of foreign policy. Already in August 1991, on the occasion of the victory over the putsch organizers the foreign minister of the Russian Federation, A. Kozyrev, declared that in support of a democratic Russia the United

States and other Western democracies are the natural partners and allies just as they had been the natural enemies of the totalitarian USSR.[7] In practical policies conditioned by these perceptions he delineated a "course from careful partnership to friendly, and in the future alliance, relations with the civilized world and its structures, including NATO, the UN, and other organizations."[8]

Awareness by the new Russian leaders of their eastern neighbor was very weak. Russian ministers underestimated the level of development of China. For instance, chairman of the Committee on Foreign Economic Relations, P. O. Aven, during his visit to China in 1992 seriously proposed supplying Russian electronic goods, which were not even in demand in Russia, to China. However, soon Russia was obliged to reconsider. In Beijing on January 27, 1994, Kozyrev declared Russia's readiness to approach relations from a strategic character.[9] This "discovery" of China was made by the Russian leadership under the influence of those circles that were very critical of Moscow's China policy and its foreign policy as a whole. Representatives of Russia's military industry, seriously suffering under the economic policies of Gaidar, expressed their strong interest in cooperation with China. Having cut the military budget, the Russian government was not in a position to pay for military orders, which threatened to leave hundreds of thousands of workers without a means of livelihood. Exports became the only reliable source of financing the Russian military-industrial complex, and China expressed great interest in purchasing Russian weapons. According to one expert, "already in 1992 China had become one of the main objects of a campaign to transfer Russian weapons to new 'untraditional' foreign markets."[10] The influence of the military-industrial lobby, very interested in close ties with China, gradually increased as awareness rose in the leadership of the country that the sale of arms to China really could play an important role in replenishment of the budget and partial resolution of social problems. Income from the export of weapons financed more than 50 percent of Russian military production, and a significant part came from sales to China.[11]

The growing role of the military-industrial complex was evident in the fact that its representatives appeared in every government after the departure of Gaidar. Evidence of its influence in relations with China is found in the selection of Vol'skii, well-known propagandist for the Chinese model, as chairman of the Russian section of the Sino-Russian Committee for Peace, Development, and Friendship in the 21st Century. This formally non-governmental organ, whose establishment was announced at the April 1997 summit of Jiang and Yeltsin, was assigned the task of "actively involving in strengthening ties between Russia and China wide circles of the public and business circles of the two countries."[12]

In the Yeltsin period the confusion over the program of weapons production was simple: "to sell to anyone practically anything they wanted."[13] Formally, there operated a system of control over arms exports, and the Ministry of Foreign Affairs asserted that "military-technical cooperation with China is developing on the basis of completely observing the international responsibilities that Russia has assumed and the interests of its own security."[14] In practice, however, according to evaluations of experts, "The Ministry of Defense and the special services were not in a position to establish exactly what was exported and what was not, especially in 1992, when in the opinion of many, there was practically no control."[15]

Another source of influence on the leadership of the country, acting in favor of improved relations with China, was political forces in the State Duma. Here, especially in 1995–99, the CPRF and its allies exerted significant influence, and also (in matters of foreign policy) the Committee on International Affairs, which actively spoke on behalf of strengthening ties with China. Although the Duma did not have any direct tie to practical foreign policy, it availed itself of the possibility of lobbying through various channels, including meetings of its chairman, G. N. Seleznev, a member of the leadership of the CPRF, with the president; conducting hearings on questions linked to China; formulating the positions of the deputies and factions in the process of discussing treaties that were submitted for ratification; presentations of representatives of the deputies in the mass media, and so on. Finally, simply the criticism of the Ministry of Foreign Affairs by the leader of the CPRF, G. A. Zyuganov, for insufficient activeness in the direction of China prodded the latter into more decisive actions.

The influence of the scientific community on the policies of Russia toward China also should not be underestimated, although it was more often expressed indirectly rather than directly, through presenting the results of publications in the press and presentations on television that helped to shape public opinion. There was also a direct influence. First, some internationalist scholars actively entered the political elite. For example, long-term supporter of Chinese reforms, O. T. Bogomolov, in 1993 was elected to the State Duma, where he occupied the post of deputy chairman of the Committee on International Affairs. Well-known internationalist A. G. Arbatov (now corresponding member of the Russian Academy of Sciences) became one of the best-known deputies taking a position on questions of security. An expert on the Chinese economy, S. S. Tsyplakov, worked as the head of the Department of International Cooperation in the Administrative Apparatus of the Russian Federation and then headed the Russian trade delegation in China. Second, periodically during Yeltsin's presidency various consultative organs were created with the participation of expert internationalists. Finally, scientific institutes continued to prepare analytical reports and informational bulletins directed to a wide circle—the presidential administration, parliamentary committees, and the government—; they conducted "roundtables" and "situational analyses" with the participation of representatives of ministries and offices. Some scientific institutes forged unofficial ties with political parties.

An influential pressure group that took a guarded position toward China in the 1990s were the leaders of some border regions, especially Primorskiii and Khabarovskii krai. Exaggerating the danger of the "Chinese invasion" for use in domestic politics, local administrations put the blame on the Chinese, and additionally on the federal center, for the serious situation caused by their own inability to resolve problems of development. They insisted on strict border controls, aimed at Chinese immigration. In the 1990s, the possibilities for regional authorities to influence Sino-Russian relations were so great that they often attempted to take one-sided measures against the border regime. For instance, the governor of Khabarovsk of his own accord disallowed the movement of Chinese ships in areas of the Amur river, the Primorskii and Khabarovskii administrations often introduced their own local restrictions for invitations to Chinese tourists, and they spread rumors of a planned Chinese "demographic expansion." Administrations of Siberian and some Far Eastern regions actively exploited anti-Chinese sentiments, linked to migration, to raise their local popularity. In 1996 in Vladivostok a book with the title *The Yellow Peril* was issued, in which chapters on the nineteenth and early twentieth centuries were juxtaposed with photographs of the recent arrests of Chinese traders by the Primorskii police. Overall, the influence and energetic anti-immigration propaganda of the authorities in some border regions created obstacles in the path of bilateral relations, which, combined with convulsions in Moscow, led to great confusion over border questions.

Anti-Chinese sentiments found only limited support inside Moscow, although from time to time one leader or another spoke of a "yellow peril." In 1995 in an interview with *Russkaia gazeta*, the Minister of Construction, E. V. Basin, discussing the situation in Amurskaia oblast, said, "The krai is well-endowed, fertile, with a moderate climate. And the land yields as much as one wants. Settling this land can make the krai rich. Chinese and Koreans very quickly understood this, actually settling our Far East. Then look and they will declare it a sovereign republic of narrow eyes."[16] Minister of Defense I. N. Rodionov once counted China among the governments of Asia that raise serious concern in Russia over the approaching possibility of the buildup of their armed forces (although at that time efforts were growing to sell arms to Beijing).[17] In June 2000 the State Duma Committee on Federation Affairs and Regional Policies spread information on the situation in Amurskaia oblast', noting imagined "hidden expansion" of Chinese into Russian territory; however at the federal level such sentiments did not acquire a mass character and did not reflect the basic direction of Russian foreign policy.[18] Despite the splash, it became ever clearer that they represented the political or mercenary interests of individuals or groups.

From the mid-1990s in the Russian leadership the Eastern direction began to be used as a counterweight to relations with the West that were not always smooth. Both the Russian president and the leadership of foreign policy organs in official documents and declarations began to pay noticeably more attention to the role of the APR and China for Russia.[19] If in 1993 the APR was placed sixth among the foreign policy priorities of Russia (after relations with the CIS, control over arms and international security, economic reform, and relations with the United States and Europe),[20] in February 1996 Minister of Foreign Affairs Primakov raised the region to third place (after the CIS and Eastern Europe).[21]

In the mid-1990s the official position toward China and Asia began to be expressed in terms of balance and "equidistance" among the centers of power. Speaking at the Kremlin in July 1995 Yeltsin drew the following conclusion. "China is an important state for us. It is our neighbor with which we have the longest border in the world and with which we have been judged to live and work side by side. The future of Russia depends on success in cooperation with China. Relations with China are extremely important for us and from the standpoint of global policies. We can lean on China's shoulder in relations with the West. Then the West will come to treat Russia with great respect."[22]

Explaining the new approach, Deputy Minister of Foreign Affairs G. B. Karasin constantly noted that the Russian two-headed eagle should look to the East and to the West,[23] and the director of the First Asia Department E. V. Afanas'ev and a department head in that department L. Logvinov made it clear that, given its unique geographical position, there is no alternative, and, moreover, these choices do not contradict each other.[24] We read that the "strategic partnership with China objectively serves the national interests of Russia and the demands of world development,"[25] "Russia and China are two of the greatest powers—poles that form a multipolar world,"[26] and that a powerful and stable China answers Russia's security interests and is a useful economic partner.[27] In the evaluation of I. A. Rogachev, ambassador to China, there is simply no alternative to the policy of closeness to China. "All other methods would be counterproductive."[28] By increasing cooperation with China, Russia aimed to resolve both strategic and economic problems. In every possible way, Russia sought to improve relations, including joint activities in international relations and to cooperate with China at the United Nations and other international organizations. Registering a shared desire to avoid U.S. world hegemony, the April 1996 Russo-Chinese Declaration on a multipolar world and establishment of a new international order did not impose on the two sides formal responsibilities; yet it was important as an expression of the objectives the two would pursue together as relations developed.

The goal of creating a multipolar world testifies to the shared perception of the two countries of the world order worth supporting. At the basis of this lies serious concern about the strengthening of the United States, which threatens to undermine the world order that emerged as a result of World War II. The U.S. desire to establish unipolarity in the world, seen in China as hegemonism, meant weakening the role of the UN and its Security Council, and alienation of the permanent members of the latter which were not part of U.S.-led alliances (namely Russia and China) from making decisions on important international questions. The meaning of multipolarity, in the words of Rogachev, is there is no place for one or a few powers dictating to others.[29]

In April 1996, during the visit of Yeltsin to China, both sides declared their desire to develop "relations of an equal trustworthy partnership aimed at strategic partnership in the 21st century."[30] Yeltsin explained that there are no more controversial questions between Russia and China, and from that time the "strategic partnership became the official policy recognized by the two countries."[31] But this Sino-Russian agreement could never be associated with some kind of "anti-American" front. The Russian side, interested in stable cooperation with the United States, constantly explained that "development of the Russo-Chinese constructive partnership is not directed against the interests of any country or bloc of countries; it does not signify and cannot signify the creation of some kind of bloc or alliance."[32] The Chinese always spoke of this even more clearly.

Explaining the official position of Moscow to China in the Yeltsin period, it is necessary to make an important observation connected to the political system of Russia as a whole. In foreign policy, as in most other spheres, coordination was seriously lacking, and toward China the state's course often was not observed or was ignored by various offices and regional authorities, not to speak of independent or private institutes. Even in the area of strategy the remarks of various leaders often contradicted each other. Sometimes Yeltsin himself made remarks that could be interpreted as attempts to forge an alliance with China and shift to openly anti-Western policies. It is sufficient to recall the very emotional remark during his visit to the PRC in December 1999: "Clinton, apparently, for several seconds forgot what Russia is. Russia possesses a full arsenal of nuclear weapons, but Clinton decided to show his muscles. I want to say to Clinton let him not forget in what world he lives. There was not and will not be a situation where he can dictate to people how to live, to rest. We will dictate, and not he."[33] Taking into account that, in accord with official statements, during this visit Russia and China came out "as a united force for maintaining security and stability in the world,"[34] naturally the above remark created a shock in the West.[35] However, it was soon explained that it was only the result of a burst of emotions and did not signify a fundamental reexamination of Moscow's foreign policy course.

"Unusual" assertions always distinguished the Russian ministers of defense P. S. Grachev and Rodionov. During his visit to China in the spring of 1995 Grachev, apparently without agreement from the Ministry of Foreign Affairs and without prior consultation with the Chinese side, proposed creation of a system of collective security in Northeast Asia with the participation of Russia, China, the United States, Japan, and the two Koreas. Never having entered into a multilateral relationship in military security, Beijing politely demurred.[36] And this same Grachev in the same year gave a warning that Chinese were trying through peaceful means to conquer the Russian Far East.[37] Replacing Grachev in the post of Minister of Defense, Rodionov long confused Beijing either by listing it among the states which are "trying to widen the zone of their influence and reduce the political significance of the countries of the CIS in resolving critical regional questions," or appealing for a long-term partnership with the PRC, or speaking of plans for military cooperation with the United States and Japan in the Far East, the growth of the military potential of which was considered in Beijing to be a source of threat to its security.[38] In the sphere of practical cooperation, interested offices and individual officials often simply placed their own interests ahead of those of the state. One example was the scandal over Taiwan in 1992 when, breaking with the official position of Moscow, a close advisor to Yeltsin, O. I. Lobov, convinced the president to sign a document establishing practically official representation of Russia in Taiwan as a means for obtaining credit from Taiwan (the order was retracted after a few days due to protests from China and the Russian Ministry of Foreign Affairs).[39]

Changes in Russo-Chinese Relations under Putin

Regularization of the system of administration realized by Vladimir Putin was favorably reflected in Russo-Chinese relations. In China, especially after the "Cultural Revolution," people value order. Besides, in the 1990s they seriously worried about the unpredictable "northern neighbor." Coming to power, Putin emphasized the development of relations with Asiatic states. In a November 2000 article "Russia: New Eastern Perspective," he particularly noted, "We never forgot that the main part of Russian territory is located in Asia." At the same time, the new Russian president, noting that Russia had not always used its advantage, called for increasing political and economic cooperation with the countries of the APR.[40]

Currently, China views Moscow as the most important of its Asian partners. Putin declared in July 2000 during his visit to Beijing, "We know that Russia is a European and an Asian state. We give our due to European pragmatism and Eastern wisdom. Therefore, the foreign policy of Russia will be balanced. In this sense, relations with the People's Republic of China will certainly be one of our main priorities."[41] Among the positions the two sides fully shared in the international arena, Putin noted "our tendency to support and strengthen a multipolar world, our combined forces in the area of preserving strategic equilibrium and balance in the world, and also the creation of conditions for peaceful, progressive, and effective development of both of our states."[42]

Inasmuch as official Moscow recognized that insufficient attention was given to practical ties with Asia in the 1990s, the new Kremlin leadership gave no less significance to rapid development of these relations than traditional ties to the West. In January 2001 at the Ministry of Foreign Affairs Putin accentuated the importance of Asian policy, calling for the maintenance of a balanced approach in international affairs. "I would say, right away, it would be incorrect to measure where we have a greater priority—in Europe or in Asia. We cannot tilt to the west or the east. The reality is that powers with the geopolitical position of Russia have national interests everywhere. We must continue to pursue that line consistently."[43]

In July 2000 Putin referred to China as a strategic partner in all spheres of activity. Also that year, Foreign Minister I. S. Ivanov declared that, "In the strategic sense we have no problems today, and in the coming years we do not predict that they will arise." He added, "Relations between Russia and China are steadily developing on a rising track."[44] In April 2001 Putin spoke of relations having a "very good dynamic."[45] Working in favor of closer relations was what Ivanov called "the special significance that Russo-Chinese joint activity has in such critical areas as raising the authority and role of the UN, insisting on the primacy of international law in world affairs, supporting strategic stability, and in the forefront, preserving the anti-ballistic missile treaty, and creating a just, equal world economic order."[46] These shared goals arose from mutual nervousness about NATO's bypassing of the UN to bomb Yugoslavia. Both sides were concerned about Islamic terrorism and separatism. Putin made it clear that he viewed interference in the internal affairs of other states for humanitarian reasons as dangerous, and that he was committed to preserving a balance of forces and interests in the international arena. China had become critical for realizing these goals.

Evidence of the new level of Russo-Chinese relations was the Treaty of Good-neighbor Relations, Friendship, and Cooperation signed in Moscow in July 2001. This document aroused great interest along with the most contradictory commentaries in Russia, as in the world. Some asserted that the two former communist giants were heading toward a new alliance directed against the United States and the West, while others, in contrast, declared that the document was purely declarative with no practical significance. Both of these reactions were, it turned out, superficial. In fact, the new treaty does not create an alliance, even less a military one. There is no obligation to come to each other's defense from aggression, which, for example, was included in the Sino-Soviet treaty with Chiang Kai-shek in 1945 or the alliance formed in Moscow in 1950 with the communist government of China that became the basis for the well-know "eternal brotherhood." The careful text of 2001 avoided any ideological statements and unfulfilled obligations, as leaders consciously strived not to repeat the mistakes of the past. This does not mean that the new treaty does not have significance. It strengthens the tendency for closer cooperation of two powerful world powers, partners in the "nuclear club," and permanent members of the Security Council.

The treaty, as Sino-Russian cooperation in general, has two aspects: international and bilateral. A high degree of consensus in views on international problems is an important engine for improvement in bilateral relations, and Russian and Chinese leaders often declared that close bilateral ties are not directed against any third party, including the United States. And this is completely true in the sense that the United States and the West, as a whole, are not considered in Russia or China as the enemy. On the contrary, both countries are extremely interested in cooperation with the West; it is an important factor for the development of both states, and fully corresponds to their strategic goals. However, it is true also that Sino-Russian closeness is stimulated, to a certain degree, by a series of negative (in the view of each) tendencies in international development, connected with the inclination of certain states (above all the United States) to depart from the principles of contemporary international law. This means, first of all, to reduce the role of the UN as the central element in the system of international relations; attempts by NATO to usurp the function of the UN Security Council; the line of interference in the affairs of sovereign states on the basis of a humanitarian pretext; the practice of double standards in international affairs; continued expansion of NATO to the east; the departure of the United States from the anti-ballistic missile treaty; its inclination to create a one-sided system of missile defense, and so on. After the end of the cold war, the United States, pretending to the role of sole world leader, feels itself constrained within the limits of existing international law, contrasted with a weakened Russia and a China, not yet having reached its anticipated power, striving to coordinate their energies in order to make a stand for a world of sovereign nations and its organs, above all the UN. The Sino-Russian treaty presents a program for the preservation of the postwar system of international law. This is also the meaning of "multipolar world," about which the two countries signed a separate declaration.

While the treaty should not be construed as a sign of interest in an anti-American alliance, we should recognize that the meaning of the treaty for bilateral relations has been great. China values the expression of support for each country choosing its own path of development, which testifies to Russia's refusal to try to teach China about "human rights," as occurred at the beginning of the 1990s when Russia's own system was far from being in order. Article 9 is about the important mutual interest in the struggle with separatist movements, which are supported by international organizations or third countries. However, its formulation can be interpreted broadly. For example, could a Russian organization or branch of an international organization act on behalf of Tibetan independence? The Russian constitution does not prohibit this, but according to the treaty (which has priority over domestic legislation), China now has the right to demand that it be outlawed. Chinese authorities refer precisely to this article when they attempt to prevent the Dalai Lama from visiting Russia. The decision to issue him a visa, taken at the end of 2004, undoubtedly was properly grounded. There is no doubt that Russia is not at all interested in the collapse or destabilization of China; yet as a sovereign and democratic state, she can hardly allow the programs of its nongovernmental organizations and, even more, decisions about granting visas, to be determined abroad.

For Russia Article 6 has great significance, recognizing the existing state border and the necessity of preserving the status quo where unresolved areas remain. This reduces any speculation that China may find some pretext to claim Russian territory or to conduct planned settlement of the Russian Far East, although China has constantly reminded its citizens to obey all Russian laws and abide by all measures proposed by Moscow for an orderly regime on the border. The problems of the Russian Far East connected to China were not provoked by that country. These were Russian problems: the neglect of national interests during the restoration of bilateral relations at the turn of the 1990s; the ineffectiveness of local authorities who under the guise of pseudo-patriotism ran their economies into an extremely lamentable state; and the corruption of law enforcement organs that allow illegal migration; the past confusion in Federation relations whereby local authorities could without consequence for themselves change the border regime in contradiction to Russia's international circumstances.

The explosive growth of China's power doubtlessly poses a serious problem for Russia, and today's Russian leadership understands it. Speaking on July 21, 2000 in Blagoveshchensk on the needs of the Russian Far East and the possibility that "even the indigenous Russian population in a few decades will speak mainly Japanese, Chinese, and Korean,"[47] Putin was just raising a new question; already Nicholas II's Prime Minister P. A. Stolypin, appealing to stimulate the settlement of the Far East by Russians, warned that nature abhors a vacuum.[48]

Although the current Chinese leadership does not have territorial pretensions toward Russia, nobody knows what will happen in the quite distant future. In Chinese society the dominant view is that the territory of Russia's Primorskii krai was gained by Russia through an "unequal" treaty. Not long ago a scandal was provoked by an article in an unofficial journal to the effect that China lacks "living space."[49] However, this problem results not from perfidious Chinese machinations, but from Russian laxity and inability to develop rich Far Eastern lands. In a strong and rich Russia nobody could threaten the Far East and the population would not flee from there, but, on the contrary, it would flow inward from other parts of the country, as during the Stolypin reforms. However, to date almost nothing is being done to improve the situation there.

Outlook for Trade and Economic Relations with China

Broad economic cooperation with China may emerge as an important factor for Russia's economic growth, including the development of its Far East region. However, Sino-Russian relations in the economic sphere have yet to match the political ties. These relations have long been impeded by the plight of the Russian economy and confusion in the country as a whole. After 1999, the Russian economic situation began to improve, and economic cooperation with China was given the highest priority. Both Moscow and Beijing clearly understand that without relying on common economic interests, " strategic cooperation" will prove to be short lived. As a result, in recent years the economic sphere of bilateral relations has been marked by a trend toward stabilization and growth, although the situation is still far from ideal. First of all, its scope and scale do not match the capabilities of these two neighboring great powers that boast one of the longest land borders in the world. Although the task of increasing the volume of bilateral trade to $20 billion by 2000 was set under Yeltsin, throughout the 1990s this indicator never reached more than $8 billion, and even dropped at the end of the decade. This figure was more than ten times less than China's trade with the United States, and China is far from being Russia's priority trading partner. Much of the blame for this falls on the Russian side. Amidst the corruption, general economic crisis, and confusion in the legal sphere, it is difficult to count on serious cooperation with foreign partners.

The Chinese are unhappy with the unreliability of Russian suppliers, who often fail to meet delivery terms, and with the difficulties of operating in Russia, where Chinese businessmen have to contend with the arbitrariness of law enforcement agencies and the mafia. Yet the Russian side is also often dissatisfied with its Chinese partners. Large Russian companies complain that tenders in China are often a purely formal affair, and that Russian companies are treated with disrespect and are effectively barred from many contracts, even though they offer better terms compared with their Western competitors. A case in point is the tender to supply generators and turbines for the Three Gorges hydro-engineering complex, which was estimated to be worth $3–5 billion, and which Russia lost to a consortium of West European companies. Furthermore, there is concern in Russia over the proclivity of some

Chinese companies and individual businessmen operating on the Russian market to illegal activity and tax evasion, and over excessively tough regulations for Russian investors in China.

All of these problems are being tackled by various intergovernmental agencies on economic cooperation at all levels, including regular meetings of heads of state. Recently, these meetings have been producing positive results. This is largely related to the general political and economic stabilization in Russia, but also to the fact that both sides have gained experience and have learned to move away from empty declarations to deal with specific problems of cooperation more effectively. Sino-Russian trade has grown steadily since 1999, which, no doubt, is connected to the general state of the Russian economy. In 2003 bilateral trade reached $15.76 billion, an increase of 32.1 percent over 2002, including a 15.7 percent rise in Russian exports to $9.73 billion and a 71.4 percent increase in imports to $6.03 billion. The tempo continued in 2004, bringing trade above $20 billion. In the Beijing summit of October 2004 it was declared that by 2010 the volume of trade should climb to $60 billion. Yet, what would seem to be striking indications of growth conceal an insecure reality. First, the goal of $20 billion was achieved only after a delay of four years. Second, given the scale of the two states and their proximity, the amount should be much higher. Third, the role of Russia in overall Chinese trade is quite meager. Not only in 2003 was it only China's ninth partner, its share was falling from 2.1 percent in 2001 to 1.85 percent in 2003. Meanwhile, China climbed from sixth to fourth in Russian foreign trade, rising from 5.1 to 6.1 percent of the total from 2001 to 2003.[50] Thus, in trade China is much more important for Russia than Russia is for China, and the imbalance is growing.

Other tendencies are of concern. In Russian exports the weight of machinery and equipment is continuously falling, while that of raw materials is rising. If not long ago China was seen as one of the few countries in the world interested in large-scale purchases of Russian machinery, in 2004 the composition of Russian exports was monotonously that of raw materials: the four main trade groups (oil and oil products, ferrous metals, wood products, and chemical goods) comprised 67 percent of all exports in comparison to 59 percent in 2003. In one year machine exports dropped more than 50 percent, constituting only 4.8 percent of Russian's exports to China.[51] Chinese producers now have a full line of the products traditionally supplied by Russian producers for export. These machines are cheaper and more competitive not only on the domestic market but also in the markets of third countries. Also, the competition from other countries has grown more intense. Not only do they provide more favorable financial terms, often it is their joint enterprises that are involved.

The situation with investments is even more lamentable. According to statistics of the Minister of Trade of China to August 2004 there were registered in Russia 549 projects with Chinese investments with a contracted sum of $582 million. At the end of 2004 Chinese investments in Russia were roughly at the level of $700 million. In total this was about 5 percent of Chinese capital investment abroad. In China there were 1644 enterprises registered with Russian capital involvement, consuming just $414 million or 0.08 percent of the total investment in China. In September 2004 the two states chose a figure of $12 billion as the goal for investment cooperation in 2020; however concrete measures for reaching it are unclear, and considering the long time frame that level would not look very impressive for two great neighbors.

From the Chinese perspective, another problem of bilateral trade is that Chinese imports exceed exports. However, Russia is also unhappy with the fact that the bulk of its exports consists of arms and raw materials. Arms account for 15–20 percent of total Russian exports to China, which is hardly surprising given that China can buy products from Russia that are not available from the West. This trade is very important to Russia insofar as it helps address major social problems by providing jobs and a source of income to tens of thousands of defense industry employees, and taps the technological potential that is concentrated in the defense industry, for which state funding is clearly insufficient. There is some concern in Russia over the fact that Russian weapons that are sold to China could be used against the country should relations between the two states turn sour, yet there are no grounds for such concern. Experts believe that the Chinese army today is too far behind to pose a threat to Russia in the foreseeable future, and in addition, its main efforts are focused on the resolution of the Taiwan problem, which could take decades. In this situation, officials think that it would be short sighted to give up these lucrative defense contracts. Russia would also like to sell China civilian products, in which the latter shows far less interest, often preferring to buy from the West, even though the prices are higher. Moreover, there is considerable controversy, both in Russia and abroad, over the transfer of Russian high technology to China. There are serious concerns over this, and in this context the diversification of Russian exports is very important.

There are also other problems. China has been much dissatisfied with the situation regarding the projected oil pipeline from Siberia to China.

An agreement on feasibility studies was reached in July 2001 during the visit of Jiang Zemin to Russia, and two months later the two premiers signed a corresponding agreement. It was expected that the pipeline (2400 km in length with an anticipated cost of $1.7 billion) would connect Angarsk in Russia's Irkutsk region with Daqing in Northeast China, and would supply at least 20 million tons of Russian oil every year starting from 2005 and 30 million tons of oil a year from 2010. In 2002, however, Russia started discussing an oil pipeline between Russia and Japan, and an agreement on feasibility studies was reached during a visit of Prime Minister Koizumi (it was expected to be 3885 km long and its cost was assessed to be $5–6 billion). Some have voiced the opinion that the Japanese project is more attractive than the Chinese, because it would offer access to the United States and the Asia–Pacific region. However, it is much more expensive than the Chinese project.

The Angarsk–Nakhodka (later the Taishet–Perevoznaia) option was suggested by the Russian state-owned pipeline monopoly Transneft, and involves building not just oil pipelines with a planned efficiency of 50 million tons a year, but also oil terminals for tankers of up to 300 thousand tons. The plan is to move Russian oil to Japan through the Russian Far Eastern port of Nakhodka. In addition, according to preliminary estimates from the Russian Ministry of Energy, the Angarsk–Nakhodka pipeline could be very profitable if South Korea and Taiwan buy Russian oil as well as Japan, which is actively promoting this project. According to analysts, Japan's interest is caused by military and political problems in the Persian Gulf zone, from which Japan receives over 55 percent of its oil. Discussions or, more precisely, struggles between various interest groups for building the oil pipeline in the east proceeded until December 2004, when the Taishet–Perevoznaia line was approved with an offshoot to China from Skovorodino in Amurskaia oblast. There remains great doubt both about the presence in Siberia of enough oil and the possibility of attracting enough investment. In the Far East, ecologists are very critical.

It is quite natural that Russia should guide itself by its economic interests when dealing with trade and economic problems; yet this should be carried out consistently, without u-turns and the cancellation of already concluded agreements. The abandonment of the Angarsk–Daqing project, which was approved at the very top level in both countries and which, according to former Chinese ambassador to Russia Zhang Deguang, could increase the annual turnover between the two countries by $6 billion, would cause deep incomprehension in China, and would demonstrate that Russia's policy in the sphere of foreign economic cooperation lacks consistency.

The privatization of Slavneft, a state-run oil company, has also seriously damaged Sino-Russian economic relations. The main problem is not that the Chinese National Oil and Gas Corporation did not manage to purchase the state-owned block of shares (74.95 percent) that it wanted, but that the "strategic partner" was treated in a humiliating way. According to press reports, the Chinese side inquired about the coming tender during Putin's visit to Beijing in December 2002, and was obviously encouraged. This must have been taken as official approval of Chinese participation, or the otherwise cautious Chinese would never have bothered. However, when it came to the tender, the organizers did their best to keep the Chinese company out, despite the fact that the Chinese might have paid between $1 and 1.5 billion more than the eventual winners did.

The Chinese obviously concluded that Russia was not yet ready to enter into serious economic cooperation while the state was too weak to defend its interests against the powerful private oil corporations. Of course, nobody declared this openly, but if Russian companies again lose important tenders in China it would be hard to blame such a failure on biased Chinese organizers (something that the Russians are fond of doing), particularly when one considers that several weeks after the Chinese failure, BP managed to obtain a considerable part of the Russian oil market. Those who were against China entering the Russian oil market once again raised the myth of the "China threat." They again accused China of allegedly populating Russia with millions of illegal immigrants and of buying Russian raw materials at low prices. In the case of Slavneft, the China threat argument was used to grab state property at a low price.

Regional Cooperation

The June 2004 meeting of the Shanghai Cooperation Organization (SCO) brought Sino-Russian cooperation on a multilateral level to a new peak. It took place in Tashkent, and it signaled the eagerness of Uzbekistan, which has no border with China, for close cooperation in a wide array of areas linked to security. An organization that had started with a limited focus on border problems had been transformed into a body for the pursuit of many common interests, highlighting counterterrorism but ranging well beyond it. Already in June 2001 at the Shanghai summit after two years of preparation of a Convention on Terrorism, Separatism, and Extremism, there was agreement on the meaning for these difficult to define terms. The participants also envisioned the establishment of an anti-terrorist structure in the SCO. The addition of Uzbekistan to the "Shanghai Five" at that 2001 meeting formally launched the SCO, and at the following year's St. Petersburg summit a document was adopted that set the aims and principles of the organization. Having facilitated Kazakhstan, Kyrgyzstan, and Tajikistan in settling almost all their border issues with China, the organization also served as a boost to Sino-Russian relations and their successful resolution of the lingering dispute over three islands. The October 2004 bilateral summit produced that dramatic result, reflecting not only the broader trust achieved between China and Russia but also the rising importance of China in Russian strategic thinking. According to the border agreement, the disputed islands were divided roughly in half. Putin remarked, "We have made an important political step, finishing the border problem between our states. We have resolved a problem of 40 years."[52] This agreement gave a boost to bilateral ties and to cooperation in dealing with regional issues.

Another signal of an upgraded relationship was the holding of joint military exercises in August 2005 off the northern coast of China. As part of the SCO program of activities, this signaled to the Central Asian regimes in the organization the seriousness of Sino-Russian cooperation in their support. At the same time, the location far from Central Asia suggested that the meaning of this joint effort is not limited to the original purposes of the SCO. Sino-Russian strategic cooperation extends to East Asia. In addition, the SCO had come to signify a cooperation mechanism that opposes trends leading to a unipolar world. A joint statement at the summer 2005 SCO meeting called for the removal of U.S. bases in Uzbekistan and Kyrgystan, suggesting an alteration in the power balance of the area. In addition, the SCO complements the cooperation that exists within the CIS. For example, Uzbekistan is a CIS member, but it is not party to the Collective Security Treaty. Only as part of the SCO is it linked with Russia in a multilateral regional security system.

Sino-Russian Relations and the Fight against Terrorism

The events of September 11, 2001 in New York and the subsequent antiterrorist operation had no serious impact on the character of the bilateral relations between Russia and China. The two countries did not need to pool their efforts in the fight against international terrorism, as they had long since done this. Sino-Russian cooperation in the security sphere merely became more target-orientated and effective. At first,

Beijing was apprehensive over a possible Russian shift toward the West. Many in China believe that although Russia has given its unstinting support to the United States in the antiterrorist operation, it has received nothing in exchange. Beijing fears a Russian return to Kozyrev's foreign policy of unilateral concessions to the West or even participation in the U.S. "hegemonic" course. If this were the case, then China would have to deal with the United States on its own, which is not what Beijing wants. Beijing's worries have been fueled by Russian diplomacy, which after September 11 was extremely active on the Western front, but somehow forgot about China. It is not that contacts with China were cancelled or limited, indeed, in this sense it was business as usual. However, the very lack of extraordinary activity sharply contrasted with the significant intensification of Moscow's dealings with the United States. This situation obviously contradicts the officially proclaimed Russian policy of two equally important heads of the Russian double-headed eagle. While Putin was the first to call Bush, he did not speak with Jiang Zemin until a full week later. Russian and Chinese leaders met in October at the APEC Summit in Shanghai, but this was largely a protocol encounter. Besides, in Shanghai the Chinese were trying to divert the attention of the world leaders (although somewhat unsuccessfully) from international terrorism to regional economic cooperation, which they believed to be a more appropriate topic for the occasion. The Russian and Chinese leaders had telephone conversations on November 19 and December 13, but such conversations at a frequency of about one a month had earlier become the norm. Thus, Russian contacts with China remained at the pre-September 11 level against the background of a radical intensification of Moscow's relations with the United States, NATO, and Western Europe.

Since early 2002, however, Russian diplomacy has become more active. In January, an extraordinary meeting of the foreign ministers of the SCO member states was held in Beijing. In a joint statement, the ministers stressed the common position that Afghanistan in the future should be a "peaceful and neutral country." They also maintained that the activities of the international forces there should be conducted "in accordance with the UN Security Council mandate and with the consent of the legitimate government of Afghanistan." They expressed the opinion that the global anti-terrorist system should be based on regional, sub-regional, and national structures. In June 2002, the SCO summit in St. Petersburg finally adopted the SCO Charter, which is the organization's official founding document. On January 15, 2004, the SCO Secretariat officially began its work in Beijing, and the Executive

Committee of the SCO Regional Anti-terrorist Structure was simultaneously launched in Tashkent. Thus, although Chinese doubts about the future course of Russian foreign policy remain, Sino-Russian cooperation continues to increase. Sino-Russian cooperation stagnated somewhat in the first months after September 11, but the subsequent development shows that it has in fact been stimulated by events, especially in the field of security and the coordination of antiterrorist activities within the framework of the SCO.

On the issue of Iraq, China, Russia, France, and Germany shared a common stance, which ran contrary to the position of the United States. Beijing was quite satisfied with Russia's more balanced foreign policy and its position on Iraq, and up until the last moment both China and Russia tried to find a peaceful solution to the Iraqi crisis, and firmly insisted on a political and diplomatic solution in full conformity with Resolution 1441 of the UN Security Council and on continued international weapons inspections in Iraq. At the same time, Moscow and Beijing called on Iraq "to completely fulfill the corresponding resolutions of the UN Security Council" and to "recognize to the full extent the importance and urgency of these inspections." The joint communiqué of the foreign ministers of the two countries that was signed on February 27, 2003 confirmed this position. Unlike during the Yugoslav crisis, however, the Russian and Chinese insistence on the primacy of the UN was shared by key European states.

Conclusions

The increasing closeness of Russo-Chinese relations, reflected in a strategic partnership that keeps adding more dimensions, has an objective basis in the way Russians view international relations around the world and especially in Asia. Russian leaders, and most others who follow world affairs, recognize that their country's interests around the world largely correspond to those of China, leading to common approaches to handling international problems. Both Moscow and Beijing are interested in establishing a multipolar world, objecting to U.S. attempts at hegemonic domination as the lone center. These objections have intensified as U.S. conduct grew more assertive, especially under the George W. Bush administration. Both Russia and China are also striving harder to strengthen their role and influence in the world, the former as its economy has rebounded and the more energetic and forward-looking leadership of Putin took charge. Of course, rapid and stable economic development is needed. Increasingly, this has become possible without pronounced dependency on the West, for instance, as energy prices have climbed and Russia has freed itself from new borrowing from international organizations. Constructive partnerships with industrially developed countries are essential, as with all neighboring states. Yet, it became increasingly clear that something more was needed to counter the U.S. strategy that marginalized Russia. While the "strategic partnership" with China is not an alliance, it strengthens Russia's voice along with China's on a global scale and within Asia it provides the core of a significant combination. Their collective voice is expressed through the SCO in Central Asia and can be heard on other matters, as the situation warrants. For instance, Russia often supports China's position in the six-party talks dealing with the nuclear crisis, as U.S.–North Korean tensions threaten to destabilize the region. The bilateral treaty of 2001 and further agreements in 2004 and 2005 reflect a strengthening partnership with increased influence.

Russian strategic thinkers recognize that the partnership would be on firmer footing if economic ties with China were strengthened. Yet, serious problems remain. Despite an increase in trade, Russia is increasingly turning into a supplier of raw materials and a customer of finished products. Yet, Russian leaders are, for the most part, moving away from the fear that closer cooperation suits China's purposes and will lead steadily to dependency in which Russia will lose its influence. Instead, strategic thinkers are putting credence in the argument that a rapidly developing China is interested in a strong and developed Russia as one possible pillar in balancing the extreme influence in the world of the United States and the West as a whole. China accepts the fact that cooperation with Russia is essential for realization also of some problems in its development. A weak Russia loses its strategic appeal for Beijing, and would be of interest only as a source of raw materials needed to accelerate its own rise as a center. Cooperation and not antagonism answers the fundamental interests of Russia, and is required in order really to have a multidirectional foreign policy.

Some observers and even a small minority in Russia argue that by drawing ever closer to China the Russian government is showing a lack of long-range strategic thinking. This presumes either that Russia is endangered by China's rise within the short- or mid-term or that Russia has some credible alternatives that would secure its interests along its borders and beyond. Neither of these premises is credible. For the past decade the evolving strategic partnership has served Russia's interests well—for instance, in Northeast Asia, Central Asia, and with the United States—and there is ample reason to expect the same will hold through the coming decade and beyond. Indeed, apart from a short period in the early 1990s, all of Moscow's leaders—Gorbachev, Yeltsin, and especially Putin—have valued a closer relationship with Beijing. This is a keystone in efforts to expand the range of strategic steps in the coming years. Overall, Russian foreign policy toward China deserves praise. Gorbachev valued it and had good success. If Yeltsin underappreciated it at first, he and Primakov put a high priority on it later with positive results. Finally, Putin has given the most weight to China, and achieved much for Russia's policy in Asia. The strategic partnership idea is not to the detriment of Russia's overall relations with the United States and the West. It is part of a pragmatic set of policies that extend beyond China. In contrast to concerns raised elsewhere in this volume about Russia leaning too heavily on China, this chapter makes the case for a balanced approach.

Notes

1. Alexander Lukin, "The Initial Soviet Reaction to the Events in China in 1989 and the Prospects for Sino-Soviet Relations," *The China Quarterly*, No. 125 (March 1991): 119–36.

2. *Krasnoe znamia*, July 13, 1994; *Novosti*, August 9, 1994, p. 1; *Utro Rossii*, April 5, 1996, p. 1; *Krasnoe znamia*, March 23, 1996, p. 2; *Vladivostokskoe vremia*, January 30, 1996; *Vladivostok*, November 28, 1995, p. 1; *Vladivostok*, June 21, 1996, p. 2.

3. V. L. Larin, "Rossiia i Kitai na poroge tret'ego tysiacheletiia: kto zhe budet otstaivat' nashi natsional'nye interesy? Vzgliad s Dal'nego Vostoka," *Problemy Dal'nego Vostoka*, No. 1 (1997): 25.

4. E. A. Plaksen, "Integratsiia Primor'ia v ekonomicheskuiu strukturu ATR: obshchestvennoe mnenie naseleniia i osobennosti vzgliadov rukovodstva," *Rossiia i ATR*, No. 2 (December 1993): 40.

5. Egor Gaidar, "Rossiia XXI veka: Ne mirovoi zhandarm, a forpost demokratii v Evrazii," *Izvestiia*, May 18, 1995, p. 4.

6. Vladivostok, March 11, 1995, cited in V. G. Gel'bras, *Aziatsko-Tikhookeanskiii region* (Moscow: Institut mikroekonomiki pri Minekonomiki RF, 1995), p. 43.

7. A. V. Kozyrev, *Preobrazhenie* (Moscow: Mezhdunarodnye otnosheniia, 1995), p. 211.

8. "Preobrazhennaia Rossiia v novom mire: Nauchno-prakticheskaia konferentsiia MID RF," *Mezhdunarodnaia zhizn'*, Nos. 3–4, (1992): 92.

9. *Izvestiia*, March 7, 1992, p. 4.

10. *Segodnia*, February 2, 1994, p. 3.

11. "Rossia v mirovoi torgovle oruzhiem: strategia, politika, ekonomika," cited in Pavel Fel'gengauer, "Oruzhie dlia Kitaia i natsional'naia

bezopasnost' Rossii," in *Rossiia v mirovoi torgovle oruzhiem* (Moscow: Carnegie Moscow Center, 1996), p. 128.

12. Alexander A. Sergounin and Sergey V. Subbotin, "Sino-Russian Military Co-operation: Russian Perspective," *Regional Studies*, Vol. 15, No. 4 (1997): 24.

13. G. B. Karasin, "Rossiia i Kitai na poroge tret'ego tysiacheletiia," *Mezhdunarodnaia zhizn'*, No. 6 (1997): 16.

14. Pavel Fel'gengauer, "Oruzhie dlia Kitaia i natsional'naia bezopasnost' Rossii," p. 135.

15. *Rossiia*, March 1997, p. 14.

16. Pavel Fel_'gengauer, "Oruzhie dlia Kitaia i natsional_'naia bezopasnost_' Rossii," p. 136.

17. *Rossiiskaia gazeta*, January 1, 1995, p. 16.

18. *Nezavisimaia gazeta*, December 26, 1996, p. 1.

19. "O situatsii v sfere prigranichnikh sviazei s Kitaem: Soobsheniia press-sluzhbi Gosdumi FS RF," July 3, 2000.

20. *Diplomaticheskii vestnik, 1993*, (Special edition, January 1993): 15–16.

21. Alexander A. Sergounin and Sergey V. Subbotin, *Russian Arms Transfers to East Asia in the 1990s* (Oxford: Oxford University Press, 1999), pp. 44–70.

22. E. P. Bazhanov, *Aktual'nye problemy mezhdunarodnykh otnoshenii* (Moscow: Nauchnaia kniga, 2002), Vol. 2, p. 419.

23. G. B. Karasin, "Vzgliad dvuglavnogo orla na Zapad, i na Vostok," *Rossiiskie vesti*, December 19, 1996, p. 7; S. Tsekhmisterenko, "Dvuglavyi orel otkvyl glaza na Vostok,"*Delovye liudi*, No. 73 (January 1997): 17.

24. E. V. Afanas'ev and G.S. Logvinov, "Rossiia i Kitai: na poroge tret'ego tisi-acheletiia," *Mezhdunarodnaia zhizn'*, Nos. 11–12, 1995, p. 53.

25. S. Tsekhmisterenko, "Dvuglavyi orel otkryl glaza na Vastok," *Delovye liudi*, No. 73 (January 1997): 17.

26. Ibid.

27. *Rossiia*, March 1997, p. 14.

28. *Nezavisimaia gazeta*, April 19, 1997, p. 1.

29. Ibid.

30. "Sovmestnaia Rossiisko-kitaiskaia deklaratsiia," in *Sbornik Rossiisko-kitaiskikh dogovorov 1949–1999*, p. 333.

31. *Izvestiia*, April 26, 1996, p. 3.

32. E. V. Afanas'ev and G. S. Logvinov, "Rossiia i Kitai: na poroge tret'ego tisi-acheletiia," p. 60.

33. *Moskovskii Komsomolets*, December 10, 1999, p. 1.

34. Ibid.

35. *Moskovskie novosti*, May 21–28, 1995, p. 5.

36. Galina Vitkovskaya, Zhanna Zayonchkovskaya, and Kathleen Newland, "Chinese Migration into Russia," in Sherman W. Garnett, ed., *Rapprochement or Rivalry? Russia-China Relations in a Changing Asia* (Washington, DC: Carnegie Endowment for International Peace, 2000), pp. 348–49.

37. *Nezavisimaia gazeta*, December 26, 1996, p. 1; *Izvestiia*, May 29, 1997, p. 3; *Segodnia*, September 17, 1992, p. 6.

38. *Izvestiia*, September 17, 1992, p. 6.
39. http://www.president.kremlin.ru/appears/2000/11/10/0000_type63382_28426.shtml
40. Renmin ribao, July 16, 2000, cited in http://www.ln.mid.ru/ns-rasia.nsf/1083b7937ae580ae432569e7004199c2/432569d80021985f4325699c003b6021?OpenDocument
41. http://www.kremlin.ru/appears/2001/01/26/0000_type63378_28464.shtml
42. *Rossiiskaia Federatsiia*, Vol. 10, No. 155 (July 2000): 3.
43. http://www. pravda.ru/abroad/2001/04/29/25552.html
44. www.ln.mid.ru/ns-rasia.nsf/1083b7937ae580ae432569e7004199c2/432569d80021985f43256cda00436de7?OpenDocument
45. http://www.president.kremlin.ru/appears/2000/07/21/0000_type63378_28726.shtml
46. P. A. Stolypin, *Rechi v Gosudarstvennoi Dume* (Petrograd Tipografiia Ministerstva vnutrennykh del, 1916), p. 132.
47. Wang Xiaodong, "Dangdai Zhongguo minzuzhuyi lun," *Zhanlue yu guanli*, No. 5 (2000): 69–82.
48. http://www.rusimpex.ru/index1.htm?varurl=Content/Economics/; www.ln.mid.ru/ns-rasia.nsf/1083b7937ae580ae432569e7004199c2/432569d80021985f43256cda00436de7?OpenDocument
49. http://www.interfax.ru/r/B/exclusive/260.html?menu=8&id_issue=10745875
50. http://www.president.kremlin.ru/appears/2004/10/14/2120_type63380_77989.shtml
51. http://www.mid.ru/website/ns-russia.nsf
52. www.ln.mid.ru/ns-asia.nsf/1083b7937ae580ae432569e7004199c2/432569d80021985f43256cda00436de7?OpenDocument

CHAPTER 7

The Policy of Russia toward Japan 1992–2005

Alexander Panov

From the Soviet Union to the Russian Federation

After the Soviet Union ceased to exist, before the new Russian leadership loomed the problem of forging a foreign policy course for the new government, both conceptually and in relation to a wide circle of concrete countries. Japan was not excluded from this plan. Already in the period when Russia still was part of the Soviet Union, the Ministry of Foreign Affairs (MID), showing great interest in the development of Russo-Japanese relations, began actively to mend bilateral ties. In the leadership of MID Russia were a number of specialists on Japan, among whom those who had transferred from MID USSR. To the extent that the Russian Federation, finding itself a part of the USSR, had a border with Japan, they assumed that it would be impossible without Russian leadership to discuss questions of relations with Japan, above all the territorial problem. In their opinion, the leadership of the Soviet Union, including President M. S. Gorbachev, was taking an unjustifiably harsh position on the territorial question; it followed that showing flexibility and a willingness to compromise on this matter could lead to a path to its quick resolution and, thus, to begin building principally new relations with one of the most important states not only in Asia, but also in the world.

In the second half of 1991 the Russian leadership repeatedly sent the Japanese leadership signals of its readiness to take a "new approach" to the resolution of the territorial problem; however, there was no specific plan or even conception of what concretely it should consist. At the beginning of September 1991, as chair of the Supreme Soviet of the Russian Federation, Ruslan Khasbulatov visited Japan and transmitted a personal message from President Boris Yeltsin at a meeting with Prime Minister Kaifu Toshiki. In the message the Russian president spoke in favor of the maximum possible development of Russo-Japanese ties in all areas. The readiness of the Russian leadership, unlike the example of the Soviet one, was underscored to accelerate the negotiating process for concluding a peace treaty, conducting it under the guiding principles of law and justice, and refraining from any concept of a division between the victor and vanquished in the Second World War.

At the beginning of November 1991 President Yeltsin gave an address to the citizens of Russia dedicated exclusively to the theme of Russo-Japanese relations. In this address he repeated the intention of the Russian leadership to find a solution to the problem of a peace treaty with Japan, the "presence of which interferes with the development of Russo-Japanese relations, not permitting the new democratic Russia to overcome the legacy of its past." Determination was declared to approach the question of a peace treaty with Japan, guided by the principles of justice, legality, international law, and humanism. Among the specialist-internationalists and in a wide circle of Soviet public opinion such an extraordinary address by the president of Russia to Russian citizens was perceived as a signal of the readiness of the Russian leadership for territorial concessions to Japan. Meanwhile, events moved rapidly, and already at the end of 1991 the collapse of the Soviet Union occurred.

The Initial Year after the Emergence of a New Russia

After the emergence of a democratic Russia its leadership was faced with deciding an enormous quantity of problems, among which were those connected to the practical realization of a new foreign policy course. However, at the first stage there was no holistic, conceptual view of this course, and a foreign policy doctrine for the new state was absent. Not coincidentally, it was precisely in this period that the diplomacy of Russia was distinguished by lack of follow through, impulsiveness, and competing approaches. All of these inadequacies appeared in the activity of Russian diplomacy in the Asian–Pacific direction as a whole and also in relations with the critical countries of the region.

It was not decided how to build relations with Russia's great neighbor China. On the one hand, China was viewed as a communist state, different from democratic Russia, but on the other hand, there was also an understanding of the necessity of laying a general base for the development of relations and the resolution of practical problems of bilateral ties, which were becoming ever more numerous. Relations with India, especially on the political level, were practically frozen. A little-contested decision was taken not to have, as the Soviet Union did, any "special partnership" relations with Delhi. But it was unclear what form new relations should take with what was traditionally one of the most important countries for Russia. Relations with North Korea worsened especially sharply. A critical attitude toward the political system existing there was not concealed, and political, economic, military, and maritime contacts were practically severed. There was not sufficient attention to mending relations with the countries of ASEAN, and participation in its regional arrangements was considered unrealistic. Dialogue with such important states of the region as Australia and New Zealand practically was not developed. In general a negative-passive attitude prevailed toward the inclusion of Russia in Asia-Pacific regional organizations and forums. All the above relates to the beginning period of the establishment of new Russian diplomacy—1991–94.

Then, gradually, step by step, began the second stage, characterized by the elaboration of a foreign policy doctrine and the formation of a diplomatic course toward separate governments. In the first stage Russo-Japanese relations developed to a significant degree spontaneously, with a "romantic-dramatic scenario." In an atmosphere of "revolutionary euphoria" supporters of building new relations with Japan, above all in the leadership of MID Russia, started from the fact that conditions had been created for rapid resolution of the territorial problem. These inclinations were understood in Tokyo. Already on January 27, 1992 the minister of foreign affairs, Watanabe Michio, visited Moscow and repeated to the Russian Minister of Foreign Affairs Andrei Kozyrev the proposal for resolving the territorial problem that former Minister of Foreign Affairs Nakayama Taro had articulated when he visited the Soviet Union on October 12–18, 1991. The essence of that proposal was that if Russia agrees to recognize the sovereignty of Japan over the four islands—Habomai, Shikotan, Kunashir, and Iturup—then Japan will be ready to show flexibility regarding the time and conditions of their direct return.

The tempo of bilateral relations began to accelerate. In February 1992 agreement was reached on the first official visit of the President of Russia Boris Yeltsin to Tokyo in mid-September. For the purposes of preparation for this visit in March Foreign Minister Andrei Kozyrev visited Japan. During the visit a narrow circle around Kozyrev and Watanabe held a meeting, the contents of which the sides did not reveal. But eventually in the Japanese press information was leaked to the effect that at this meeting the Russian side proposed to conclude a peace treaty on the basis of the transfer to Japan of the islands of Habomai and Shikotan, and after the treaty was signed to continue negotiations on the two other islands. However, the Japanese side declared that if in the future there would be no guarantee of the transfer of Kunashir and Iturup, then it would not be possible to sign a peace treaty.[1]

In April 1992 the Japanese government clearly indicated that at the summit Japan would insist not only on the return of two islands in accord with the 1956 Declaration but also on recognition by Russia of the "residual sovereignty" of Japan over the two other islands. In Tokyo it was assumed that achieving the indicated goal was fully possible. Such an impression was formed to a significant degree under the influence of the meeting of Kozyrev–Watanabe, and as a result of subsequent contacts through the foreign ministries of Japan and Russia.

It should be noted that at this time the conclusion prevailed in Russian public opinion that MID Russia on the whole was favorably disposed to the transfer of the islands. Viacheslav Kostikov, the former press secretary of Boris Yeltsin, writes precisely about this in his book *Novel with the President*. He cites a document, which was prepared in August 1992 by the Service for Operational Information of the Administration of the President of Russia, in which it was noted that, according to the evaluation of the Russian press, the activity of MID Russia on the problem of the Southern Kuriles is either "favorable for relations with Japan" or "pro-Japanese." Kostikov adds, "Similarly, the President himself was afraid that MID already at that stage of working out the problem had committed a mistake, giving cause for hopes for a rapid resolution of the territorial problem."[2] At the same time, from the spring of 1992, in Russian public opinion the rejection of any territorial concessions to Japan became dominant. Political figures, deputies, scholars, and journalists with very rare exception rejected the possibility of the transfer to Japan of any islands. What was the reason for this mounting wave in "defense of Russian territory from Japanese pretensions?"

Above all, after the collapse of the USSR, when Russia acknowledged its repudiation of a significant amount of territory, Russian public opinion responded to this necessary process very painfully, and all reminders of the possibility now of what would be a "voluntary" transfer of any other territory were treated extremely negatively. Moreover, to a significant degree Japan was seen, as before, through "the eye of past relations," which in the historical memory of the Russian nation carried not a little resentment. It is worth mentioning that even the Japanese side in this period did not concentrate serious forces in order to demonstrate a course for the construction of principally new relations with a new state—democratic Russia. In Russia the opinion gained strong support that Japan "simply wants to use the time of weakness of the Russian state in order to get territory for itself, and was not seriously interested in developing Japanese–Russian relations." The basis for such views was the Munich G-7 summit in July 1992 when Japan insisted on the inclusion in the political declaration of a point in support of "full normalization of Japanese-Russian relations by means of resolution of the territorial problem." As Kostikov writes, such a Japanese position "produced an unpleasant impression on the entire team of the President and, naturally, on Yeltsin himself."[3]

More important was the fact that the Japanese government did not demonstrate any readiness to refrain from the strategy of: "linkage of politics with economics," that is to agree on large-scale cooperation with Russia in its most difficult period for the development of wide-ranging economic cooperation without linkage to resolution of the territorial problem. Not coincidentally, at the press conference of August 21, 1992 President Yeltsin noted that among the Western countries Japan offers the least economic assistance to Russia, paying attention to the fact that in the Japanese approach the principle of the "inseparability of politics and economics" is preserved.

This approach was repeated by the minister of foreign affairs of Japan Watanabe Michio at a meeting in Moscow with the president of Russia. Watanabe, writes Kostikov, "did not bring from Tokyo anything new. The disappointment of Yeltsin was extraordinarily high. Yeltsin was extremely irritated and dissatisfied with this meeting."[4] As a result the Russian side made the decision to postpone the visit of the president of Russia to Japan, about which there was a statement four days before the planned beginning. The cancellation of the visit had the "effect of a shock" in Japan, where it was perceived extremely negatively, "as an insult." All of this was, to a significant degree, the consequence of the absence of any clear understanding in Japanese political circles, above all in the Ministry of Foreign Affairs, of the processes taking place in Russia; a correct understanding of the position and intention of the Russian leadership in regard to Japan was missing. The relationship of Japan to all of the processes occurring in Russia was formulated exclusively through the prism of "the fastest possible resolution of the territorial problem." The sentiments of Russian public opinion, coming out practically united against "the simultaneous and rapid transfer of the islands" were not seriously taken into consideration.

From the Shock to the Pause

After the "shock of the postponement of the visit of the President of Russia" Russo-Japanese relations entered a period of "pause." The "frozen" relations of Moscow and Tokyo contrasted all the more with the active development of Russian ties with the countries of Europe and the United States, where the new President Bill Clinton took a clear position of support for Russian reforms and spoke in favor of an improvement in relations between Russia and Japan. Under the influence, not least of all, of the United States, the Japanese side began to soften its position. An agreement was reached for a visit of President Yeltsin to Tokyo in October 1993.

The visit transpired and was concluded with the adoption on October 13 of two important documents—the Tokyo Declaration and the Declaration on Economic and Scientific-Technological Cooperation. The Tokyo Declaration has special significance as the first political document on such a high level in relations between Russia and Japan. In the Declaration were set forth the principles on the basis of which the new Russia and Japan intended to build their relations. Especially meaningful was the statement that Russia and Japan "share universal values of freedom, democracy, the supremacy of law, and respect for basic human rights." In other words, it was acknowledged that the epoch of Russo-Japanese opposition was over, and now both states could construct principally new relations and advance to "full normalization of relations" by means of concluding a peace treaty with resolution of the territorial question.

There was agreement also on principles, on the basis of which the sides would continue negotiations "on the question of the sovereignty over the islands Iturup, Kunashir, Shikotan, and Habomai." Among them were historical and legal facts and the principles of law and justice, which had been set forth in documents between the two countries. As for the latter, the Russian side did not offer a reminder in the Declaration of its acknowledgement that the Joint Declaration of the USSR and Japan of 1956 was in effect for the Russian side, as the Japanese side had insisted. The Russian side agreed only to record that Russia "is the state that is the successor to the USSR and all treaties and other international agreements between the Soviet Union and Japan will continue to apply in relations between the Russian Federation and Japan." Thus, it remained unclear whether the Russian side is legally bound by the ninth statute of the Declaration, according to which the transfer to Japan of the islands of Habomai and Shikotan is envisioned after the signing of a peace treaty.

At the same time, it was evident that the Russian side acknowledges that the subject of negotiations is the four islands. They are a subject for negotiations, but not more than that. However, some Japanese scholars, political scientists, and even high-ranking diplomats began to treat the declared position of the Tokyo Declaration as if it were an affirmation by the Russian side "of the fact that all four islands are Japanese territory," and "in as much as the problem of the islands Habomai and Shikotan was resolved in the Joint Declaration of 1956, then the subject of negotiations from now on would be the conditions for the transfer of the islands Kunashir and Iturup." Toward this there followed and follows even today the explanations of the Russian side to the effect that in the Tokyo Declaration the Russian side recognized the real situation that the question of sovereignty over the four islands in an international-legal form between Russia and Japan has not been conclusively regulated. However, this in no way signifies agreement by the Russian side that these islands are Japanese territory, including even "potentially" so.

The first official visit of the president of Russia to Japan allowed Russo-Japanese relations to stabilize, laying a foundation for their further development. However, after the Tokyo meeting high-level contacts on a political level did not grow more active, and trade and political ties continued to stagnate. On the whole, no serious changes occurred in the character of bilateral relations. For the Japanese political elite it became clear that in the near future they could not, as they had done in 1992, count on the rapid return of the "northern territories." On the whole, the opinion prevailed that there was no rush in relations with Russia, and they should wait for stabilization of the political and economic situation. Cooperating with the Russian reform forces had reached its limit.

In Moscow they saw this approach by Japan toward the development of relations with Russia, and they answered the "Japanese passive approach" with a no less passive Russian one. The conclusion prevailed that Japan is only interested in resolution of the territorial problem on its terms, and is not ready for building new relations with a democratic Russia. Thus, in Russo-Japanese relations after a short "romantic period" (from January to September 1992) a "period of passivity" ensued, lasting almost five years. Only from the middle of 1997 begins the activization of bilateral ties, which entered into a period of unprecedented development in intensity and in achieving results, which lasted to the end of 2001.

Unprecedented Activization of Bilateral Ties

Through 1997 the fundamental principles of Russian policy in the APR were formulated and began to be operationalized. The main objective of this policy was creation in the east of the country of a "belt" of good-neighborliness, trust, and security in the interest of establishing favorable conditions for the economic and social development of Russia and successfully realizing the policies of reform. The task was set forth to develop bilateral relations with the countries of the region to the maximum possible degree, proceeding in this as far as would be agreeable to Russia's partners. Great meaning was attached to the inclusion of Russia in the activities of all regional organizations and forums. As a result of the realization of these policies in quite a short time span not a few successes were achieved. Relations fundamentally changed for the better with China, with which already in the spring of 1996 a declaration of strategic partnership was signed. The political dialogue was restored with India, as the atmosphere in Russo-Indian relations began to improve rapidly. Appropriate attention began to be given to relations with Mongolia, Vietnam, Laos, and Cambodia. Contacts were started with the DPRK. Relations were formed with the countries of ASEAN. Russia was included in the dialogue with ASEAN as an organization, and Russia applied for entrance into APEC.

Within the framework of this policy direction more attention began to be paid to relations with Japan. It was seen as unnatural that, participating in the summits of the G-7, Russia had the least developed ties with one of the most important and developed members of this "club" Japan. In the Japanese political elite at this time there also occurred certain changes in attitudes toward relations with Russia. The conclusion began to prevail that the process of democratization and the transition to a market economy in Russia had acquired an irreversible character, that Russia shares democratic values in common with Japan and other Western countries, and that it is worth developing relations with Russia in various spheres and in the course of their activation to seek a resolution to the territorial problem.

In its conceptual plan the new approach of the Japanese side toward relations with Russia was set forth by Prime Minister Hashimoto Ryutaro on July 24, 1997 in his presentation to the Keizai Doyukai. This approach foresaw an improvement in Japanese-Russian relations on the basis of three principles. First was the principle of "establishing genuine trust among those who directly sit across the table in the negotiations." As part of this, Hashimoto had in mind his relations with President Yeltsin. Second was the principle of mutual benefit, assuming the absent of attempts to gain one-sided advantage. Third was the principle of a long-term approach, having in mind the necessity of establishing a firm base for the improvement of bilateral relations. In the end, it was anticipated, developing Japanese–Russian relations on the basis of the indicated three principles would make it possible to find a way forward to resolve the territorial problem. On the whole, the approach set forth assumed that the search for a way out in resolving the most complicated—territorial—problem was through the all-around development of Japanese–Russian ties, giving them, according to the expression of Hashimoto, a "multi-layered character."

The speech by the prime minister of Japan, which articulated a new approach to the development of relations with Russia, was met with the most positive evaluation by the Russian leadership, inasmuch as it corresponded to the very sentiments that had congealed in Russian public opinion regarding "the most rational" manner of conducting affairs with Japan. Winning respect also was the approach to regularizing the territorial problem. The "Hashimoto doctrine" opened the way to active development of Russo-Japanese relations. Already at the beginning of November 1997 in Krasnoyarsk there occurred the first informal meeting on the highest level—that of Yeltsin and Hashimoto—which concluded with the realization of a series of important agreements. First, there was agreement on an unfolding plan of gradual development of Russo-Japanese economic relations, dubbed the "Yeltsin–Hashimoto plan." Japan, in response to an appeal from the Russian side, declared its readiness to provide direct credits on the scale of $1.5 billion for rendering cooperation to Russian reforms. Second, the Japanese side informed Russia of its decision to support Russia's membership in APEC. To this time, the Japanese position actually blocked the entrance of Russia into APEC. Third, an agreement was reach to make more active the dialogue on questions of stability and security in the APR, to broaden contacts and exchanges between military departments in the two countries.

But most attention was focused on the agreements related to negotiations over a peace treaty. An agreement was reached to the effect that, while conducting negotiations, the sides would actively develop the entire complex of bilateral ties, to make efforts to resolve practical questions which have a relationship to the disputed territories. And finally the main point: "the two leaderships agreed to apply all of their energies in order to conclude a peace treaty by 2000 on the basis of the Tokyo Declaration of 1993." It was, in fact, Yeltsin who introduced this proposal.

After the Krasnoyarsk meeting quite a few versions and guesses appeared for why Yeltsin made such an extraordinary and unexpected proposal. Yeltsin himself subsequently never commented on his decision. At the same time one can conjecture that, taking the initiative on the peace treaty, Yeltsin acted in his own characteristic style. Often he startled his partners—leaders of many states—with unexpected statements and proposals. He did this, it is assumed, including with remarks "to the utmost degree to bring the situation to a head" in order to have a clearer understanding inasmuch as it would mature for realization of a concrete result. The Krasnoyarsk proposal by Yeltsin can be interpreted as an "invitation" seriously to examine whether it was realistic in principle to conclude a peace treaty in these concrete historical conditions and what is required for creating the circumstances in which it would be possible to achieve results. And if one proceeded toward the conclusion of a peace treaty within the allotted time and did not succeed, then the expenditure of energy would not be in vain—the sides would probe variations for resolving the problem, and, what is most important, would significantly move forward in the development of bilateral relations.

Subsequent events affirm this conclusion. The sides put forward a proposal for resolving the problems of a peace treaty—the Japanese side, at Kawana in April 1998, and the Russian side, in Moscow in November 1998. And although by 2000 they did not succeed in concluding a peace treaty, bilateral ties began to develop at a tempo never before seen in the history of Russo-Japanese relations. The essence of the "Kawana proposal," made at the second informal Yeltsin–Hashimoto meeting at the little Japanese resort town of Kawana consisted of the following. The Japanese side proposed to write into the peace treaty that the Japanese–Russian border would pass between the islands of Iturup and Urup, but for a certain period of time (until the realization between Japan and Russia of a separate agreement) Japan would recognize the legality of Russian administrative control over the islands of Iturup, Kunashir, Shikotan, and Habomai. In other words, talk turned to recognition by the Russian side of Japan's "residual sovereignty" over the four islands.

For the Russian side recognition of residual Japanese sovereignty over the four islands would signify actual recognition of the correctness of the Japanese position on the territorial problem and the eventual transfer of the islands to Japan. The Russian president could not go that far. Already in September 1997 in one of his public presentations Yeltsin declared that the "islands cannot be transferred to Japan as long as Russian society does not accept that decision." In a survey of public opinion in Russia conducted on the eve of the visit of Prime Minister Obuchi Keizo to Moscow in November 1998, 60 percent of Russian citizens spoke out against the idea of recognizing the sovereignty of Japan over the Southern Kuriles with the actual transfer to occur in the future. On the

Southern Kuriles themselves and also on Sakhalin the number of opponents of this idea turned out to be even greater—corresponding to 75 and 83 percent.[5]

The Russian side at the Moscow negotiations of Yeltsin–Obuchi in November 1998 in response to the "Kawana proposal" of the Japanese side put forward its own proposal, which was characterized as a "compromise." The Russian side suggested agreeing on and signing by 2000 a Treaty of Peace, Friendship, and Cooperation, in which it would be stipulated that the sides would continue searching for a mutually acceptable formula for resolving the question of the border. In this way, it actually had in mind signing two treaties: first, on peace, friendship and cooperation, second on the border. In the first treaty wording was suggested to indicate that in pursuit of establishing favorable conditions for a final settlement of the territorial demarcation the sides would stimulate and develop broad contacts between residents of the islands, Sakhalinskaia oblast, and the residents of Japan, and also work out a special legal regime, which, not causing any loss to the state interests and political positions of the two countries, would facilitate the establishment of a favorable atmosphere and legal basis for joint economic and other activity on the islands. In the treaty would be fixed the obligations of the sides to conduct negotiations about the conclusion of a separate treaty on the establishment of a line for the border passing between Russia and Japan in the region of the islands.

In this way, the Russian side, assuming that the situation was not yet ripe for a final settlement of the problem of territorial demarcation, offered to conclude what in essence was an "interim treaty." This could be the "means" (*michisuji*) for a way to a final settlement of the problem of territorial demarcation, about which Prime Minister Hashimoto spoke in his talk in July 1997. The "Moscow proposal" consisted not of setting the territorial problem aside, but of reaching a staged resolution. The Treaty on Peace, Friendship, and Cooperation had in mind fixing the intentions of the sides on resolving the territorial question, and in a different treaty to specify the concrete passage of the border line. Moreover, the Russian side went to the unusual step of proposing jointly with the Japanese side to work out a special legal regime for assuring judicial and other conditions for joint economic and other activity on the four islands. In international practice one can scarcely find examples when one state offers to another jointly to work out the status for a part of its own territory. This was a genuine, compromise step for the Russian side.

The Japanese side did not accept the "Moscow proposal," considering it insufficient. Nevertheless, the Russian and Japanese sides, advancing the corresponding "Kawana" and "Moscow" proposals, defined their "starting positions" in the negotiations for a peace treaty. After this, it was necessary to bring matters toward convergence, looking for a mutually acceptable compromise. The Russian side in the direction of such a compromise made a series of very important steps. During his official visit to Japan in September 2000 Vladimir Putin orally repeated that for the Russian side the Joint Declaration of 1956 is in effect in its entirety, including the ninth statute—the territorial one—, bringing to everyone's attention the fact that this document was ratified by both sides and has an obligatory character both for Russia, as the state that is the successor to the Soviet Union, and for Japan. And at the end of the negotiations between President Putin and Prime Minister Mori Yoshiro on March 25, 2001 the Russian side agreed to include in the Joint Statement mention of the Joint Declaration of the USSR and Japan of 1956 as the basic legal document, which had been established as the starting point in the process of negotiations for the conclusion of a peace treaty after the restoration of diplomatic relations between the two countries. Thus, for the first time after 1956 the Russian side put on record in an official document that the Joint Declaration is in effect for Russia without any qualifications. In this way one can proceed on the basis that after this the position set forth in a note from the Soviet side of 1960, that the "territorial statute" of the Joint Declaration is not in effect in connection with the conclusion of the Japanese–American Security Treaty, was relegated to history. The acknowledgement that the subject of negotiations is four islands as agreed in the Tokyo Declaration was also confirmed in the March Joint Statement.

The Negotiations at an Impasse

In connection with the position of the Russian side in Japanese political and academic circles as well as in the Ministry of Foreign Affairs a discussion ensued regarding how to react to this. Supporters appeared of the idea of an "interim treaty" or a "dual track formula" of "two islands plus two islands." The meaning of this could amount to the fact that, based on recognition by the Russian side that the "territorial statute" of the Joint Declaration of 1956 is in effect, first there should be signed a treaty on the return of the islands Habomai and Shikotan with the understanding that negotiations on the transfer of the islands Kunashir and Iturup would be continued and completed through the signing of a corresponding treaty. However, in the final analysis the supporters of the "traditional approach" on the "simultaneous return of all the islands" won. Prime Minister Koizumi Junichiro after his election to this post in April 2001 declared that "Japan would win from Russia recognition that all the Southern Kuriles are Japanese territory. Only after that would Japan be prepared flexibly to advance to the conditions and timing of their transfer." In other words, adherence to the "Kawana variant" was affirmed. The "traditional approach" was reconfirmed in the spring of 2002 by the change of personnel dealing with Russia in Japan.

If in the "two track approach" one could notice the appearance of some degree of inclination of the Japanese side toward compromise, then the "traditional approach" did not leave room for maneuvering. In essence, it was proposed to discuss concrete conditions for the transfer of the islands Habomai and Shikotan, and also the sovereignty—read the transfer—of the islands Kunashir and Iturup "in one package," inasmuch as the four islands are for Japan "a single entity." The Russian side cannot proceed to a continuation of the negotiations on such a basis, and they were in fact broken off. This is the situation that remains right up to the present.

Moreover, in Russia people have paid attention to the fact that recognition by the Russian side that the Joint Declaration of 1956 is in effect was perceived in Japan either with passive neutrality or, more often, negatively, as insufficient. Such an approach created in Russia the impression that in the conduct of negotiations with the Japanese side it is necessary to keep in mind a very important circumstance. Each "concession" or "step to meet Japan halfway" was taken as "expected" and "natural," and led to it beginning to strive for new concessions. At the same time Japan itself did not demonstrate an interest in welcoming steps or in compromise.

It is noteworthy that at the Soviet–Japanese negotiations at the highest level in April 1991 Prime Minister Kaifu over several hours tried to persuade President Gorbachev to recognize that the Joint Declaration of 1956 was fully in effect. And the disappointment of the Japanese side was great when it did not succeed in this. But here without any pressure from "outside" the Russian side took such a step and again there was "disappointment" from the Japanese side, but already of a different order. Undoubtedly, such an approach did not stimulate the inclination of the Russian side to actively conduct negotiations.

Neither by 2000, as the sides agreed in Krasnoyarsk, nor to the present day has there been success in advancing to sign a peace treaty. However, for a relatively short period in relations between the two countries there occurred an unprecedented positive transformation, a negotiating process for a peace treaty characterized by unparalleled activeness. This was the period 1997–2001.

From 2002 a slowing of the tempo of development of bilateral ties can be observed; however on the whole that which was achieved to this high level of relations has been preserved. The search continues, however so far without success, for a mutually acceptable basis to conduct negotiations for a peace treaty. Speaking on December 23, 2004 at a press conference President Vladimir Putin underlined that it is in both Russian and Japanese national interests to resolve as soon as possible all problems which interfere with the development of bilateral relations. This, first of all, refers to the problem of completing a peace treaty. "The Russian Federation," he observed, "is the legal successor of the Soviet Union, and we, it is understood, will strive to fulfill all international-legal obligations which were assumed by the Soviet Union, however burdensome." In this connection the president recalled the Joint Declaration of 1956 and concretely the ninth statute, where, as he pointed out, "It is written that as required by prior conditions the transfer of two islands would be made possible by the signing of a peace treaty that was considered synonymous with settlement of all remaining territorial disputes . . . . Second, there is stated that the Soviet Union is ready to transfer two islands. It is not stated under what conditions to transfer them, when to transfer them, and whose sovereignty extends to this territory. These are all subjects for our careful study and joint work with our Japanese colleagues." That for the present is how the Russian position on the territorial problem is formulated. The Russian side affirms its readiness to act in accord with the territorial statute of the Joint Declaration of 1956, to conduct negotiations on the conditions for its realization and to consider as in any way well-founded the Japanese pretensions to the islands of Kunashir and Iturup. The Japanese side retains its own well-known position.

Russia–Japan Relations from a Broad Perspective

As world experience shows, territorial differences are not resolved simply on the basis of legal, historical, or geographical evidence. Very serious stimuli of the economic, political, or strategic order are necessary in order for the leaders of the respective states to agree to mutual conces-sions and to reach a compromise, overcoming strong opposition inside each of the countries, which always arises with regard to such patrioti-cally tinged problems. With this conclusion of the well-known Russian scholar and politician Aleksei Arbatov it is difficult not to agree.[6] To the present, unfortunately, mutual stimuli for resolving the problem are few. For a significant part of the Russian political elite it is still little understood how, in a major way, Japan, which on principal questions closely follows the United States, can be useful to Russia. Would it not be better to devote more attention to Washington? New Russian businessmen also do not have great interest in Japan, looking mainly to the West, where they better orient themselves and have an easier possibility of forging business ties.

In Russia the declarations are well known of official Japanese representatives to the effect that "true economic cooperation between the two countries is impossible without signing a peace treaty." This gives rise in Russia to the opinion that Japan is trying "to play the economic card in the form of an enticement for the return of the islands." And to the promises that after the signing of a peace treaty a "golden age" in bilateral relations will commence, few believe that it is really this that will bring a massive inflow of Japanese capital into the Russian market. Among Russian politicians and scholars practically nobody shares the reasoning of many Japanese political scientists, politicians, and businessmen to the effect that Russia faces the prospect of being threatened by the danger of "losing its Far East," since on the basis of a complex socioeconomic situation the dissatisfaction of the local population is growing in the face of simultaneous expansion of Chinese influence and presence. The thesis on the "China threat" in Russian society is not gaining ground. On the contrary, cooperation with China in the Far East brings concrete political and economic benefits. It is precisely conditions of large-scale and voluntary cooperation that have made possible the final settlement in the summer of 2005 on a compromise basis of the problem of the course of the Russo-Chinese border in the region of Khabarovsk.

If in the early period of the existence of the new Russia in the Far East there were calculations about substantial Japanese investment, then to the degree that not one more or less substantial investment project has been successfully realized, expectations that Japanese business would make much of the Russian Far Eastern market have practically disappeared. Local authorities have learned to find their own sources of investment for realizing quite substantial, including infrastructural, projects.

Now across broad circles of Russian public opinion—and this is a fundamental difference from the Soviet period—there is not only an understanding of the existence of a territorial problem in relations with Japan, but also knowledge of its details. In recent times in Russia a large quantity of related research has been published. They, as a rule, with a strong foundation and argumentatively engage in polemics with the Japanese position, which only supports the conclusion that this position is far from uncontroversial and "100 percent justified," as the Japanese side insists. Now the Russian position looks much more well-founded and convincing than the Japanese one. This is connected, first of all, to the acknowledgement of the Russian side that the Joint Declaration of 1956 is fully in effect. At present this is the only document of an international character, which was ratified by the legislative organs of both countries. It is worth making it the starting point for negotiations.

Moreover, the Russian side undertook one more "strong step." On September 4, 2001 at the fiftieth anniversary of the conclusion of the San Francisco Peace Treaty MID Russia made a declaration in which the Russian side for the first time gave a positive evaluation of this document. Let's recall that in the treaty Japan renounced the rights, legal basis, and pretensions to the Kurile Islands. The Soviet Union, more precisely Stalin, made a mistake not signing the San Francisco Peace Treaty, which then required the completion first of the Soviet–Japanese Joint Declaration of 1956 and later a peace treaty. A positive assessment by the Russian side of the San Francisco Treaty of course strengthens the position of Russia in the negotiations with Japan. Judging by everything, it is precisely for this reason that this step of the Russian side remains practically "unnoticed" even in Japan.

The Russian side considers it principally important to find a mutually acceptable solution to the territorial problem. As Russian Minister of Foreign Affairs Igor Ivanov underscored in his presentation of March 13, 2002 at a session of the State Duma, "Russia does not have a border with Japan which was fixed in the international-legal order. A peace treaty is also absent. Therefore, it is natural that these problems are an important part of our negotiations with Japan." The territorial problem is the only essential question in which the positions of the two sides are still opposed. Russia really is striving to build lasting good-neighborly relations with Japan. However, it starts from the position that this in equal measure serves Japanese national interests.

The appearance in 1991 on the international arena of a new Russia as a sovereign state created conditions for the formation of bilateral relations of a principally new character. With the end of the "Cold War epoch" between Russia and Japan antagonism and confrontation, which had been caused by the position of the two countries in two enemy camps—"socialist and capitalist"—ceased. Russia and Japan are interested in supporting peace and stability in the Far East and in the APR, which is necessary for the successful resolution of domestic problems in both countries. The correspondence or similarity of the positions of Moscow and Tokyo on many pressing international problems permits very concrete close cooperation of the two countries in a whole series of directions.

It is not accidental that the Russian side practically immediately supported the concept of six-sided negotiations on the problems of guaranteeing peace on the Korean peninsula that was put forward in March 1998 by the minister of foreign affairs of Japan Obuchi. Russia subsequently is supporting Japan's candidacy for entrance into the United Nations Security Council in case it is reformed.

In Soviet military strategy Japan was regarded as a forward beachhead for the deployment of American military forces, targeted against the Soviet Union, and as an American military ally which possessed a contemporary, well-equipped army. Starting from this view of the situation, the Soviet leadership attempted to strengthen its Far Eastern land forces, but not with as much energy or contemporary technology as its European ones, since a land military confrontation with the United States and Japan in the Far East was perceived as improbable. Therefore, the main efforts were directed at strengthening the naval forces with the goal of achieving in this sphere, if not parity with the powerful Pacific fleet of the United States, then to approach that. As a result, even in the Far East the Soviet Union was an active participant in the arms race. Significantly reducing Russian armed forces and naval presence in the Far East,[7] and establishing Russian–American relations on new principles eliminated the "problem of the Russian threat" for Japan. Conditions arose for advancing a dialogue on military matters and exchanges between the militaries of Russia and Japan, of which the two sides actively made use.

The Russian side changed its attitude toward the Japan–American security treaty. In the course of the first visit in the history of bilateral relations to Japan in May 1997 of a minister of defense of Russia the Russian side declared that Russia is not concerned by the close alliance of Japan with the United States, and it starts from the position that these relations will have a defensive character, will not be directed against the interests of third countries, will not broaden the sphere of their inclusiveness and functions, will be transparent, and will not arouse anxiety in neighboring countries.

On August 16, 1999, at the level of the leaders of the defense ministries of the two countries a memorandum was signed in which it is remarked that development of relations between the military ministries would serve to deepen mutual understanding and trust between Russia and Japan and also to strengthen peace and security in the APR. An understanding was reached to continue intensive, regular contacts at all levels and in the most varied forms. It is worth noting that previously the Japanese side signed documents of this type only with the United States, its strategic military ally. After the passing in May 1999 by the Japanese Diet of a packet of laws with new wording on the basic direction of Japanese–American cooperation in the area of defense, in accord with which Japan would no longer limit itself to supplying American armed forces only with military bases and would directly provide support for the military forces of the United States in case of the occurrence of extraordinary circumstances in regions contiguous to Japanese territory, the Russian side came forward with a statement of its position on this matter. It underscored that military alliances should have a deeply defensive direction, should not disrupt the regional balance of forces, should adapt to multisided forces in the sphere of security and avoid widening this sphere, and should not substitute for or act without authorization by the UN and the Security Council. Recognizing that the new laws caused concern among a variety of countries, including Russia, the Japanese government offered some explanations, putting stress on the fact that the new laws are intended to improve the system of support for the security of Japan, and also to serve in the capacity of a mechanism for containing conflicts, and are not directed against any other countries.

The Russian side from the very beginning did not conceal its negative attitude toward the plans for creating a Japanese–American system of antimissile defense whose theater of military activity would be adapted to the region of East Asia. Although the Russian side does not see in such a system a direct threat to its security interests; nevertheless it starts from the fact the creation of a system of theater missile defense could destroy the existing regional balance of power and would facilitate a missile arms race. Therefore, Russia proposes in this region, as in Europe, to take a different path, namely with joint, multilateral efforts to establish a system of defense against rocket attacks. But, on the whole, Russo-Japanese contacts and exchanges in the sphere of defense policies and security provide a good example to other countries of the Asia–Pacific region, serving to strengthen the region's stability and opening the possibility for movement toward a multilateral effort to maintain it.

Ways Ahead

In the postwar era Japanese–Soviet and then Japanese–Russian relations gained experience for developing and finding a way to the conclusion of a peace treaty with the resolution of the territorial problem along three paths. The first path, identified by the Soviet leadership in the mid-1950s, foresaw the possibility of a compromise solution to the problem—conclusion of a peace treaty and transfer to Japan of two islands. This variant Japan did not accept either at that time or at the start of the 1970s when it was in essence repeated by Moscow. The second path is that of "armed opposition." The Soviet Union denied the existence in bilateral relations of a territorial problem, built up its military presence in the Far East, including with the aim of pressuring Japan. Japan responded by strengthening its military–political alliance with the United States in opposition to Soviet policies, especially in the APR. This path brought relations to a dead-end, and the search for a way out began in the mid-1980s with the "Gorbachev team" coming to power in the USSR. The third path—that of resolving the problem by "getting it out of the way"—was approved in the first year of the appearance of the new state of Russia. It has not provided the results on which Moscow and, even more, Tokyo counted.

There remains a fourth path, which the two sides began to test at the end of the 1990s. This is the path of intensive development of relations, raising them to a principally new level, the results of which can be carried over to the settlement of the problem of territorial demarcation. On this path certain successes were reached, but clearly not enough to lead to a concrete result. For Russia full normalization of relations with Japan, naturally with the resolution of the territorial problem, would mean a significant strengthening of its global position, and above all in the APR. Signing a peace treaty would resolve the problem of fixing in international legal terms the border of Russia in the Far East and provide in Japan for a long historical period a friendly state. Russia starts from the fact that also for the national interests of Japan it is important to draw closer to Russia, since this would make possible its entry into the international arena with a more autonomous and weighty role.

Over the past decades in relations between Russia and Japan there has occurred a positive transformation unprecedented in their entire history. As a result, their level has risen immeasurably. Nonetheless, that conclusion is drawn in comparison to the "point of stagnation" or the "frozen point" that existed earlier. In reality Russo-Japanese relations have still not reached the level that exists between Russia and Japan with their close partners. By this, I have in mind the level of intensity, trust, and depth of contacts. The historical tendency for the movement of Russia and Japan to meet each other has appeared. Now there are objective preconditions for the two countries to draw closer. These are such shared values as freedom, democracy, a market economy, and respect for a diversity of values and interests among various states. However, on the other hand, both sides, as before, are still not linked by a tight network of concrete mutual interests. The guarded, negative perceptions of each other are far from fully overcome. The main problem persists: how to realize the historical opportunity to build truly friendly Russo-Japanese relations and to take action for resolving the concrete questions of bilateral interaction and cooperation.

Notes

1. *Asahi shimbun*, May 21, 2002.
2. V. Kostikov, *Roman s Prezidentom* (Moscow, 1997), p. 92.
3. Ibid., p. 104.
4. Ibid.
5. *Asahi shimbun*, October 31, 1998.
6. *Nezavisimaia gazeta*, November 30, 1998.
7. The commander of the Pacific Fleet of Russia Admiral Valdimir Kuroedov at a symposium in Tokyo in November 1996 presented dated showing that from 1991 to 1996 the number of ships of the Pacific Fleet was reduced almost two and one-half times, the number of personnel by two times, and the activity of the ships on the ocean dropped by 50 percent.

CHAPTER 8

Russian Strategic Thinking toward North and South Korea

Vasily Mikheev

When we consider strategic thinking in Russia, we should be aware of three levels: (1) the political authorities of the country; (2) the diplomatic, military, and other bureaucratic elites; and (3) scholars, specialists on Korea and, more broadly, on Asian and global problems. The 1980s were the critical moment of transformation in Moscow toward the Korean peninsula. Roughly half of this study is devoted to the Putin period, since this offers the timeliest insight into where strategic thinking is heading after the transitional decade of the 1990s.

The 1980s: Years of Slow Transformation in Perceptions of North and South Korea

As the 1970s gave way to the 1980s in the USSR qualitative changes occurred in the strategic understanding of North and South Korea. At their root lay two principal factors: the processes of differentiation of the former "world socialist system" (WSS) and change in the correlation of economic forces between North and South Korea.

The complexity of processes inside the WSS and Sino-Soviet contradictions did not permit the Central Committee of the Communist Party of the Soviet Union (CC CPSU) to follow a single political line in relation to the European socialist countries, China, and the so-called non-European socialist countries. As the ideological foundation for a differential approach by Moscow to the various members of the WSS in the middle of the 1970s the concept of the "core" of the WSS was advanced, or the *sotsialisticheskoe sodruzhestvo* (the socialist concord) understood to mean the members of the Warsaw Pact and Mongolia. Vietnam and Cuba were placed in the ranks of the "non-European members of the SEV" (COMECON). Yugoslavia and Albania, with which the USSR did not maintain diplomatic relations from the beginning of the 1960s, remained outside the framework of the *sotsialisticheskoe sodruzhestvo*. China was considered an antagonistic "social-democratic" power. The DPRK also was considered a country outside this framework, and moreover, with a pro-Chinese, "Maoist" inclination. In practical policies it was required that the North take sides with whom it stood—with Moscow or Beijing. Pyongyang all the same continued to maneuver between the USSR and the PRC, seeing precisely in such maneuvering the main road for guaranteeing the security of the ruling regime of Kim Il-Sung.

The restructuring of the WSS had real political and economic consequences. Supporting the policies of Pyongyang, Moscow held back from broad military-technical cooperation and made the North Korean leadership understand that it would not take Pyongyang's side if Pyongyang undertook military action against South Korea. In the economic sphere at the turn of the 1980s the USSR toughened its approach to the DPRK, demanding that Pyongyang fulfill its commercial obligations before the Soviet side and exerting pressure on the North through cutbacks on the supply of oil in response to the unconscientious fulfillment of these obligations.

Official Moscow did not regard South Korea to be a sovereign state, considering it a "satellite" of the United States and not a full-fledged "country," but only a "territory." Nevertheless, at the turn of the 1980s in Moscow the conclusion was reached that beginning from the middle of the 1970s North Korea had started to lag behind South Korea in economic development. The USSR began to look on South Korea as a potential economic partner, capable of making a contribution to the development of the economy of the Russian Far East. Politically, Moscow began to pay attention to the fact that South Korea could have its own foreign policy interests, not always corresponding to the interests of the United States. In this context, in Russian scientific and political circles it started to be considered that "South Korea's own interests" could be used in order to oppose the intensifying influence of the United States in Northeast Asia.

A turning point in the approach of the USSR to the Korean situation could have been the short period of administration by Iury Andropov

(1982–83). In this period the Soviet military elite, striving to find an answer to the intensifying military–political cooperation of the United States, Japan, and South Korea started to consider the DPRK a part of the united system of defense of the Far Eastern border of Russia. In this context the USSR was ready to strengthen its military cooperation with North Korea, which, on its side, demanded from Moscow help in the modernization of North Korean armed forces in response to the modernization of the South Korean army with the assistance of the United States.

This conception of a new military–political partnership of the USSR and DPRK was predicated on real loyalty of Pyongyang to Moscow. Yet, among the Soviet leadership there were serious suspicions that Pyongyang, having received large-scale military assistance, would continue its tactics of "sitting on two stools"—the Russian and the Chinese. In order to clarify the situation, Andropov made the decision personally to meet Kim Il-sung and to put the question sharply with whom he wanted to stand—Moscow or Beijing.

As a lever for pressuring Pyongyang the South Korean card was played. On the one hand, in 1983 the USSR introduced strict prohibitions on indirect trade with South Korea, that is, trade through a third country (direct trade did not exist). On the other hand, it prepared to begin an economic dialogue with Seoul. The USSR planned to send a delegation to the seventieth session of the Inter-Parliamentary Union, which was scheduled for the beginning of October 1983. The delegation was supposed to bring with it serious trade-economic proposals for South Korea. However, there was no talk at that time of diplomatic recognition.

Together with the Soviet delegation all European socialist countries were preparing to go to Seoul. Pyongyang interpreted the measure under preparation as a serious threat to its security and a break from the international isolation of South Korea. At the beginning of August the North Korean leadership made desperate attempts to press its East European partners and insist that they not go to Seoul. The answer from all of the capitals of Eastern Europe was negative. Sophia, Prague, and Warsaw pleaded that the Soviet delegation was going to Seoul and they had to go together with it. Berlin alluded to the fact that it could not let this pass since Bonn was participating. Budapest sharply declared that this is its internal matter and Pyongyang should not interfere. And Bucharest suggested to Pyongyang that it too go to Seoul and together struggle against "American imperialism."[1]

The shooting down over Soviet territory at the end of August 1983 of a South Korean Boeing passenger plane complicated the situation in the region and the question of a trip to Seoul by the Soviet delegation, as by the delegations of other socialist countries, no longer arose. Soon Andropov died, and the visit of Kim Il-sung to Moscow occurred anyway in 1984. The Soviet leadership, with Chernenko at the head, softly "reproved" the North Koreans for their pro-Chinese position; however, they made it understood that they were ready to proceed to the development of military cooperation with the aim of including the DPRK in the Far Eastern arc of opposition to American influence in Northeast Asia.[2]

The Trap of Gorbachev

The possibilities under consideration for Pyongyang were used already under Gorbachev in 1985–86. North Korea succeeded in playing on the previous approach of the military leadership of the USSR, which desired to see in the DPRK a part of the Far Eastern military outposts to counterbalance, as tit was written then, the "triangle of Washington–Seoul–Tokyo," and to receive from the USSR in 1986–90 military assistance unprecedented over the entire postwar period, and even commitments for the construction of a nuclear reactor in North Korea. In doing this in the "soft" Gorbachev style the "deal" was devoid of its initial logic: in exchange for the military assistance and assistance in development of atomic energy Pyongyang did not provide any concrete promises to "cut" off Beijing and to undertake unambiguous pro-Russian and anti-Chinese positions—, which was what had been conceived at the first conception of the "deal."

The large-scale widening of military cooperation between the USSR and the DPRK in the Gorbachev period contradicted the entire course of Moscow on relaxation of tensions in relations with Washington and dialogue with the United States on questions of disarmament. However, in my opinion, it would be incorrect to see in this discrepancy some kind of "conspiracy" of the Kremlin. It was more a matter of the absence of a political, strategic vision by the Soviet leaders toward North Korea, which was used by the political leadership in Pyongyang, intensifying its party-bureaucratic pressure on Moscow with the goal of gaining access to military technologies and a nuclear reactor. In this, such pressure corresponded to the interests of the Soviet military elite, which continued through "inertia from the beginning of the 1980s" to look at the DPRK as a military outpost against the American military presence in Northeast Asia.

As for the nuclear reactor, Moscow understood the risk of cooperation with the DPRK in the nuclear field; therefore as a prerequisite

Pyongyang had to accept corresponding types of obligations within the framework of the International Atomic Energy Agency (IAEA) and the Non-Proliferation Treaty (NPT). They were accepted.

Despite the breakdown at the end of the 1980s, Moscow continued, with distrust, to deal with Pyongyang, despite continuing to suspect it of cooperation with Beijing against the interests of the USSR. The Gorbachev leadership was upset also with the hostility by the North Korean authorities toward Soviet perestroika, spreading active internal propaganda against "new thinking" and glasnost. Pyongyang saw in the "reforms" of Gorbachev a threat to socialism, to the USSR, and even to the DPRK itself. Following from this, there occurred both technological restrictions (to North Korea the newest technology was not transferred), which Moscow imposed on military cooperation, and slowness of work on the nuclear reactor, which finished with only the selection of an area for construction of the reactor.

At the same time the "new thinking" of Gorbachev permitted a part of the Soviet academic and bureaucratic elite to spread broadly its new approaches to South Korea as a powerful and long-term economic partner of the USSR. The decisive foreign stimulus, prodding Moscow to move toward a meeting with Seoul, was the Seoul Olympics of 1988. The boycott of the Moscow Olympics, and following it of the "socialist sodruzhestvo," dealt a powerful blow to the Olympic movement that was reinforced by the boycott of the following Olympics in the United States (1984). And this already contradicted the overall course of Gorbachev for the relaxation of tensions.

In the period of discussion about whether or not to participate in the Olympics in Seoul, the Kremlin was subjected to active lobbying from the South (unofficial contacts) and the North (official pressure). Seeing that it would be difficult to restrain Moscow from going to Seoul by political means, Pyongyang undertook some strong measures. The main one was the leakage of information in the summer of 1988 to the effect that North Korea could use nuclear cooperation with the USSR for military objectives.[3] And although inspections by special forces did not confirm the fact that Pyongyang had conducted nuclear military work, the very possibility of this caused irritation in Moscow. The Kremlin saw in the actions of North Korea a threat to its own dialogue with the United States on questions of nuclear disarmament, in the framework of which North Korea privately was relegated to the zone of "Soviet influence." During preparations for the Seoul Olympics Moscow viewed as a threat to the security of its athletes in South Korea the North Koreans, who were continuing their work on behalf of a boycott of the Olympics by the socialist countries.

The perception of Pyongyang as, although not obvious but all the same, a threat to the interests of Moscow created a favorable atmosphere for the advancement among part of the academic and bureaucratic elite of the USSR the idea of normalization of relations with South Korea and weakened the position of those, above all in the higher leadership of the Foreign Ministry, who spoke out against official recognition of Seoul by Moscow. This situation was effectively used by Seoul, in fact exchanging in 1990 $3 billion of commercial and economic credits in return for diplomatic recognition of South Korea by Moscow.

Thus, on the eve of the collapse of the USSR, Moscow perceived North Korea as before as a "socialist partner," but a "bad" one, not accepting perestroika and causing problems in the areas of security and relaxation of tensions, and South Korea as a potential economic donor, which, by the way, gave rise to well-known overexpectations in relation to economic cooperation with Seoul, which manifested themselves in the 1990s as serious disappointment.[4]

The 1990s: Years of Sharp Fluctuations

The break-up of the USSR and the collapse of the world system of socialism were accompanied by a worsening of relations between Moscow and Pyongyang and an intensification of the overexpectations of Russia in relation to South Korean capital. The Yeltsin leadership, relying on democratic slogans, regarded North Korea, if not as an enemy, then as an opponent of change, not as a friend, as an economic partner with no future, and in political relations, as an undesirable partner, capable of relations of "friendship" only if it undercut the newly acquired international democratic image of Russia. An additional factor in the disappointment of Yeltsin's Kremlin was the fact that Pyongyang maintained active ties with the communist opposition to the Yeltsin regime.[5]

As a result of the break-up of the USSR, economic and military ties of Russia with the DPRK fell to nothing. Political-diplomatic ties began to assume a more official and formal character. Pyongyang, seeing that in questions of providing security for the ruling regime it could not rely on Moscow and it could rely significantly less than before on Beijing, which had in 1992 established diplomatic relations with South Korea, advanced a new strategy of security. Its essence consisted of attracting the United States into direct dialogue through nuclear blackmail and providing in this way for the survival of the regime, and not introducing change in the closed and authoritarian character of North Korean society. This policy to an even greater degree aroused anxiety in the Kremlin, which was concerned at the time with preserving the authority of Yeltsin and did not desire to get involved deeply in international problems that did not touch on Moscow's principal interests. Moscow considered Pyongyang's nuclear pretensions to be unsupported by its technological possibilities and left it to the United States to resolve how best to get out of the crisis.

In parallel, in Russian–South Korean relations disappointment was mounting over the fact that the economic partnership that had formed earlier was not bringing the expected results. Seoul cited the bad conditions for foreign business in Russia and was distressed about the fact that, in essence, it had "bought" diplomatic relations with Moscow in 1990 when in 1992 the collapse of the USSR could have produced the same effect for free. Moscow, in turn, blamed Seoul for inactive investing in the Russian economy.

A new turning point in strategic perceptions in Moscow of North and South Korea occurred in the mid-1990s following changes inside Russia—the Chechen War, the rise of nationalism—, and in relations between Russia and the West—plans for the expansion of NATO and the EU to the East, creation of a national missile defense system—, and on the Korean peninsula—the Agreed Framework between the United States and the DPRK on nuclear energy in 1994, and the idea of four-party talks on Korea (the two Koreas, the United States, and China, but without Russia's participation). In Moscow the possibility was seen, first of all, of attempting somehow to play the card of North Korean anti-Americanism, and secondly, of "pressuring" Seoul through one or another variant of warming relations with Pyongyang in the hope of nudging South Korea into more active investment behavior inside Russia and recognition of a political role for it in Korean affairs.

As a result, an unofficial conception of "parallel" development of relations with North and South Korea emerged in diplomatic circles. Its goal consisted of somehow putting a stop to the decline in relations with the North of the first half of the 1990s and also, where it was in Russia's interest, to develop relations with Pyongyang "parallel" to relations with Seoul, that is, two sets of independent relations neither of which was dependent on the other.[6] This would also mean, when possible, using relations with one or the other Korean state to put pressure on the other.

In this, Russian political and expert elites started from a pragmatic perception of the North and the South. In North Korea nobody saw a real economic partner, and in political terms Pyongyang was considered by part of the elite as a totalitarian enemy with which it would be better not to have dealings and which should be destroyed, and by another part as currency "just in case" in Russia's "games" with the United States, China, and South Korea. The South continued to be regarded as a potential important, although already without the former overexpectations, economic partner. Politically, Russia regarded Seoul as a pro-American element in international relations and made no special plans toward the South.

With Putin's arrival the tendency strengthened of Moscow to use the North Korean card in the global game with the United States over the expansion of NATO and the establishment of a National Missile Defense System, and in the games with South Korea and China for recognition of Russia's right to participate in determining the fate of the Korean peninsula.

The Putin Period

Coming to power, Putin in foreign policy faced the problem of the expansion of NATO and the establishment of a National Missile Defense System. One of the first experiences was Putin's first summit of the G-8 in Japan in the summer of 2000. A visit to Pyongyang—at that moment drawing the focus of world attention after the inter-Korean summit in June of that year—on the eve of the meeting of the G-8 allowed Putin to find himself, for a certain time, at the center of attention of the other leaders, none of whom had been in North Korea.[7]

However, further attempts to play the "North Korean card" in the game with the United States did not bring success. Pyongyang waited for Moscow military assistance when Moscow was proposing on account of North Korea to strengthen its negotiating positions in the dialogue over security with the United States. As a result, the two sides decided to maintain the appearance of good relations: the DPRK in order to have additional possibilities for diplomatic maneuvering; and Russia in order to demonstrate its presence in handling Korean affairs. A rational strategy by Moscow toward Pyongyang, thus, remained unformulated.

South Korea continued to regard Moscow as a potential economic partner and, politically, as a participant in the North Korean conflict on the side of the United States; however as striving for more independence for Washington in its policies toward Pyongyang. The new nuance consists of the fact that now—on a foundation of rapidly developing economic relations of Russia with China and new hopes for cooperation in investments from Japan—South Korea was relegated to a secondary role in resolving the economic problems of the Far East sector of the Russian economy. Moreover, political differences between Seoul and

Washington, although a matter of attention by Moscow, were considered to be insubstantial. Only experts of the most anti-American disposition spoke about their practical use in the diplomatic game.

Over the course of Putin's administration, Russian policy toward Korea has undergone certain changes These changes were a consequence of changes in Russian policies as a whole, and in Northeast Asia in particular of changes in the situation on the Korean peninsula as a result of the Korean nuclear crisis. In the process, the question of whether the influence of Russia in Korea has grown or, on the contrary, declined cannot be answered simply. On the one hand, Russia does not have the necessary influence over the DPRK sufficient to insist that the North Korean leadership return to the nonproliferation regime. But, even in the Soviet years when the USSR provided large-scale economic and military assistance to the DPRK, Moscow often could not oblige Pyongyang to act in its interests. On the other hand, the personal contacts of Putin and Kim Jong-il increased the diplomatic respect for Russia from other participants in regulating the Korean situation and objectively strengthened the political position of today's Russia in comparison to Russia in the time of the Yeltsin administration. Fundamental changes in Russian foreign policy occurred after September 11, 2001. Having supported the United States at that moment, Russia chose a course of drawing up new relations between Moscow and Washington. At their core were the questions of support for strategic stability, the battle against terrorism, and nonproliferation of weapons of mass destruction. The problem, however, was that the logic of the new foreign policy thinking of Putin—mutual influence with the United States and the West in matters of support for strategic stability and battles with the new threats—did not automatically carry over to the other directions of Russian foreign policy. Here there are still operating old bureaucratic inertia and old impressions—on the level of ideological lines that have entered into the consciousness of diplomats—of the world as a struggle for domination between the United States and Russia. And now there is China.

In recent years, Russia has made corrections in the line of the 1990s for parallel development of relations with North and South Korea. The policy of developing relations with each according to the plan that "each direction would proceed in accord with its own isolated logic" could not be effective because both Pyongyang and Seoul jealously follow the development of Russian relations with the opposite side of the Korean conflict. In this Moscow understands that an isolated North and the South, which is an active factor in the development of world markets, are not at all equal partners in either an economic or political sense.

The goal of Russian diplomacy of intensifying Russia's influence in Korea by means of giving priority to strengthening relations with the North was not realized. Initiating the nuclear crisis, Pyongyang put Moscow in a delicate position. The diplomatic activity of Russia in Korea in recent years did not lead Pyongyang to begin to listen more keenly to voices from Russia. And Russian diplomacy found itself prisoner to two types of logic—the logic of action of a nuclear power, responsible for nonproliferation of WMD, which objectively demands from Moscow the same toughness that the United States shows in relations with the DPRK; and the logic of having improved Russian–North Korean relations as a result of summit diplomacy, which elicits restraint in Moscow on questions of pressuring Pyongyang.

In this, the objective (although official not yet recognized by Moscow) interests of Russia in Korea in their contemporary reading consist of drawing closer the moment of absorption of North Korea by the South Korean market-democratic social system on the basis of:

1. transformation of the North Korean regime and society in a market-democratic direction;
2. creation of measures of trust on the peninsula;
3. establishment—as an intermediate phase in the movement toward absorption of the North by the South—of diplomatic relations between the DPRK and the Republic of Korea;
4. resolution of the nuclear crisis.

In order to realize these aims balanced or parallel policies are not needed, but other actions, and, above all, active work by Russia for creation of a mechanism of coordination of the policies of the United States, Russia, China, the EU, South Korea, and Japan toward the DPRK. For this official Moscow is not yet ready.

In practice today the Kremlin looks at North Korea and the Korean situation in the context of global relations with the United States and China. The Kremlin does not have its own view of the concrete problems of the Korean peninsula and it relies on the opinion of the Ministry of Foreign Affairs, the power structures, and experts. Recently the relationship of Moscow to Kim Jong-il has changed: at first Russia regarded Kim as a politician "with whom one could do business," then it became irritated with receiving constant requests from Kim for assistance. At the end of 2002 and beginning of 2003 Kim, exiting from the Treaty on the Non-Proliferation of Nuclear Weapons and refusing to cooperate with the International Atomic Energy Agency, put the Kremlin in an uncomfortable position before the White House, with which there had already been reached an agreement making common cause in defending the nonproliferation regime.

Not yet having a plan of action in relation to Kim Jong-il and seeing that Pyongyang rejected the intermediary services of Russia in normalization of the situation on a multilateral basis (Kim turned down the "package agreement" proposed by Russia), and made it clear that it did not regard Russia as a guarantor of its security, Moscow took a pause on the Korean problem. It wanted the United States by itself to regulate the situation with North Korea, and then it could perform the role of guarantor of the security of the North Korean regime. However, Russia did not want on its own to perform this role since this could be construed by the United States as a rebirth of the alliance of Russia and the DPRK against the United States. Therefore, the Kremlin already at the end of 2002 advanced the still weakly worked out idea of triangular cooperation and the concept of a guarantee of security of the DPRK by Russia, China, and the United States. At the same time, Moscow continued to maintain with Kim Jong-il good relations, supporting Kim "as a reserve" in case of a change in the situation in Korea and in case there should arise the necessity for a new trade-off in relations with the United States or China over Korea.

Moscow still does not consider it necessary for harsh actions to be taken against the DPRK. The moment for active inclusion of Russia in the game and a change of Russian policies toward the DPRK from soft to hard could be either the testing by Pyongyang of a nuclear weapon (which is improbable) or the firing of a ballistic rocket. It is not coincidental that the Russian Ministry of Foreign Affairs is constantly trying to persuade Pyongyang not to undertake a test of a long-distance rocket.

Among Russian experts there is unanimity that the DPRK has a nuclear weapons program. However, the opinions of nuclear experts regarding whether Pyongyang has the nuclear bomb are divided. Some consider that it has 1–2 nuclear mechanisms. Others assume that although the DPRK wants very much to have an atomic bomb, it cannot make it for technological reasons. Politically, Moscow finds it advantageous to take this approach to the extent that in case of recognition of the fact of the North's possession of nuclear weapons, Russia would have to sharply harden its approach to Pyongyang, to which it is still not ready by force of the "second logic" of behavior toward Korea.

The Kremlin does yet have its own vision of the path to Korean unification. The official position of Moscow consists of support for the unification of Korea by peaceful means without interference from outside; however, Russia does not believe in the unification of Korea according to the formulas proposed by Seoul and Pyongyang, and, secondly, is afraid of unification of this sort.

Russia considers that in reality unification will occur by means of absorption of North by the South and the establishment in a unified Korea of the economic and political laws and institutes of South Korea. Regarded as a stage in this is the policy of "engagement" of the North and penetration of South Korean capital into the DPRK. At the same time, in Russia people are certain that in the lifetime of Kim Jong-il unification will not occur.

Russian experts consider that unification of Korea is not beneficial either to Russia or to China in as much as, politically, it will introduce on the borders of China and Russia a powerful pro-American state (the factor of the new quality of Russo-American relations experts do not yet take into account) where there will be found American forces. And, economically, South Korea will need to focus its energy on the reestablishment of the economy of the northern part of the country, which objectively reduces the financial possibilities of the South in regard to investment in Russia. The basic approach of the Russian leadership toward the unification of Korea consists of the fact that it would be beneficial to preserve the status quo on the peninsula as long as possible.

At the same time, in case of real market reforms in the DPRK beginning and processes of privatization of state property or in case of unification of Korea on market-democratic foundations, Russian private business has an interest in participation in privatization of those seventy industrial objects that were built in the DPRK with the assistance of the former USSR. Such a turn of events could attract the attention to North Korea of the Russian president, actively lobbying for the foreign policy interests of big business in Russia, and color the diplomatic activity of Russia in the direction of Korea.

Russian experts consider the variant of the collapse of the DPRK a consequence of the death of Kim Jong-il. Distinct from Kim Il-sung, who in his lifetime succeeded in preparing his political heir, Kim Jong-il still does not have an heir—which makes the variant of collapse real.

The main threat of a negative scenario in the development of events would be chaos inside North Korea, a humanitarian catastrophe, and the outflow of refugees. In Russia it is understood that the main blow under such a scenario would be felt by South Korea and China, however there is fear for the situation in the Russian Far East.

Overall the position of Russia toward the unification of Korea remains passive. Its ostentatious (political-demagogic) activity in the near future could be induced by the tendency of Moscow in its turn to play on the theme of Korea and its future as part of a regional trade-off with the United States. Real activity would ensue only in a situation where Russian business would display its privatization interests.

Recently one can observe some correction in Russia's approach to the DPRK. In Moscow irritation is growing with the North Korean regime, which does not want to bring the situation back to its former peaceful track. The declaration of Pyongyang of February 10, 2005 that it possesses nuclear weapons exacerbated this irritation—by the way, without any subsequent logical conclusions for introducing correctives into the strategic perception of Pyongyang. These nuances do not signify that Russia really can change its passive behavior toward Pyongyang. The reasons for this are as follows.

First, despite personal contacts with the higher Pyongyang leadership Russia does not have any real levers of influence on Pyongyang. Moreover, Pyongyang stopped seeing in Russia a guarantor of its security, assuming that only the United States can give a real guarantee of security. Second, Russian business has no interest in North Korea in as much as North Korea has no market reform and, correspondingly, programs of privatization in which Russian business could participate. Investments in gas pipelines, oil pipelines, or a railroad are too risky due to the lack of clarity in the political situation.

Third, Russia does not see real threats originating from Korea. It reasons as follows. (1) The regime of Kim Jong-il controls the political situation in the country and the threat of an internal "explosion" does not exist. (2) The probability of military action of the United States against the DPRK is trivially small since Seoul finds itself in the position of a fore-doomed hostage, and China would be drawn into a military conflict in accord with the Armistice Agreement of 1953 and the Sino-North Korean treaty of mutual assistance. (3) The DPRK technologically cannot create a nuclear weapon on the level of Soviet and American standards and cannot create a contemporary ballistic missile [in as much as it uses modified technology of old Soviet rockets with a short range (SCUD)]. (4) The threat of the spread from the DPRK of radioactive materials or the creation of a "dirty bomb" Russia considers not very dangerous for itself.

Russia supports the six-party mechanism of Beijing meetings on North Korea and in principle is prepared for its preservation and conversion into a wider forum on security and cooperation in Northeast Asia. However, remaining within the limits of a passive approach, it will not take the necessary initiatives by itself, preferring as before only to react to the situation.

The Korean Nuclear Crisis

Expert opinion in Russia is divided over whether North Korea possesses a nuclear weapon or can it build one. There is no possibility for reliable technical analysis of the problem. All discussions about the nuclear program of North Korea are built on rumors, indirect indicators, and evaluations of American and former Soviet special services. This heightened measure of skepticism lowers the sense of urgency, as does the calculation that Russia lacks much influence over either the North or the United States.

Russians also consider it unlikely that, given the limits of the views affirmed within the framework of the six-party process, there will be a resolution of the crisis. The United States starts from the position that the DPRK is a nuclear power, while the DPRK uses its nuclear program as an instrument of political bluff and blackmail. Its aim is to draw the United States into dialogue and to gain the maximal political and economic dividends. This suggests that Pyongyang will not look for a compromise since the negotiating process in and of itself allows it to realize its interests for regime survival, including economic assistance from China and international organizations, and South Korea invests hundreds of millions of dollars in cooperation with the DPRK even in conditions when the nuclear crisis remains unresolved. This combination of rigidity from the two main antagonists and incentives from the two closest economic partners leaves Russia averse to taking any action of its own, which would be more likely to draw criticism than to help to resolve the crisis.

Many Russians are aware that the essence of the problem is the nature of the North Korean regime. Concentration on the nuclear crisis does not focus on the essential issue of market reforms and openness or on the event of a regime crisis after the death of Kim Jong-il, which could bring chaos to the country. Yet, because of the diversity of strategic views among the "five" who are calling on North Korea to abandon its nuclear program there is no prospect of addressing the essentials. Such doubts set limits on Russian strategic thinking.

Moscow is in a complicated situation. It sees Washington taking a strict position to Pyongyang, demanding unconditional proof that the latter has stopped its nuclear program. In a less strict form, analogous demands are repeated by Tokyo and Seoul. Beijing, in turn, repeats its adherence to the idea of the preservation of the Korean peninsula as a zone free from nuclear weapons. Having over recent years actively played the card of improving bilateral relations with North Korea in order to lift the role of Russia on the Korean peninsula, Moscow has a complicated choice. It can, of course, take a passive position, perhaps motivated by the fact that Pyongyang is bluffing, in the hope that the conflict will resolve itself. This could occur if the North is not capable of conducting a successful nuclear test and wants only to "scare" the United States into changing course. Alternatively, Moscow could see the possibility of increasing its role in Korea and the Northeast Asian region by actively joining with the countries that demand from Pyongyang clear proof that it is returning to a nonproliferation regime. Either way, aggravation of the situation negatively influences regional economic cooperation, from which Russia would benefit.

While others are alarmed by the North's threats—rocket-nuclear development for the United States and Japan, a rising flow of refugees for China, and dashed hopes for the political interests of the "new elite" in South Korea intent on unification of the country—Russia is further removed. Yet, it should be considering how to emerge advantageously from the unfolding situation. The axis of economic integration is Japanese–South Korean cooperation, to which China in the last 2–3 years is drawing all the closer. With Russia, especially its Far Eastern flank, experiencing a dearth of investment and demand, it is extremely important to find its place in this integration. Neutralization of North Korean instability and a turn of that country to development would correspond to Russian interests.

Pyongyang is unlikely to test a nuclear weapon, because that would cost it the possibility for further use of the politics of nuclear blackmail. If it did, both Russia and China, which still refrain from support for the American idea of sanctions against the DPRK, would have to support a Security Council resolution in favor of sanctions against Pyongyang. In the absence of that step, Moscow, like Beijing, would not resort to sanctions.

Russian trade with North Korea is growing, especially through rising imports, but in comparison to China and South Korea Russia lacks the resources or motivation to provide substantial economic assistance. Given the narrow (17 km) and well-fortified border with the North, Russia also lacks the worries of China about a flood of refugees. These factors limit Russia's involvement.

Pyongyang officially declared on February 10, 2005 that it has nuclear weapons and that it would stop participating in the six-party talks. In Moscow, views differed on how to react. The Ministry of Foreign Affairs meekly said that this "cannot but cause regrets." The response from the Minister of Defense was firmer, calling this a "step in an incorrect direction." These approaches hardly corresponded to the spirit of Putin's overall response to the problem of the spread of WMD. Last December at a press conference, he said that in questions in the battle with terrorism and proliferation Russia and the United States are not simply partners, but "allies." A firmer response could have been expected when on Russia's border a nuclear state arose under a totalitarian regime. At the root of the passivity and flexibility is probably a deep conviction that Pyongyang is bluffing and does not really have nuclear weapons. In addition, there is a desire to refrain from wrecking the emerging if unstable equilibrium that gives Russia its role.

It is the process that draws Russian interest. The majority look to the six-party talks as the basis for an institutionalized security structure in the region. Even those who doubt that North Korea under its current regime is prepared for a constructive role envision the remaining five states emerging as a regular forum, which would always invite Pyongyang to meetings but not be afraid to proceed without it. Over time, the agenda would broaden to include other questions of regional security. With the North's decision to return to the talks in July, Russians were eager to have their country fully involved in the bilateral and multilateral consultations to make progress on the nuclear issue and, on that basis, advance beyond it.

The fourth round of the six-party talks in July confirmed Pyongyang's tactics of splitting the other parties and looking for ways to gain financial support without serious concessions. By my calculations, it obtained about $500 million in goods from South Korea (rice and fertilizer) as well as commercial credits from China for the simple fact of agreeing to participate in the meeting. This was an economic victory. The refocusing of the talks on the problem of denuclearization of the Korean peninsula as a whole and the right of Pyongyang to a peaceful nuclear program could be construed as a political victory, while the switch to a bilateral format (Pyongyang and Washington) in essence constituted a diplomatic victory for the side that had insisted on this from the very start.

Russia's behavior in these negotiations was the most passive of all the rounds of the six-party talks. The head of the Russian delegation even left the talks for a time. Yet, in this passivity can be observed not only the weak interest of Moscow in participating in regulating the Korean situation in the absence of any sources of pressure on North Korea, but also well-known diplomatic wisdom: sometimes in diplomacy it is better to refrain from any activity than to display an irresponsible course of action.

Conclusion

Despite the various epochs from the 1980s to today, strategic thinking in Russia in regard to Korea reveals odd coincidences. North Korea somehow falls outside the general political logic of Russia. Such was the case to Gorbachev when the DPRK was perceived as, although a socialist partner, extremely unreliable and pro-Chinese, and in the time of Gorbachev when North Korea from the point of view of military cooperation began to fall outside the general course of Moscow in its interaction with the United States in questions of global disarmament. This is what is happening even today when the interests of alliance of Russia and the United States on contemporary security threats do not lead to corresponding logical steps by Moscow in relations to North Korea.

One possible exception to these coincidences was the start of the 1990s when communist and totalitarian North Korea did not subscribe to the logic of the democratic revolution in Russia, but that period led to a sharp worsening of relations between Moscow and Pyongyang, which was induced in parallel by disappointment as a factor of overexpectations from cooperation with South Korea.

The reason for such a discrepancy is in the system of making political decisions in Russia. In both the Soviet period and now North Korea is located on the periphery of Russian political, economic, and security interests, which focus on the United States, Europe, and Central Asia. Thus, South Korea did not become the focus of the economic interests of Russia, which is especially noticeable against the background of rapidly growing Sino-Russian economic cooperation and new investment expectations of Moscow in regard to Tokyo.

The dynamic of the strategic vision of South Korea consists of the fact that in the 1970s–80s this country was regarded as bundled into the harsh context of the relations of Russia with North Korea and the global standoff with the United States. In the 1990s South Korea at the beginning was given a clear economic and political priority as an independent factor for the development of the Russian economy, and then—as a result of mutual disappointment in the stormy economy cooperation— a period of cooling in Russian–South Korean relations began and, as a result, a fall in the strategic interest of Moscow to Seoul. In the Putin period there has been preserved a perception of South Korea as a real, but also not the main, potential economic partner of Russia in Northeast Asia and as an important but not the decisive player in Korean affairs, in which it is striving for, but without benefit for Russia, more political independence from the United States.

On the whole, Russia, both before and now, regards Korea in the context of its relations with regional leaders in Northeast Asia—the United States, China, and Japan. Precisely this aspect of a strategic perception by Russia of Korea is unchanging over the duration of the past decades, and it is this that delineates the limits of Russian activity in the direction of Korea.

Notes

1. B. Lim, *Vzlet bez posadki: Taina gibeli Iuznokoreiskogo samoleta KE-007* (Moscow: Izdatel'stvo "Luch", 1992), pp. 153–54.
2. Vasily V. Mikheev. "Reforms of the North Korean Economy: Requirements, Plans and Hopes," *The Korean Journal of Defense Analysis*, Vol. 5, No. 1 (Summer 1993): 93.
3. Vasily V. Mikheev, "Koreiskaia problema i vozmozhnosti ee resheniia" (Moscow: Moscow Carnegie Center, 2003), p. 14.
4. Vasily V. Mikheev. "Soviet Policy Towards the Korean Peninsula in the 90s," *Korean Studies*, Vol. 15, (1991): 31–49.
5. Vasily V. Mikheev. "Russian Policy towards the Korean Peninsula after Yeltsin's Reelection as President," *The Journal of East Asian Affairs*, Vol. 11, No. 2 (Summer/Fall 1997): 348–77.
6. Vasily V. Mikheev "Russian Policy towards North Korea," *New Asia*, Vol. 7, No. 4 (Winter 2000): 137–40.
7. Vasily V. Mikheev. "South-North Reconciliation and Prospects for North Korea–Russia Relations," *Asian Perspective*, Vol. 25, No. 2 (2001): 37.

CHAPTER 9

Russian Strategic Thinking toward Central, South, and Southeast Asia

Joseph P. Ferguson

Strategic thinking toward the Central Asian region undoubtedly occupies the minds of Russian leaders more so today than at any time over the past century. A large part of Central Asia had been under Russian—or Soviet—domination for close to 130 years. This changed almost overnight at the end of 1991. The collapse of the Soviet Union, and the subsequent emergence of the independent states in Central Asia, brought this heretofore-isolated region to the forefront of international diplomacy and global politics in the 1990s. The emergence of Central Asia as a geopolitical arena of competition has dramatically affected Russia, and strategic thinking among Russian leaders. Today nations such as China, India, Iran, Turkey, and the United States are vying for influence throughout Central Asia. Although somewhat politically eclipsed in the region compared to past decades, Russia still maintains deep connections in Central Asia and wields some influence over the five nations of the region.[1] In 2004–05 the Russian government undertook serious efforts to reestablish its power and influence in the region. Moscow's interest in South Asia also remains strong, although its position in the sub-continent is also considerably weakened compared to fifteen years ago. Southeast Asia still remains a distant region in the eyes of Russia's leaders, and is accordingly given little attention. Nevertheless, several nations in the region represent potential economic partners in the strategic industries of armaments and energy.

Since September 11, 2001, regional and global events have highlighted the strategic importance of Central Asia, not just to Russia, but also to other nations such as China, India, and the United States. This is due not only to the importance of the region as a potential alternative source of natural resources, but also to its central geographical position in the war on terror. Since that time U.S. bases have been established in two Central Asian countries, China has increased its regional profile dramatically, several of the states in the region have been confronted with serious domestic political instability, and Russia has attempted to rebuild its position in the region. All of this transpired against the background of the wars in Afghanistan and Iraq.

Additionally, the independence of the Central Asian states and the changes brought on by the global war on terror have forced strategic thinkers in Russia to consider the South Asian region in a much more complex way. With the ending of the constraints of the cold war, traditional relationships and alliances have been dramatically reshaped in South Asia. Russia's traditional ally in the region, India, now looks elsewhere for strategic cooperation. The war on terror and the U.S. invasion of Afghanistan have created more flux in the region. Moscow now has to consider the potential for serious instability, and perhaps even nuclear war in South Asia. As was the case during the cold war, Russia's primary focus in South Asia has been India—for strategic and political reasons—, but leaders in Moscow now must consider different means of exerting influence in the region.

Southeast Asia has been important to Russian (and Soviet) leaders over the past several decades only in the sense that it was a geopolitical arena of competition with the United States and, to a lesser extent, China. But after the substantial drawdown from Cam Ranh Bay in the early 1990s and the eventual closure of that naval asset, Russian interests in the region have been primarily about arms sales (primarily in Indonesia, Malaysia, and Vietnam). Russia, however, could reemerge in the region as a supplier of both conventional and nuclear energy, and is along with growing also seem interested in a heightened diplomatic profile in Southeast Asia, as their interest and commitment toward multilateral institutions across Asia.

This chapter explores Russia's strategic dilemmas and options in Central, South, and Southeast Asia, with a primary focus on Central Asia due to geographical and geopolitical considerations. How has the Russian leadership dealt with the sudden incursion of U.S. strategic power in the once Soviet-dominated region of Central Asia? How is Russia coping with China's emerging political and economic role in

Central Asia? What role will collective security organizations such as the Collective Security Treaty Organization (CSTO) and the Shanghai Cooperation Organization (SCO) play in the future in this region? What does India's new partnership with the United States mean for Russian strategy in South Asia? What are the prospects for Indo-Sino-Russian trilateral strategic cooperation? Can Russia find a new role for itself in Southeast Asia? These are among the major questions confronting the Russian leadership in Asia in the early twenty-first century.

Central Asia

Although the five new Central Asian republics (Kazakhstan, Kyrgyzstan, Tajikistan, Turkmenistan, and Uzbekistan) became independent nations in 1991, in the early half of the 1990s they were still heavily influenced by Moscow, more due to geographical proximity than to Russian designs. In each case, these nations—after brief experiments with liberal reforms—settled back into a familiar autocratic system of government, likely owing as much to pre-colonial traditions as to the rule-from-the-center policy instituted by Moscow in the tsarist era, and continued by the Soviets.[2]

In the first years of the Yeltsin presidency, Prime Minister Egor Gaidar and Foreign Minister Andrei Kozyrev wanted Russia to distance itself as much as possible from what was perceived as a backward and authoritarian group of leaders in Central Asia. Yeltsin appears to have initially concurred with this view and took little interest in the region, preferring to let his second Prime Minister Viktor Chernomyrdin act as Moscow's face in the region.[3] In 1992, however, Moscow found itself having to respond to the deteriorating situation in Tajikistan, where the civil war became an extension of the lawlessness and tribal warfare that marked Afghanistan throughout the 1990s. Russian troops had never left the Afghan–Tajik border after the Soviet withdrawal from Afghanistan in 1989, but they were now much less capable and less properly supplied to carry out their mission (of maintaining peace in Tajikistan). As much as the Yeltsin team in the Kremlin may have wanted to distance itself from the region and focus on Russia's relationship with the Euro-Atlantic community, Central Asia continued to play (and will always play) a major role in Russian strategy and geo-political considerations, due to the basic, yet vital facts of geography and demography.

Russian interest in the region has never waned, in spite of where the interests of Kozyrev and Gaidar may have steered their energies. This is due to reasons besides politics alone; there is a substantial Russian population of more than 8 million that still resides in the region and numbers more than 8 million. These ethnic Russians and the nation of Russia share what could be called a "common cultural space" with the peoples and nations of Central Asia.[4] Russia is a member of no less than half a dozen multilateral political, military, and economic groupings in Central Asia that vary in their influence and prestige.[5] Russian troops today occupy bases in Kyrgyzstan, Uzbekistan, and Tajikistan, and Russia has a bilateral defense treaty with Kazakhstan. Russia's economic links with Central Asia, however, are a mere shell of what they were in the 1980s. In some cases, two-way trade is one-tenth of the level that it was between the Soviet center and the various republics in 1990. Technical credits from the center no longer link Moscow with the "near abroad." The establishment of a "new" ruble in 1993 pushed the Central Asian nations out of the ruble zone and forced them to create their own currencies, which caused tremendous economic difficulties (because of the price-support structure the ruble zone had maintained).[6] Economic links, however, still do exist, particularly small-scale trading. The potential for increased trade turnover is tremendous, given the existing transport infrastructure. Russia, of course, also remains the primary supplier of armaments for these nations. Last but not least, there are more than 12 million Muslims in Russia proper that share close cultural, ethnic, and linguistic links with the nations of Central Asia.[7]

The focus of Russian thinking toward Central Asia during the early years of the 1990s was on a much more elementary issue than grand, national strategy. The focus remained on those ethnic Russians remaining in the former Soviet states. As early as 1993 the Russian government applied pressure on the governments of Central Asia to recognize the rights of ethnic Russians, and hence played a role as "guardian" to Russians in the "near abroad." Russia also made strong efforts in the mid-1990s to guarantee the rights of these Russians abroad to maintain dual citizenship (although Kazakhs, Uzbeks, and others remaining in Russia were not granted this right).[8]

By 1994 the influence of Gaidar (who had long since been replaced as prime minister by Viktor Chernomyrdin) and Kozyrev (still foreign minister until 1996) within the Yeltsin administration was essentially dead. Russian inattention toward Central Asia was quickly rectified under the guidance of Chernomyrdin and soon-to-be Foreign Minister (and eventually Prime Minister) Yevgeniy Primakov. Primakov has always been known as an "Eurasianist," and he recognized Central Asia as part of the first concentric circle, adjacent to the Russian core.[9] Additionally, Primakov argued for tighter political and economic integration of the states of the Commonwealth of Independent States (CIS) in order to maintain Russia's influence in the region.[10]

Meanwhile, after the independence of the nations of Central Asia in 1991–92 the United States began a concerted diplomatic push in an effort to heighten the U.S. profile in the region. In the first four years of the Clinton administration, the United States engaged Central Asian nations in a broad effort to promote democracy throughout the region, and to cultivate the leaders of the various governments. Part of this effort was meant to help U.S. and Western energy firms develop the dilapidated energy infrastructure of this geologically rich region. Russia's concern with the rise in the interest of the United States in Central Asia in the early 1990s was not as pointed as it was in the South Caucasus, where fears about NATO expansion and the permanent stationing of U.S. troops, accompanied concerns about the tremendous expansion of U.S. capital and investment in the energy sector. In Central Asia in the early to mid-1990s such concerns were not as pointed as it had been west of the Caspian Sea. It was perhaps understood by strategic thinkers in Moscow, that in spite of Russia's marginalized role in the region, the United States was also operating under serious constraints in Central Asia, not the least of which is geography. The United States did make a show of strategic reach to the region in September 1997 when soldiers from the famed 82nd Airborne Division were airlifted and dropped into Kazakhstan. There they participated in joint exercises with the Central Asian Battalion, with included soldiers from Kazakhstan, Kyrgyzstan, and Uzbekistan. This exercise was witnessed with great concern in Moscow.[11] But until late 2001 the U.S. role in the region was limited.

By the second half of the Clinton administration, the authoritarian bent of the various "republics" had become clear and the U.S. government threw up its hands in despair, while the Western energy firms turned most of their attention to Azerbaijan and, to a lesser extent, Kazakhstan. Washington was more and more disillusioned with the progress of democracy in Central Asia. Furthermore, as the situation in Afghanistan deteriorated, it became clear by 1997 that the U.S. firm Unocal's plans for a pipeline, linking Turkmenistan with Pakistan and the Arabian Sea through Afghanistan, were likely unattainable. Through the 1990s, Russia watched with some concern U.S. efforts to experiment with democratic nation building in Central Asia. Nevertheless, the real strategic angst was centered, west of the Caspian Sea and Russian leaders and strategic thinkers seemed inclined to view U.S. efforts in Central Asia with less concern.

Vladimir Putin recognized the strategic importance of Central Asia to Russia, and when he was still Prime Minister the Russian government began to seek a fresh approach. In a speech in the fall of 1999, acknowledging the region's vital place in Russia's foreign policy and national strategy, Putin stated that Russia was first and foremost a "Eurasian Power."[12] As president of Russia, Putin understoods the constraints that Moscow faced in the region, pragmatically deciding to embrace the introduction of U.S. troops and power into the region in late 2001. Early in the war on terror Putin realized that in certain ways a U.S. presence could be beneficial to Moscow's strategy in the region. He went so far as to convince Central Asian leaders to accept the U.S. role and to acquiesce to basing rights.[13] Nevertheless, there was great concern expressed in many circles in Russia during this time about the decision.[14] Putin, was able to override any opposition to his new "strategic partnership" with the United States for the first few years. He came to rethink his views on the U.S. presence in the region from 2003–04 onward.

Russia's relations with the various states of Central Asia vary. Not surprisingly, Moscow has maintained a close relationship with Kazakhstan, the nation with the largest number of ethnic Russians, and the only nation in Central Asia that shares a border with Russia. Some have accused Moscow of nefarious tactics in order to keep Kazakhstan under its wing. Moscow uses access to energy and electricity as a lever with all of the states of Central Asia, and in the case of Kazakhstan, RAO-UES, the partly state-held Russian United Energy System gained equity in a Kazakh hydroelectric station in return for debt forgiveness.[15] But leaders in Moscow and Astana undoubtedly see eye-to-eye on a variety of issues including the threat of Islamic fundamentalism, concern about China's increasing role in the region, and transborder issues such as drug trafficking and environmental degradation.

Russia has also maintained cordial relations, for the most part, with Tajikistan, where the primary issues of cooperation are military and strategic. Russia became embroiled in the civil war there in 1992, and has been a primary power broker there since a precarious peace was established by the late 1990s. The 201st Motorized Rifle Division has maintained watch over Tajikistan's border with Afghanistan since Soviet days, and although it is primarily made up of ethnic Tajiks, it is under Russian command. Additionally, Russian border guards augment this force.[16] As Tajiks are ethnically Persian, and not Turkic like the rest of Central Asia, Tajikistan's leaders feel that Russia is the outside power that can guarantee a certain amount of stability in this strife-torn region.

The past few years have seen a major increase in Russian attempts to upgrade its military presence in Central Asia; one focus of which is the Tashkent Collective Security Agreement, originally signed on May 14,

1992, but damaged by the withdrawal of Uzbekistan in April of 1999.[17] In response to numerous incursions into Kyrgyzstan, Uzbekistan, and Tajikistan from 1999 by an extremist terror organization, the Islamic Movement of Uzbekistan (IMU), Moscow saw the need to take a more proactive role, lest the contagion of Islamic extremism spread throughout the region, and potentially into Russia. The revamped organization was renamed the CSTO and includes Russia, Armenia, Belarus, Kazakhstan, Kyrgyzstan, and Tajikistan. Although it has little real power, it does indicate Moscow's concern about the dangers of insurgency getting out of control in the region. In line with this, Moscow has also negotiated with Tajik President Imomali Rakhmonov an agreement to upgrade the 201st Motorized Division from its primary role as a border protector and peacekeeping force to a regular military force to be stationed at a full-fledged army base.[18]

Moscow has also made recent inroads in shoring up defense relations with Kyrgyzstan, a nation that had distanced itself considerably from Moscow in the 1990s. In December 2002, Putin and Askar Akayev signed an agreement that writesoff or reschedules portions of Kyrgyzstan's state debt to Moscow in exchange for granting Russia the rights to the former Soviet flight-training airfield at Kant.[19] The March 2005 coup (or "tulip revolution") in Kyrgyzstan and the resignation of Akayev (and his exile in Moscow) did little to shake Moscow's determination to enjoy good relations with whoever is in power in Bishkek.[20] Russian leaders want to assure continued access to the air facility in Kant. In addition, there are also indications that the Russian government is negotiating with the new Kyrgyz leadership to gain access to a second facility at Osh, under the auspices of the CSTO.[21]

Despite Russia's intense interest in maintaining a tight relationship, Uzbek leaders did their best to keep their distance from Moscow in the 1990s, seeking to become the new center of cultural, social, and political power in Central Asia.[22] They were supported in this notion to some extent by the United States which hoped that an enlightened leadership in Tashkent could act as a bulwark and an example to counteract fundamentalism and extremism in Islam in the region. This proved to be illusory, and by the end of the 1990s leaders in Tashkent and Washington were at severe odds over the progress of democratization. Since that time Uzbek leaders (and leaders in other Central Asian nations) have been tilting back toward Russia in an effort to counterbalance the growing U.S. strategic power in the region, and also the U.S. penchant for "lecturing" the leadership on democracy and civil society.[23] Uzbek President Islam Karimov demonstrated his desire to improve relations with Russia during his April 2004 successful summit with Vladimir Putin, even calling for a "strategic alliance."[24] Russia benefited from the further deterioration of relations between Tashkent and Washington, following the violent crackdown by Karimov on protestors in the city of Andijan in the spring of 2005. Many Russian leaders now see any lessening of U.S. influence in the region as a plus for Moscow. While the United States harps about democratic reform in the region, Moscow prefers to maintain the status quo, as the best means to assure stability and is loath to criticize Karimov for the March 2005 crackdown.[25] Karimov again visited Moscow in June 2005, and called for stepped up strategic cooperation. He publicly accused "foreign elements" (i.e., the United States) of fomenting the unrest at Andijan, and suggested that Russia would be allowed access to any number of military facilities in Uzbekistan.[26] At this time Karimov made overtures to both China and India, as well.[27] Shortly after this, the Uzbek government announced that the United States had six months to withdraw from its air base at Karshi-Khanabad, much to the satisfaction of Moscow. The suggestion was quickly made (both in Tashkent and Moscow) that Russian forces occupy the base once U.S. forces were withdrawn.[28]

Turkmenistan has, due to its geographical location, been able to keep itself somewhat distant from the intrigues and politics of the region. The iron grip maintained by President Sapuramat Niyazov and the small, scattered population help keep the nation out of the mainstream of regional politics. The enormous reserves of natural gas have allowed Niyazov to build his personal fiefdom of self-worship. Niyazov maintains cordial relations with Moscow, and Putin visited Turkmenistan in May 2000, as part of his first official travel abroad.[29] But Niyazov has shown himself to be a prickly partner, briefly suspending gas exports to Russia at the end of 2004, and resuming them again only in January 2005. Moscow, however, has been pushing in recent years to deepen relations with the Turkmen. This paid off in the spring of 2005 when Niyazov invited the Russian energy firm Lukoil to develop an offshore oil deposit in the Caspian Sea.[30]

The September 11 terror attacks fundamentally altered the strategic situation in Central Asia, after the United States invaded Afghanistan with the cooperation of the governments in Kyrgyzstan and Uzbekistan, where U.S. troops were deployed. Additionally, the United States placed a small team of airmen in Tajikistan who are responsible for tracking the airspace in the region and for refueling.

The Kremlin initially acquiesced to the sudden U.S. presence in the region, but a primary cause for the support was the ability of the United

States to stabilize Afghanistan to a certain extent, and thus alleviate the festering conflict in Tajikistan and in the Fergana Valley. For the period 2001–03 U.S.–Russia relations seemingly prospered in the global war against terrorism. This cooperation also existed in the non-proliferation area, where U.S.–Russian joint nuclear clean-up and material security efforts were institutionalized through the Nunn-Lugar program (known as the Cooperative Threat Reduction program) earlier in the 1990s (including in Kazakhstan). In exchange for Russian acquiescence to the new U.S. presence in Central Asia, Washington turned somewhat of a blind eye to Russia's actions in Chechnya. Additionally, during this eighteen-month period U.S.–Russian energy cooperation (including the first energy summit in Houston in 2002) added to the good will. This was symbolized at the highest levels by the seeming camaraderie displayed by Bush and Putin.

In spite of the improved atmospherics, there remained a good number of irritants, not the least of which were NATO expansion, arms control, and the issues of human rights, democracy, and civil society in Russia itself. In Central Asia, however, these issues were of minimal consequence and were subsumed by the greater strategic effort aimed at eradicating terrorism and establishing a cooperative regime in Afghanistan. The fissures in the foundation of the new U.S.–Russian strategic partnership, nevertheless, were laid bare with the U.S. invasion of Iraq in March 2003. Although Russia's objections to the U.S. war in Iraq were less vocal than those of some of Washington's NATO allies, relations would continue to deteriorate to the extent that by 2004–05 there was no longer a debate about "whether" Russia should attempt to limit the U.S. influence in the region, but "how" Russia should limit it.[31]

At the same time there was also some concern in Moscow about China's growing role in the region. China's links with and interest in Central Asia go back centuries, diplomatic and economic forays have grown in number over the past few years. The establishment of the SCO[32] is seen by some in Moscow as nothing but a Chinese Trojan Horse, utilized to raise China's profile and influence. One prominent strategic thinker in Russia claims that the SCO is "testimony to the Kremlin's awareness of its own limitations, China's ambitions, and the new states' [of Central Asia] independence."[33] In August 2004, China completed a gas pipeline linking Shanghai with its western borders in Central Asia, where there was an expressed desire to connect it with gas fields in Kazakhstan and Turkmenistan. In the fall of 2004, China began construction on an oil pipeline linking fields in Kazakhstan to Xinjiang province. The Chinese have also become involved in hydroelectric projects in Kyrgyzstan and Tajikistan.[34] Additionally, the government moved quickly to extend a friendly hand to embattled Uzbek President Karimov, who visited Beijing just two weeks after the violent suppression of protestors in Andijan.[35] Lastly, in September 2005 the Chinese state-owned firm China National Petroleum Corporation (CNPC) gained a controlling share in the Kazakh firm PetroKazakhstan.[36] China is clearly concerned about its rising energy consumption and views Central Asia as a potential supplier for decades to come.

Russian leaders have expressed concern about Chinese designs in the region, and Russian leaders have been careful not to allow China to turn the SCO into an organization used to increase China's influence.[37] Consequently, ideas that China and Russia will collude in Central Asia and the Middle East in some kind of "axis of energy" are unfounded.[38] Nevertheless, Beijing and Moscow share concern about U.S. designs in Central Asia and in the adjacent Middle East. At the 2002 St. Petersburg SCO summit (between Putin, Hu, and the other leaders of the SCO member-states) the organization became more institutionalized and a permanent anti-terror center was opened in Bishkek, Kyrgyzstan. What had originally been established as a sort of confidence building mechanism to fix borders and engage neighbors had become an institution that pledged itself to deal with regional threats such as terrorism and drug trafficking. Although, in reality, no one of the Central Asian states is apt to ask for Chinese security cooperation in the form of troops, the Chinese have taken a heightened role politically, and Chinese troops have conducted joint exercises in the region in Kyrgyzstan and most recently in Kazakhstan. Additionally, Hu Jintao's visit to Russia from June 30 to July 2, 2005 demonstrated that Moscow and Beijing could cooperate if the two felt that the U.S. presence was as a direct threat to the strategic balance in the region. There has also been talk in Moscow of a strategic "troika" between China, Russia, and Uzbekistan, in order to balance against U.S. influence in Central Asia.[39]

The SCO has played a heightened political role in Central Asia. This was demonstrated at the July 2005 summit in Astana, the capital of Kazakhstan. Although the focus of the summit was ostensibly anti-terror cooperation, the most visible resolution was a call by all members for the United States to set a deadline for withdrawal of U.S. forces, and the closing of U.S. bases in Kyrgyzstan and Uzbekistan.[40] It is unclear whether this declaration was made at the urging of *all* SCO members; the speculation has been that Beijing and Moscow were behind it and pressured the other SCO members to go along. The Chairman of the U.S. Joint Chiefs of Staff General Richard Myers accused Moscow and

Beijing of "bullying" their junior partners in the SCO to go along with the call for a deadline for withdrawal.[41] Russia has announced that it looks to double the number of troops at its Kyrgyz base. But is unclear that the new Kyrgyz leadership is all that enthusiastic about these new plans, or about the call for a deadline for a U.S. withdrawal from that country. President Kurmanbek Bakiyev—as well as his Prime Minister Felix Kulov—have since made cautionary statements about the future of foreign military bases on Kyrgyz soil. They have been careful to not direct those statements toward any one nation (suggesting that *all* foreign bases will have to be removed at some point).[42] When U.S. Secretary of Defense Rumsfeld visited Bishkek in late July 2005, the Kyrgyz leadership assured him that U.S. bases could remain in that country until anti-terror operations in Afghanistan ceased. Tajik leaders gave the secretary the same assurances.[43]

Putin and leaders in the Kremlin administration have been trying to revitalize the CIS and the CTSO (which both exclude China) in an attempt to revamp Russia's marginalized position, and to balance against both the Chinese and U.S. presence.[44] Recently Russia joined the Central Asia Cooperation Organization (CACO), the only non-Central Asian state to be a member.[45] Russia continues to maintain a prominent regional profile, as evidenced by the frequent state visits between the leaders of the Central Asian states and Vladimir Putin. Putin's interest in the region seems to manifest itself more than that of his predecessor, although this is no doubt in part due to the war on terror and the continuing morass in Chechnya. Nevertheless, Putin recognizes that Russia has a deep interest in Central Asia, and that strategic necessity will dictate some sort of active Russian role in the region. In early April 2005 Russia led a series of CSTO military exercises known as *Rubezh*, which took place in Tajikistan and which involved Russian air and ground forces based in Kyrgyzstan.[46] Also, Moscow understands the importance of Russian "soft power" in the region, and the Kremlin has established a new department in the presidential administration known as the Department for Interregional and Cultural Relations with Foreign Countries and the CIS. Its strategy is to expand Russia's influence in the CIS through cultural and humanitarian programs.[47] Some Russian strategists have also debated whether Russia can become a "regional policeman" in Central Asia, supplanting the United States[48]

In 2004–05 the U.S.–Russian strategic partnership was under immense strain, Putin's domestic political decisions were seen as a threat to civil liberties and democracy. There was also tension over Russia's stand in the Ukrainian presidential election in late 2004. U.S. and

European protests succeeded in having the fraudulent elections annulled and a new round convened, resulting in the victory of a candidate supported in the West. For Russia, this was yet one more example of the "domineering" U.S. voice in world affairs. Since the early 1990s Moscow had seemingly granted Washington one concession after the other: unfettered NATO expansion in Eastern Europe and in three former Soviet republics (the Baltic states); the unilateral U.S. abrogation of the ABM treaty and the go-ahead with a missile defense system; the bombing of Yugoslavia; withdrawal of Russian bases from Cuba and Vietnam; access to Russian nuclear facilities, and a host of other "concessions" (economic, political, and strategic). Combined with the overwhelming U.S. strategic presence in Central Asia, there is a sense that leaders in Russia (and Russians, in general) have become weary of their "partner" the United States.

Russian opposition to the United States' strategy in Central Asia is clearly growing. There has been wide public debate on how a strategy should be devised in order to counter the loss of Russian power and influence in the post-Soviet space.[49] As one U.S. scholar points out: "At present . . . danger lies in the fact that Russian strategy is now cast as competing against, rather than complementing, American strategy in Georgia, Uzbekistan, Kazakhstan, and possibly Afghanistan."[50] The Russian leadership can cozy up to the regimes that have become focal points of U.S. criticism, targeting outside powers that are similarly not keen to see an U.S. dominance, such as China and India. Vladimir Putin may seek to reawaken Primakov's concept of the China–India–Russia triangle. An unprecedented meeting took place in Vladivostok among the foreign ministers of China, India, and Russia on June 2, 2005. There the ministers discussed not only joint economic cooperation, but also the need to be wary of "unilateralism," a catch phrase for the United States.[51] Yet, India is working more closely with the U.S., and it will remain aloof from such trilateralism.

South Asia

Russia's interests in South Asia have always been primarily strategic. South Asia was a region of overlapping strategic interests between Beijing, Moscow, and Washington throughout the Cold War. The existence of religious and territorial disputes threatened to result in conflict that could mobilize the world's superpowers. More recently, Moscow has come to view these divisions in South Asia as having the potential to affect security in Central Asia, as well. Additionally, it is a region that since the late 1990s has two nuclear-weapons states, standing in opposition to one another. Lastly, and perhaps most importantly, by the 1990s Russia's withering military-industrial complex had become dependent on Indian largesse to not only help keep it afloat, but to actually maintain its R&D base.[52]

India will continue to matter for Moscow because it could be a future key player not only in South Asia, but in Central Asia and the Middle East, as well. But what is of more immediate interest to some in Russia is whether the triangular relationship between Beijing, Delhi, and Moscow can actually be formulated in a plus-sum, positive way. Well-known were the Cold War parameters of this relationship, which was actually a quadrangle including Pakistan (and often a pentagon involving the United States): Moscow supported Delhi against Islamabad, Delhi supported Moscow against Beijing, and Beijing supported Islamabad against Delhi. Caught in the middle was the unfortunate quasi-state known as Afghanistan.

Beginning in the 1990s the nature of this relationship changed, due to the Sino-Russian *rapprochement*, to India's economic development and its warming ties with the United States, and to the increasing political marginalization of Pakistan. India's ties with the United States, however, did not substantially improve until the late 1990s, after the 1998 nuclear test crisis. Initially, in the early 1990s Prime Minister Gaidar and Foreign Minister Kozyrev were cool on India, and called for a policy of equidistance between Delhi and Islamabad. But Yeltsin, and the vast majority of strategic thinkers in Russia (in the Duma, the military, and elsewhere in and out of government), were quick to dismiss this notion. Yeltsin visited India in January of 1993.[53] But it was easier to proclaim friendship with India than to present concrete results. Delhi was deeply disappointed with the prior visit by its defense minister to Moscow in March 1992, where he was unable to meet with any senior Russian officials. Additionally, Moscow's refusal in July 1993 to honor a contract promising cryogenic booster engines for an Indian space launch after a twelfth hour intervention by Washington (due to concerns about the Missile Technology Control Regime), greatly vexed the political leadership in India.[54]

Nevertheless, Moscow was able to maintain a cordial relationship with Delhi throughout the 1990s driven more than anything by the sales that Russian arms manufacturers were able to push through with regularity (and still are able to do today). Russia also kept its promise not to sell arms to Pakistan, despite temptation. Indian Prime Minster Narasimha Rao's visit to Moscow in July 1994, several months before a planned Moscow summit between Yeltsin and Pakistani Prime Minister Benazir Bhutto, led Moscow to cancel Bhutto's visit. Moscow continues to support India in its claims in Kashmir.

Relations between Moscow and Delhi took a dramatic turn for the better in early 1996 when Yevgeny Primakov became foreign minister. His first visit abroad was to India, and this is when he began publicly speaking of developing a triangular relationship between China, India, and Russia.[55] Primakov visited India again in late 1998 as prime minister and was able to keep Russia's profile in South Asia active, in spite of the severe constraints posed by domestic economic and political problems. The strained relationship between Moscow and Washington over NATO actions in Yugoslavia, and NATO expansion into Eastern Europe were part of the rationale for Primakov's move toward Beijing and Delhi. The Russian Duma deemed India "a strategic ally" twice during the 1990s.[56]

Following the May 1998 nuclear tests in South Asia, Moscow refused to join the West in calling for sanctions against Delhi. After the uproar died down, and after the accession of the Bush administration in 2001, U.S.–Indian ties began to blossom. India was one of the few nations in Asia that championed U.S. missile defense plans, much to the irritation of Beijing and Moscow. Additionally, growing economic ties (especially in the high-technology sector) served as a bridge between India and the United States. India's concern about China's rise served to further bring strategic thinkers together in the two capitals, especially after Bush took office and the China 'threat' argument still had much cachet. Japan, also concerned with China's rise, similarly cultivated a close strategic relationship with India around this time.[57]

Russia found itself constrained by its lack of economic and diplomatic resources in dealing with India. During the Cold War the Soviet Union was India's number two trade partner; two-way trade averaged between $5 and $7 billion annually. In 1998 two-way trade registered barely $1 billion.[58] Additionally, by 1999 Indian strategists were concerned with what they considered Moscow's strong tilt in the direction of Beijing.[59] Perhaps in desperation Moscow was offering more and more liberal military technology licensing agreements to the Indian government. Deals that might have had to be cancelled (because Moscow could not even afford basic production costs) were kept alive because India agreed to fund the R&D costs in return for having access to the spin-off research and any resulting technologies.[60] Additionally, Moscow continued to supply India with nuclear energy technology and plants. But Russia was running out of cards. By the end of the 1990s the

Russian diplomatic compound in Delhi, once the Soviet Union's biggest, was largely empty, and weed-choked. Meanwhile, Delhi was sending its best and brightest diplomats to Singapore, Tokyo, and Washington, when they had once gone to Moscow.[61]

Vladimir Putin visited New Delhi in November of 2000. During the June 2001 visit to Moscow by Indian Foreign and Defense Minister Jaswant Singh, the two governments agreed in principle to a series of arms deals over a decade totaling close to $10 billion. This included tanks, aircraft, and even an aircraft carrier.[62] Leaders in Delhi recognize the importance of keeping the strategic relationship between India and Russia in good stead.[63]

Vladimir Putin has personally demonstrated his keen desire to reinvigorate the traditionally strong relationship between Moscow and Delhi. The agenda of his visit to New Delhi in December 2004 was dominated by arms sales, but he and Prime Minister Manmohan Singh also agreed to increase anti-terror cooperation. During the visit, Russian firms signed deals to construct two more nuclear power plants in southern India. Russian Foreign Minister Igor Ivanov, a Primakov protégé, made a tour of South Asia, visiting both India and Pakistan in the summer of 2003. Ivanov met with Indian Prime Minister Atal Bihari Vajpayee one week before Vajpayee was due to visit China. Ivanov's visit coincided with joint Russian-Indian naval maneuvers in the Indian Ocean, at the same time that Chinese diplomatic forays had been targeting Bangladesh, Burma, and Pakistan.[64] India undoubtedly shares with Russia some concern about Chinese designs in Central and South Asia, something that has prompted Indian observer status in the SCO. Russia, additionally, has voiced support for a permanent seat for India on the UN Security Council. As for the potential for a strategic triangle, Putin stated that cooperation among Russia, India, and China, "would make a great contribution to global security."[65]

One other area of potential cooperation between Moscow and Delhi is energy. India's major oil concern, the Oil and Natural Gas Corporation (ONGC) already has a 20 percent stake in Russia's Sakhalin-1 project, where it invested $1.7 billion, and is keen to bid up to $3 billion for a stake in Sakhalin-3. In early 2005, the Indian Petroleum and Natural Gas Ministry reportedly offered the Russian government up to $25 billion in investments into Russia's oil and gas industry, as ONGC seeks to secure a stake in Yuganskneftegaz, the YUKOS unit put up for auction. If successful, this would surpass British Petroleum's 2002 investment as the largest single foreign investment project in Russia.[66] Meanwhile, the Indian government also hinted that it would be interested in a gas pipeline linking Turkmenistan, Afghanistan, and Pakistan to India.[67] No matter how far-fetched this may be (the U.S. firm Unocal lobbied throughout the 1990s for a similar route), it reflects India's growing interest in Central Asia, and in particular, its desire to see stable, yet independent regimes in the region. India will be handicapped somewhat by cultural barriers due to its perceived anti-Muslim image in much of Central Asia, but it can be seen as an alternative source of capital and economic expertise to the more overbearing governments in Moscow and Washington.

Southeast Asia

By the late 1980s, Southeast Asia was a mere strategic afterthought for Soviet leaders. The war in Cambodia was viewed globally as a Soviet war of proxy against China, and indeed at one time it might have been, but by the late 1980s Gorbachev and his team were eager to put an end to that festering conflict, which involved a large-scale Soviet-backed Vietnamese presence. Once a settlement was concluded in Cambodia, the last hurdle to Soviet–Chinese normalization was cleared (the pullout from Afghanistan was concluded earlier). A scaled-down Soviet/Russian presence around Cam Ranh Bay was maintained,[68] but it was nothing like that of the heyday of the Soviet–Vietnamese strategic partnership in the late 1970s and early 1980s. Throughout this period the other, Western-leaning nations of Southeast Asia (the original ASEAN members) viewed Moscow's imperial ambitions in the region with great distrust and enmity.

By the early 1990s, Southeast Asia was gradually emerging from being a strategic afterthought for Moscow. There was little in the way of political or economic resources to devote to the region. Only in 1993 was Foreign Minister Andrei Kozyrev able to devote some attention to the region, and he did so through his appeal to ASEAN. Accordingly, Russia was invited to join the ARF in 1994. In subsequent years, Deputy Foreign Minister Alexander Panov put much energy into improving Russia's image in Southeast Asia.[69] Much time was also spent trying to recoup Soviet-era debt from Vietnam, which at one time amounted to almost $2 billion. When Russia was invited to join APEC in 1997, it gained further entrée into Southeast Asia.

Faced with the elimination of traditional arms' markets in Eastern Europe, Latin America, and Africa and with a crumbling military-industrial complex, Russian leaders began to focus on new markets for arms exports. A rapidly growing arms market was emerging in Southeast

Asia, which was also experiencing tremendous economic growth in the early 1990s. This development was not lost on Russian leaders. Malaysia—which had never been a traditional U.S. arms client—was one of the first targets. Russia was able to sell to Malaysia eighteen MIG-29s for $500 million in 1995.[70] In 1996 the Russian state-owned arms manufacturer Rosvooruzhenie made a push to sell diesel submarines to Malaysia. Another large Russian arms firm hoped to sell tanks.[71] Russian arms firms also looked on with great interest at the Indonesian market, and in 1997 the Indonesian government decided to buy twelve Su-30 fighter aircraft and eight Mi-17 helicopters.[72] Nevertheless, the Asian financial crisis, temporarily precluded any further large-scale arms sales transactions for Moscow in the region.

In 1996 new Foreign Minister Yevgeny Primakov also looked to Southeast Asia, not only to boost Russia's economic prospects, but also to boost Russia's diplomatic—and hence strategic profile—in the APR. Primakov met with ASEAN Secretary General Ajit Singh in Moscow in June of 1996 and in July, Russia was invited to become a dialogue partner along with China and India. In Jakarta Primakov declared that one of Russia's diplomatic priorities in Asia would be the improvement of relations with ASEAN. In what was perhaps a planned slight to Washington, Primakov announced that Russia supported the idea of a nuclear weapons-free zone in Southeast Asia, something the United States has long opposed due to the fact that U.S. nuclear submarines and nuclear-armed surface warships regularly transit the region.[73] In the summer of 1997 Primakov made another highly-publicized trip to the region, visiting Thailand and Malaysia.[74] He would return to Malaysia for the Kuala Lumpur APEC summit in November 1998, while his successor Vladimir Putin would attend the Auckland APEC summit in September 1999.

Although Moscow's strategic regard was focused elsewhere over the next several years, Southeast Asia never completely disappeared from the radar. In the first few years of the twenty-first century, Russian arms manufacturers were still focused on how they might increase sales in the region. In 2000 the Indonesian Army bought from Russia twelve BTR-80 armored personnel carriers, sixteen Mi helicopters and four Mi-8 helicopters, and a large stock (9,000) of Kalashnikov submachine-guns. Russia demonstrated its willingness to accept barter deals, often agreeing to take payment for weapons systems in the form of rubber, tin, and palm oil from Southeast Asia.[75] Vladimir Putin was the first leader of Russia or the Soviet Union to visit Vietnam, which he did in early 2001 in an attempt to reawaken dormant ties. There was a last push to try and keep the Russian naval asset on Cam Ranh Bay open, but that facility was eventually shut down.

Putin's Foreign Minister Igor Ivanov, made a wide tour of Asia in the summer of 2003, and included Cambodia, where he attended a summit of the ARF. In that same year Indonesian President Megawati Sukarnoputri visited Moscow, the first official visit to either country by their leaders.[76] Russia's diplomatic efforts seemed to pay off further when Malaysia signed a deal for close to $1 billion to purchase eighteen advanced Su-30MK fighters (chosen in preference to U.S. F-18 Super Hornets). Interestingly, India was connected to this deal by agreeing to provide the training of the Malaysian pilots and the servicing of the Su-30s. This was an obvious boost to India's strategic and business interests in Southeast Asia. "India has acted as a gateway for Russian arms sales to Southeast Asia," according to Alex Vaskin, director of the Indo-Russian Strategic Forum. Vaskin also pointed out that Malaysia had previously purchased Russian MiG-29 fighters and Mi-17 helicopters, after studying India's experience with these aircraft.[77] In the summer of 2004, thanks to a large presence at the Indonesian Defense Exposition by the state-owned arms export firm Rosoboronexport, Russia was also able to sell twelve Sukhoi fighters to Indonesia. At the exposition a representative of Sukhoi Air Holding announced that his firm hoped to sell 80–100 Sukhoi fighters in the APR by the year 2010.[78]

The Russian government and Russian firms have been anxious to kick start negotiations with Southeast Asian nations in the energy sphere. At the Vientienne ASEAN Summit in Laos in November 2004, the Russian delegation discussed with ASEAN members energy development schemes, including the training of personnel, pipeline construction, site surveying, and production. But apart from arms sales, Russia's economic interaction with the region remains light. Two-way trade in 2004 with the members of ASEAN amounted to only $4.4 billion—less than 2 percent of Russia's total trade volume.[79]

The fact that Putin was able to speak at the East Asia Summit in December 2005 could be seen as somewhat of a coup for Russia. When the Kremlin put out initial feelers about being invited to the summit (which was originally conceived as a meeting of ASEAN leaders, plus leaders from China, Japan, and South Korea), the reception was somewhat cool. Efforts by Russian diplomats were eventually rewarded by the host country Malaysia inviting it to attend the prior ASEAN summit and then later to speak at the East Asian Summit, although it could not be there as a member. Russian leaders see multilateral institutions as a means of inserting a Russian diplomatic and political presence into the APR, including in Southeast Asia. This is a low-cost, high-effect way of assuring that Russian interests are heard and known throughout the region.[80]

Moscow sees opportunities in Southeast Asia, but in comparison to Central and South Asia, it will remain a lesser priority for leaders who recognize that it has become a region of overlapping United States, Chinese, and Indian influence and competition. Nevertheless, Russia will continue to push arms deals and attempt to insert itself as a potential supplier of energy for the region

Conclusion

Russia's strategic position in Central, South, and Southeast Asia has undoubtedly slipped since the days of the cold war. But Russia is leveraging what tools it can—whether they be multilateral partnerships, arms sales, diplomatic forays, energy, or old political connections—to maintain an active role in these regions which in the future could be translated into a role as an honest broker, or a balancer of last resort as other nations jockey for political and strategic influence across this broad arc of geopolitical importance. Moscow will now have to learn to deal with entrenched American power, Chinese thirst for energy, and India's attempt to become engaged across this region in order to stabilize that nation's northern flank and its southern littoral. Central Asia—and South Asia to a lesser extent—will continue to occupy a central role in Russia's strategic thinking, both for historical and practical reasons.

Although, the potential for strategic cooperative efforts between Beijing, Delhi, and Moscow remains limited, there are a number of emerging bilateral and multilateral relationships across this region that offer the potential for enhanced strategic cooperation. Among these is the Indian–Sino–Russian relationship, as well as Sino–Russian–Uzbek relations, Kazakh–Russian–Uzbek relations, Kazakh–Sino–Russian relations, U.S.–Indian relations, the CSTO, the SCO, and even a potential coalition revolving around U.S.–Indian–Kyrgyz–Tajik cooperation in the region and in Afghanistan. References to a new "Great Game" in Central Asia no longer focus on strategic competition—or cooperation—between Moscow and Washington. They now encompass China, India, and a host of peripheral players, including non-state actors.[81] This, in a sense, levels the playing field for Moscow. Moscow is still constrained diplomatically, politically, and economically in Asia, and must truly ponder how far it wishes to go in designing a strategy that clearly confronts Washington, and relies more and more on the growing power of China.

Notes

1. This chapter will deal with the five nations in Central Asia that were Soviet republics prior to 1991: Kazakhstan, Kyrgyzstan, Tajikistan, Turkmenistan, and Uzbekistan.

2. Alexei Bogaturov, "International Relations in Central-Eastern Asia: Geopolitical Challenges and Prospects for Political Cooperation" (Washington, DC: The Brookings Institution Center for Northeast Asian Policy Studies, June 2004), p. 2.

3. Irina Zviagelskaya, "Russia's Policy Options in Central Asia," in Gennady Chufrin, ed., *Russia in Asia: The Emerging Security Agenda* (SIPRI; Oxford: Oxford University Press, 1999), p. 124. Also, see Kenneth Weisbrode, "Central Eurasia: Prize or Quicksand?," *Adelphi Paper*, No. 338 (2001): 17.

4. Konstantin Syroezhkin, "The Policy of Russia in Central Asia: a Perspective from Kazakhstan," in Chufrin, ed., *Russia in Asia*, p. 102.

5. Among these are the Central Asian Cooperation Organization (CACO) composing Russia, Kazakhstan, Kyrgyzstan, Tajikistan, and Uzbekistan; the Collective Security Treaty Organization—or CSTO (Russia, Armenia, Belarus, Kazakhstan, Kyrgyzstan, and Tajikistan); the Eurasian Economic Community—or EEC (Russia, Belarus, Kazakhstan, Kyrgyzstan, and Tajikistan); and the Shanghai Cooperation Organization—SCO (Russia, China, Kazakhstan, Kyrgyzstan, Tajikistan, and Uzbekistan). For a more comprehensive listing see Bogaturov, "International Relations in Central-Eastern Asia." Also, see Stephen Hanson, "Russia: Strategic Partner or Evil Empire," in Ashley Tellis and Michael Wills, eds, *Strategic Asia 2004–05: Confronting Terrorism in the Pursuit of Power* (Seattle, WA: The National Bureau of Asian Research, 2004), p. 179.

6. Syroezhkin, "The Policy of Russia in Central Asia," pp. 102–103.

7. Zviagelskaya, "Russia's Policy Options in Central Asia," p. 130.

8. Martha Brill Olcott, "Post-Soviet Kazakhstan: The Demographics of Ethnic Politics," *Problems of Post-Communism*, Vol. 42, No. 2 (March/April 1995), pp. 25–26.

9. The states of the CIS represented the inner most circle, the next circle represented former socialists states, especially in Eastern Europe. Subsequent circles represented Western Europe and the United States, then the states of Asia, including China, India, and Japan. Thanks to Dr. Ilya Prizell for pointing this out to the author in the mid-1990s.

10. Alvin Rubinstein, "The Transformation of Russian Foreign Policy," in Karen Dawisha, ed., *The International Dimension of Post-Communist Transitions in Russia and the New States of Eurasia* (Armonk, NY: M.E. Sharpe, 1997), p. 49.

11. Zviagelskaya, "Russia's Policy Options in Central Asia," p. 135.

12. Gregory Gleason, "Central Asia: State Building in the Face of Insurgent Islam," in Tellis and Wills, eds, *Strategic Asia 2004–05*, pp. 214–15.

13. Jason Lyall, "Great Games," Working Paper, Princeton University, Spring 2005, p. 18.

14. See for example, two articles in the daily *Kommersant* warning about the dangers of 'yielding' Central Asia to the United States. *Kommersant'*, January 11, 23, 2002. Also, *Izvestia*, January 23, 2002.

15. Martha Brill Olcott, "Central Asia," in Richard Ellings and Aaron Friedberg, *Strategic Asia 2002–03: Asian Aftershocks* (Seattle, WA: The National Bureau of Asian Research, 2002), p. 242.

16. Weisbrode, "Central Eurasia: Prize or Quicksand?" p. 60.

17. Olcott, "Central Asia," p. 243.

18. Kathleen Collins and William Wohlforth, "Central Asia: Defying Great Game Expectations," in Richard Ellings and Aaron Friedberg, eds., *Strategic Asia 2003–04: Fragility and Crisis* (Seattle, WA: The National Bureau of Asian Research, 2003), pp. 301–04.

19. Ibid.

20. Roger McDermott, "Moscow and Bishkek Affirm Continued Cooperation," *Eurasia Daily Monitor*, Vol. 2, Issue 62, March 30, 2005.

21. Roger McDermott, "Russia Studies Osh for Possible New Military Base in Kyrgyzstan," *Eurasia Daily Monitor*, Vol. 2, Issue 107, June 2, 2005.

22. Vitaly Naumkin, "The Emerging Geopolitical Balance in Central Asia: a Russian View," in Chufrin, ed., *Russia in Asia*, pp. 84, 91–92.

23. Gleason, "Central Asia," pp. 217–18.

24. Weisbrode, "Central Eurasia: Prize or Quicksand?" p. 59.

25. Igor Torbakov, "Moscow and Washington Pursue Diverging Policies in Uzbekistan, Central Asia," *Eurasia Daily Monitor*, Vol. 2, Issue 118, June 17, 2005.

26. *Nezavisimaia gazeta*, June 30, 2005.

27. Roger McDermott, "Uzbekistan's Relations with China Warming," *Eurasia Daily Monitor*, Vol. 2, Issue 142, July 22, 2005.

28. *Rossiiskaia gazeta*, August 2, 2005. See also, *Nezavisimaia gazeta*, August 8, 2005.

29. Weisbrode, "Central Eurasia: Prize or Quicksand?" p. 18; Gleason, "Central Asia," pp. 205–06.

30. *Itar-Tass*, May 8, 2005.

31. Lyall, "Great Games," pp. 20–31.

32. See, Alexander Lukin and Alexei Mochul'ski, "Shankhaiskaia Organizatsia Sotrudnichestva: Strukturnoe oformlenie i perspektivy razvitiia," *Analiticheskie zapiski* (February 2005). The organization was originally established in 1996 and was known as the "Shanghai Five," after the original members China, Russia, Kazakhstan, Kyrgyzstan, and Tajikistan. Uzbekistan joined in June 2001, and the organization was renamed the SCO.

33. See Ch.5 by Dmitri Trenin.

34. Chietigj Bajpaee, "China Fuels Energy Cold War," *Asia Times*, March 2, 2005.

35. Stephen Blank, "Islam Karimov and the Heirs of Tiananmen," *Eurasia Daily Monitor*, Vol. 2, Issue 115, June 14, 2005.

36. *Wall Street Journal* and *Financial Times*, August 23–25, 2005.

37. Russian Foreign Minister Sergei Lavrov, concerned about China's domination of the SCO, has even proposed SCO–NATO cooperation. See, Stephen

Blank, "Moscow Offers Muted Response to Possible End of EU Arms Embargo Against China," *Eurasia Daily Monitor*, Vol. 2, Issue 41, March 1, 2005.

38. Irwin Stelzer, "The Axis of Oil," *The Weekly Standard*, February 7, 2005.

39. *Kommersant*, June 29, 2005. Also, see, Sergei Blagov, "Karimov Travels to Moscow Discusses Andijan And 'Terrorism' With Putin," *Eurasia Daily Monitor*, Vol. 2, Issue 127, June 30, 2005.

40. *Nezavisimaia gazeta*, July 6, 2005; also, *Gazeta.ru*, July 6, 2005; and, *Vremya Novostei*, July 6, 2005. In English see, *Christian Science Monitor*, July 7, 2005.

41. *Washington Post*, July 15, 2005.

42. *Globe and Mail*, July 12, 2005; also, *Agence France Presse*, July 16, 2005. Also, for a view of how Kyrgyz political elites view this issue, see Erica Marat, "Kyrgyz Experts Oppose Bishkek's Decision to Limit US Military Presence," *Eurasia Daily Monitor*, Vol. 2, Issue 139, July 19, 2005.

43. *Washington Post*, July 27, 2005.

44. Vladimir Mukhin, *Nezavisimaia gazeta*, June 25, 2005; also, Vladimir Socor, "From CIS to CSTO," *Eurasia Daily Monitor*, Vol. 2, Issue 125, June 28, 2005.

45. See Trenin, "Russia's Asia Policy," pp. 3–4; also, Vladimir Socor, "CIS Collective Security Organization Holds Summit," *Eurasia Daily Monitor*, Vol. 2, Issue 123, June 24, 2005.

46. Roger McDermott, "Russia Plays Peace Advocate in Krygyz 'Regime Change,' " *Eurasia Daily Monitor*, Vol. 2, Issue 67, April 6, 2005.

47. Vladimir Frolov, "Soft Power Politics," *Moscow Times*, April 13, 2005.

48. See the article by Vladimir Bogdanov in the *Rossiiskaia gazeta*, June 24, 2005. Also, see the article by Vladimir Mukhin in *Nezavisimaia gazeta*, June 25, 2005.

49. For a good overview of these debates see, Igor Torbakov, "Russian Pundits Divided on How to React to the Death Throes of Post-Soviet World," *Eurasia Daily Monitor*, Vol. 2, Issue 99, May 20, 2005. For articles in Russian dailies that have covered this issue, see for example: *Moskovskii Komsomolets*, May 25, 2005; *Trud*, May 26, 2005; *Vremia Novostei*, May 27, 2005.

50. Lyall, "Great Games," pp. 31–32.

51. *Kommersant,* June 3, 2005; *Nezevisimaia Gazeta*, June 10, 2005.

52. Vladimir Moskalenko and Tatiana Shaumian, "Russia's Security and the Geopolitical Situation in South Asia," in Chufrin, ed., *Russia in Asia*, p. 229. Also, see Vinay Shukla, "Russia in South Asia: A View from the Region," in Chufrin, ed., *Russia in Asia*, p. 266.

53. Moskalenko and Shaumian, "Russia's Security," pp. 233–34.

54. Shukla, "Russia in South Asia," pp. 252–53.

55. Shukla, "Russia in South Asia," p. 252.

56. Moskalenko and Shaumian, "Russia's Security," p. 233.

57. *Asahi shimbun*, December 13, 2001.

58. Shukla, "Russia in South Asia," p. 268.

59. Ibid., p. 269.
60. Ibid., pp. 265–66.
61. This according to a Western diplomat stationed in Delhi. Interview with author in February 2005.
62. *Eurasia Daily Monitor*, June 7, 2001.
63. Ashley Tellis, "South Asia," in Richard Ellings and Aaron Friedberg, eds., *Strategic Asia 2001–02: Power and Purpose* (Seattle, WA: The National Bureau of Asian Research, 2001), pp. 255–56.
64. *Asia Times*, June 19, 2003.
65. *Asia Times*, December 7, 2004.
66. *Kommersant*, February 22, 2005; also, Moscow *Times*, February 24, 2005.
67. *Itar-Tass*, February 25, 2005.
68. While traveling in Vietnam in 1991, this author was repeatedly forced to explain to people that he was not a Soviet (*Lien Xo*), but an American (*My*).
69. Alexander Panov, *Kaminari nochi hare*, as cited in Kazuhiko Togo's chapter on Yeltsin's strategic thinking toward Asia in the latter half of the 1990s, pp. 205–228.
70. Victor Sumsky, "Russia and ASEAN: Emerging Partnership in the 1990s and the Security of South-East Asia," in Chufrin, ed., *Russia in Asia*, p. 414.
71. *Itar-Tass*, April 25, 1996.
72. Sumsky, "Russia and ASEAN," in Chufrin, ed., *Russia in Asia*, p. 414.
73. *Eurasia Daily Monitor*, Vol. 2, Issue 145, July 25, 1996.
74. *Eurasia Daily Monitor*, Vol. 3, Issue 144, July 24, 1997.
75. *Asia Times*, December 2, 2004. Also, *Russia Journal*, April 17, 2003.
76. *Russia Journal*, April 17, 2003.
77. *Asia Times*, June 19, 2003.
78. *Asia Times*, December 2, 2004.
79. Matthew J. Ouimet, "Russia and ASEAN: Tactics of Multi-nationalism in Southeast Asia," paper presented at the annual conference of the American Association of Advanced Slavic Studies (AAASS), Salt Lake City, Utah, November 5, 2005.
80. Ibid. My thanks to Matthew Ouimet for pointing out this trend to me.
81. Daniel Kimmage, "Central Asia: Is Regional Turbulence Return of The Great Game?" *RFE/RL*, July 19, 2005. Also, see M. K. Bhadrakumar, "Foul Play in the Great Game," *Asia Times*, July 12, 2005.

CHAPTER 10

Russian Strategic Thinking on Asian Regionalism

Gilbert Rozman

When Russians view the northern hemisphere they are inclined to see two grand expanses: the Euro-Atlantic region and the APR. The former appears as "the West," whose meaning resonates from historic times. The latter, however, cannot be captured by a term such as "the East." Only recently have images for looking past global forces and bilateral relations begun to reveal how to "deconstruct" this concept. In varied discourse, each concept divides into three parts. At the broadest level both expanses include the United States, suggesting a cross-oceanic region where even after the collapse of the Soviet Union Moscow faces America's great power and hegemonic inclinations.[1] At a middle level Atlantic is dropped from the Euro-Atlantic region and Pacific disappears from the Asia-Pacific, leaving a "macro region" increasingly in the hands of the European Union (EU) and what in 2005, with the first East Asian Summit, was coming to be marked as the start of the East Asian community. Closest to home, Russians grope to identify a third area separate from the space of the former Soviet republics, if still imprecise. To the east this micro region is called Northeast Asia. For each of the three levels of regional images the critical question is: Can Russia assert its presence so that gains outweigh loss of independence? Answers to the question "who is in control?" while initially troubling, have, for now at least, become sufficiently reassuring to prompt a new wave of strategic thinking. It is the still undefined space of Northeast Asia that raises both the fears and the hopes for regionalism, while a broader image of East Asia and the favored term APR together open a playing field for great power balancing.[2]

If objectives are similar to the East and West, the opportunities for strategic maneuvering differ. However wide recent differences between the United States and the major EU states have opened, they offer much less freedom of action than does the gap between China and Japan in Northeast Asia, the still tentative start-up of the East Asian community, as well as the shifting shadows of the United States, or even India, across the vast Asia–Pacific area. Moscow's search for a voice in multilateral forums has met with limited success in NATO and the EU, but in the less-institutionalized environment of the Asia–Pacific there is the prospect of a more substantial role.[3] To its east Russia finds states with quite varied notions of national interest and sympathetic views of the sanctity of state sovereignty coupled with restraint in criticism of human rights violations. Not only is regionalism weaker, but in the critical dimensions of security and energy Moscow has come to see fertile soil for forging multilateralism where its assets really do matter. In the background is a growing partnership with China through the SCO, manifested in August 2005 in joint military exercises allegedly targeted against terrorism, but held in the Yellow Sea and Sea of Japan in a manner that delivered a message to the United States and Japan on their assertiveness in the region and also on possible joint determination should North Korea become a target of pressure or military action.[4]

As for the balance among levels of regionalism, Russians have noted opposite developments at the two ends of their country. In the west, they watched as NATO and the EU drew closer, Serbs were stripped of their hold over parts of the former Yugoslavia, and elections (even in parts of the CIS) rejected Moscow's outstretched arms in favor of closer ties to the EU/US. As integration intensified, it became impossible to identify a specific area available to Russian-shaped regionalism. In contrast, to the east, six-party talks confirmed the salience of Northeast Asia as a geopolitical unit, as South Korea's enthusiastic pursuit of Northeast Asia regionalism suggested economic prospects too. The Asian Regional Forum (ARF) talks, centered in Southeast Asia, include Russia, offering a start-up, if only informal, setting for regional security dialogue. Over the horizon Russians watched ASEAN + 3 and the new East Asian Summit in December 2005, to which Russia was not invited to participate formally but Putin was allowed to speak. Even if China's rise could eventually become a problem, Russians took heart from developments at the more accessible regional level, calculating that despite a weak economic and demographic presence in Northeast Asia they could achieve quite a large voice in its evolution. At the same time as they help to forge multilateralism, they can benefit from diversity in the area and a still uncertain struggle for power as well as shared resistance to "universal" values. This is not the tired notion of "Eurasianism" that treats Russia as unique and a leader[5]; it is Russia finding a niche for itself despite a weak hand because of an unsettled region.

Strategic aspirations for Northeast Asia center on three widely accepted assumptions, even if there remain doubts about each. One, the perspective for the Russian Far East is favorable in a regional context that holds at bay some of the forces of globalization.[6] Two, Sino-Russian relations are well-established as the foundation for Russia's growing role in the region, even if there are limits on their pursuit.[7] And three, a balance of power is within reach and must be shaped by centralized control from Moscow with suspicion of the role of private business or NGOs and of the initiative of the krai and oblast leaders along the borders, something that is often disputed by analysts in the Russian Far East.[8] So far, these assumptions have taken precedence over counterarguments to the effect that more earnest globalization must overwhelm the corruption and illegality in cross-border ties, that a genuine balance of power would put less weight on China, and that decentralized energies in the Russian Far East are needed for regionalism to blossom. With Russia lacking a model of WTO integration based on market competition at home and with the United States and North Korean locked in nuclear crisis, the search for strategic thinking has yet to face severe tests over the balance between conflicting assumptions.

The course for regionalism generally anticipated in the 1990s would have left Russia on the margins. It would have built regional integration on a firm foundation of global integration, anathema to Russians still troubled by a complex transition from leading the world in opposition to the U.S.-led bloc. East Asian traditions would have privileged values linked to the Confucian past, leaving Russia as an outsider. Japan would have a major say in setting the terms for Russian entry. Yet, revisionism and reunification took center stage in Northeast Asia after 2000 in a manner that redirected regionalism. Also, the central role in the search for regionalism shifted to Southeast Asia, which held the initiative in ASEAN + 3 and then in the East Asian Summit. Under these new circumstances, Russian leaders found more room to explore diverse possibilities. They have set a new course with short-term gains for making Russia's voice heard but not with adequate preparations for the long-term opportunities should regionalism really gain ground.

The Evolution of Regional Thinking

Beckoned by proposals for regionalism, leaders in Moscow have also been frightened by fear of its impact. For a long time, the concept was sullied with the accusation it was a plot by the United States to widen and intensify its dominance. Calculating that the United States maintains hegemony over the APR, officials and analysts never seriously explored the option of entering the existing hierarchical system. If they had done so, the focus might have turned to the economic clout one brings to the table. This would have rendered Moscow's security role minimal, undermining the one asset that serves as its trump card and, even as it was diminishing, was still considered to be the nation's primary strength. In the U.S. regional order Russia would take its place after Japan and South Korea, both of which had large numbers of U.S. troops based on their territory and were substantial market economies flush with capital. If the United States and its two allies posed no apparent threat against the territory of the Russian Far East apart from Japan's claim to four islands, their economic tentacles could easily have drawn the area into a close embrace through market forces. There were doubts that Russia knew how to counteract them. Despite some language of "new thinking" toward the region from 1986, older thinking opposed to regionalism as U.S. hegemony easily prevailed.[9] Only in the late 1990s and especially after 2000 was there a sufficient reassessment of Northeast Asia to envision more balanced regionalism. Once it was determined that the U.S. role was on the decline, the prospect grew of new strategic thinking about Russia's real options.

In fact, the United States lost interest in regionalism as Japan's leadership potential became apparent and later really soured on it as a vehicle for China's rise. The initiative began to shift in the 1980s. While Soviet leaders continued to think in terms of talks that could produce a multilateral strategic framework incorporating the superpowers in a kind of regionalism from the top down, voices within the region began to eye cross-border engines of growth that might produce regionalism from the bottom up. At the start of the 1990s some in Japan called for a "Sea of Japan economic rim." From China came proposals for making the UN-sponsored Tumen river delta development program the engine for regional growth. South Koreans sought inroads to swing Russian Koreans to their side and to outshine North Korea's derelict presence symbolized by barbed-wire logging camps. As Russian borders opened to commerce and shuttle traders, there was talk of cross-border fever becoming the driving force of regionalism. This aroused fear because vested interests lacked the expertise and capital to compete. Open borders would only expose the chaotic and criminal environment on the Russian side. It did not matter that worry about plots for U.S. dominance had receded. The danger was growing of spontaneous moves by firms and migrants that could be no less devastating. If the most uproar came from the Russian Far East,[10] the mood in Moscow was not so different.

From the mid-1990s Russia has scored important successes in Asia after recognizing the failed Soviet strategy in the Brezhnev era and the unrealized hopes under Gorbachev and the start of the Yeltsin era. In these earlier periods claims to strategic thinking proved to be short-sighted. Under Brezhnev Moscow made almost no progress in improving relations with the other powers of the region, increasingly relying on North Korea as its only friend. It refused to acknowledge the reality of regional dynamism and emerging economic integration or to conceptualize the APR as a major transformative force in a world of regions. Lacking tools to influence the area, Moscow built up its military forces to a one-sided and provocative degree. Narrow blinders kept thoughts focused on supposed parallels with NATO, even as small numbers of better-informed officials and scholars began to digest contradictory information and secretly to test new strategic thinking.[11] Under the shadow of Eurocentric thinking, Gorbachev also did not give the region its due. If the July 1986 Vladivostok speech at last declared Russia's intent to discuss regional ties, it limited the terms that would be acceptable. In 1988 a national committee for Asia–Pacific economic cooperation was formed; yet, the glasnost necessary for thinking strategically came slowly in coverage of Japan, the Koreas, and China.[12] The old notion of a multilateral security structure endured as U.S. scepticism of Moscow's intentions left little chance to explore such ideas. As a result, strategy had to concentrate on bilateral relations, where, of course, much needed to be accomplished.

After making important progress in bilateral relations with China in 1988–89, South Korea in 1990–91, and, to a lesser degree, Japan in 1989–93, Moscow policymakers faced the reality that they lacked any regional policy. Abandoning North Korea, they had no say in the nuclear crisis of 1993–94. Remaining rather aloof from China after June 4, 1989, they struggled to strengthen ties after Yeltsin's December 1992 patchwork visit. While his visit to Japan in October 1993 partially compensated for the hasty cancellation in September 1992, it ushered in several years of anxious searching just to find a new path to pursue normalization. Unable to exert much control over maverick governors in the

Russian Far East alarmed by neighboring countries, central leaders feared regional proposals such as the Tumen river delta project and left their country in danger of becoming irrelevant to the surging economic integration of Japan, China, and South Korea. Of course, China's isolation after June 4 and Japan's uncompromising stance on four islands as well as the standoff between North and South Korea made navigating in this region difficult.[13] Frustration led to calls for defending national interests and taking a strategic approach, but suggestions often were unrealistic and sharply at odds with each other. Realities had to be faced, such as the maldistribution of Russian cities and population,[14] and endemic criminality at the borders.[15]

Through the 1990s there was great wariness in Moscow as well as in the Russian Far East about possibilities for regionalism. They posed a danger that distant outposts of a newly decentralized state would be turned away from Moscow toward neighboring states. Another concern was that rival cities or transportation routes would benefit, leaving the bypassed coastal corridor of the Russian Far East to wither away. The prospect also loomed that either Japan with its powerful world-class corporations or China with its hordes of small-scale entrepreneurs would gain leadership in the region. If at times local officials drew attention and modest infusions of money by feigning an interest in discussions about regionalism, the reality was that both the center and the border areas had too little confidence that they could compete in a market environment or, perhaps, desire to do so in order to go forward.[16] Strategic thinking was limited largely to ideas on the means for resistance.[17] Minus bold recognition of Russia's true problems that could last be seen in the Gorbachev era and Yeltsin's start in 1992, narrow approaches focused on bilateral matters in pursuit of deals that benefited a few.

A consensus was forming in the mid-1990s that Russia was mismanaging its involvement in the Asia-Pacific region. This was compounded by the resentment against the Western powers preparing to expand NATO. Turning east offered more promising hunting grounds. Since all of the countries of Northeast Asia were looking for ways to improve ties with Russia, opportunities were within reach. In 1995 Russia applied to join APEC, and this was welcomed by first the United States, eager to compensate for the affront from NATO expansion, and then in 1997 Japan, searching for a way to restart negotiations with territorial as much as strategic objectives in mind. Yet, it was China, above all, that gave Russia the opening it was seeking in the region. China's strategic thinking gave priority to Russia's revival as a pole in a multipolar global system. Offering a strategic partnership and reassuring rhetoric about a long-term but not aggressive challenge to the world order, China met Russia's needs best. Yet, Japan's appeal in 1997 for Eurasian diplomacy included mention of cooperation on geostrategic goals, and some prospect existed that Japan would persist and make an offer that might balance the one by China.[18] Without an economic program to regain some of its global status, Russia's leadership found the pursuit for political reasons by other powers in Northeast Asia appealing and envisioned raising their country's voice in this region to overcome the frustration of status loss. As a target for countries still groping for a path toward regionalism, Russia did not have to embrace grand ideals and principles to be welcomed.

The debate in Moscow on how to boost Russian power in Asia was full of contradictions: China loomed as both the favored partner and the primary long-term threat; Japan appeared both rigid in its demands and urgently in need of Russia to balance China; and improved ties with North Korea were expected to give Russia influence in reducing tensions even if Pyongyang was uncompromising. Calls for a consortium of India, China, and Russia stumbled before poor Sino-Indian relations, and support for the U.S.–Japan alliance as a stabilizing force clashed with China's reasoning. Playing a weak hand and testing strategic ideas that did not measure the test of reality, Russia in the late 1990s did not have a promising strategy. Relations with South Korea had slipped over a spy scandal. In the fall of 1998 Japanese Prime Minister Obuchi returned from Moscow without any sign that he took seriously the compromise possibilities in the secret offer on how to deal with the islands and strengthen relations, while Yeltsin returned from Beijing with claims that the border demarcation had been successfully completed that were premature and did not obscure the doubts about how in the face of stagnation in economic relations and divergent goals ties could be enhanced. The Asian financial crisis was raising China and Japan's interest in regionalism centered on the new ASEAN + 3 meetings, while Russia stayed on the sidelines. The urgency of a regional approach from Russia was rising, leading to the search for a strategic foundation for it.

In 1999 as the leaders of China, Japan, and Korea were wooing Moscow and the NATO states led by the United States were being blamed for aggression in Yugoslavia, Russian officials began to see a way forward. They could tighten ties with China through the SCO and outside it. Consistent with Kim Dae-jung's new engagement of North Korea, they could actively boost ties themselves in a triangular context. And as Japanese officials prepared to intensify their appeal for a breakthrough by 2000, they might benefit from a third, interested partner.

Together these separate endeavors held hope of a regional strategy for the first time in almost a decade. Disappointment with U.S. assertiveness and a new inevitability about the rise of China raised the stakes for a region-wide calculus.

Regionalist Strategic Thinking in the Putin Era

The year 2000 transformed Northeast Asia, giving Moscow new opportunities, which it seized under Vladimir Putin's more strategic calculations. In May 1999 Kim Dae-jung had visited in quest of support for what would become the sunshine policy. One Russian diplomat claims that this trip convinced Kim that the key is to gain the North's confidence, adding that again in July 2002 Kim sought Moscow's role as an intermediary to boost ties after a sea skirmish and Foreign Minister Ivanov proceeded to Pyongyang where he succeeded in calming the tension and giving a new impetus to cross-peninsula relations.[19] Similar to a decade earlier, Seoul was hoping for Moscow's intervention in bringing Pyongyang to the bargaining table, even if Russians were prone to exaggerate their significance. Although efforts to rebuild ties with Pyongyang were not far along, Kim's visit gave new impetus to them and suggested that they would put Russia into the thick of a search for long-term peace and reintegration on the peninsula without precedent. After six years of resentment over their isolation on peninsular matters, this was a chance that Russian officials were eager to seize. It brought hope that a multilateral security framework could form in dealing with the North, plus new attention to energy and transportation infrastructure that would serve reunification on the peninsula as it linked the Russian Far East to the dynamism of the region.

Through the year 2000, Putin also found Japan's leaders wooing him in earnest and even speaking of a new will to compromise on the islands. Amidst talk that the two states have remarkable congruence of strategic interests and promising economic prospects, Putin could take seriously new vistas for Russian policy in Northeast Asia. Starting in office with prospects for balancing China and Japan, Putin would be disappointed in 2001 that Japan rejected its own negotiating strategy and, yet, could still be impressed in early 2003 with a pipeline plan endorsed by Koizumi Junichiro that could create maximum outlets in the region for Russian oil. Japan's concerns about China's rise suggested a major regional role for Russia and a need to take a fresh look at region-wide changes.

If China thought he started slowly in reinforcing ties, Putin could have no doubt that Russia's foremost regional partner was waiting to upgrade relations. In November 2000 after Putin's visit to Pyongyang and his splash as messenger to the G-8 summit in Okinawa bringing news of a freeze in the North's missile tests, Moscow issued an official document on policy to APEC that clarified some regional priorities. It called for moving away from excessive orientation to Europe and the United States and more active participation in the region. Russia was to consolidate its political and diplomatic presence as well as increase its economic cooperation, including through providing stable energy supplies. The document made clear that there could be risk to Siberia and the Russian Far East of localism and regional separatism, but it insisted that the central government had the means to neutralize these without isolating the areas from international markets.[20] China could bide its time, while proving that, more than others, it welcomed these Russian goals.

In the first months of 2001 Moscow faced adjustments to its emerging regional strategy. The Bush administration came to power with the goal of making Asia its priority and slowing the rise of China, seen as a strategic competitor. It also stymied the sunshine policy, leaving South Korea in limbo as well as North Korea. In addition, as Bush courted Japan to boost bilateral relations, Koizumi abandoned Japan's negotiating position to Russia and was more willing to boost nationalism offensive to China, seen in his annual visits to the Yasukuni shrine. Putin recognized a more promising strategic environment for a country reliant on levers of power better suited for tension and shortage than for harmony and integration. Sino-Russian relations again became focused on opposition to U.S. pressure for hegemony. Russian–North Korean relations drew closer as Putin hosted Kim Jong-il. Even as most eyes focused on Putin's strong support for the U.S. war on terrorism in Afghanistan and some in China grew nervous at this potential repeat of Moscow's tilt a decade earlier, the Northeast Asia situation was moving toward multilateralism that brought Russia, China, and even North Korea closer. The fallout from changes in 2000–01 would spread over several years, leading Putin to concentrate on ways to balance U.S. and also Japanese power as, at least, a short-term priority.

After the nuclear showdown between Washington and Pyongyang was enjoined in the fall of 2002, Moscow sought to make its voice heard. The first effort was to send Alexandr Losyukov to Pyongyang in January 2003 to seek a compromise through personal diplomacy that would put Russia at the center of peninsular diplomacy. While the North Koreans quickly dismissed his effort, the United States resented it as potentially harmful since it encouraged Kim Jong-il to think that he could strike a deal rather than yielding to the pressure of the international community.

Moscow was sidelined as three-party talks proceeded in Beijing and the United States worked with Japan and South Korea in an effort to hold open the lure of dialogue while preparing the way for pressure tactics such as limiting sea traffic and even boarding ships. Russian strategy for a time suggested concern over a massive refugee flow from North Korea, but in mid-summer when China got commitments for negotiations the North Koreans requested that Russia be one of the six parties. Once present at the six-party talks Russia emerged as a secondary and rather reserved player, patiently waiting for a new stage when its voice could be better heard but at times annoying the United States because it appeared to be the strongest supporter of the North. By sustaining rapport with the North, Russia was counting on its support for the next stage of the reunification process.

For Russia North Korea represents a catalyst for building a multilateral framework in the east that has promise to accomplish at least three things. First, institutionalization of the six-party talks would stabilize multipolar great power relations in a manner favorable to Russia. The basic balance would be China and Russia versus the United States and Japan, but this would be a fluid system that Russia could exploit for leverage against China or improved ties with Japan. Russia would matter because it along with China would be needed to give the North security guarantees beyond those the United States promised and later tensions involving the North would again see others seeking its support to find an answer. Many inside Russia argue that their country is likely to be most trusted by Koreans on both sides striving for unification, since Russia is least interested in gaining a dominant position. Second, given such fears of a region under the control of one power, a process of integration on the Korean peninsula would lead to regionalism beneficial to Russia's influence and its important role in meeting energy and transport goals for the region. West Siberian oil, Sakhalin oil and gas, Kovykta or Yakut gas, and electricity grids would become driving forces in regionalism, and the Iron Silk Road would extend the Trans-Siberian Railway through both sides of Korea, becoming a quicker and cheaper means of moving goods to and from Europe. Third, North Korea's revival as a joint project of the entire region would spill across into revitalization of the Russian Far East. Coming under the control of Moscow officials and economic interests, the separate administrations in Khabarovsk, Vladivostok, and Iuzhno-Sakhalinsk would work more closely together and use the improved energy and transportation conditions for planned objectives rather than divert more money to criminal groups and capital flight.

Although there were objections from the right and the left, Putin drew widespread support for a policy toward the North Korean crisis deemed realist, pragmatic, and balanced. Most assumed that by keeping the trust of Kim Jong-il and encouraging dialogue, Putin was a force for the only positive outcome. This assumed first that the United States was being unreasonable, aiming for hegemony more than peace. It also considered North Korea to have legitimate interests that Russia must recognize in order to play a constructive role. Few considered the possibility of a contradiction between the two goals of Russia regaining its influence and Russia becoming a positive force for a compromise good for the Korean people and the region. Widespread doubts about U.S. motives made it easy to disregard charges that Russian support for Kim Jong-il made the leader less willing to compromise. Indeed, Russians saw the United States as more oriented to expanding its influence than to eliminating nuclear weapons. They insisted that the United States shared the blame for the origins of the crisis and that it had no good reason not to guarantee the security of the Kim regime and to assist in its economic development.[21]

On the basis of the history of relations between Moscow and Pyongyang and the idea that Kim Jong-il had good reasons not to trust others, Russians asserted that they are uniquely suited to persuade the North. Good relations and trust are the right means, not pressure. Even many who doubt that the North is likely to proceed with serious economic reform or escape from the crisis of its system accept the logic of gradual change with Russia avoiding any pressure. A prosperous North is less important for Russia than a friendly North suspicious of others. Gradual, top-down reunification has the likelihood of keeping security questions in the forefront and boosting Russia's voice.

The North Korean crisis appeared more as an opportunity for Russia than as a threat. Seeing the North as too poor and weak to attack, Moscow insisted that it is anxious for a way out. Collapse was not considered a realistic option. U.S. pressure over human rights violations was deemed selective and hypocritical. When eventually the United States recognized the futility of its approach, Russia would stand to gain the most by its soft stance toward the North during the crisis and the North's confidence that it could serve as one of four equal powers in guaranteeing the negotiated outcome. Russians trusted in the sound judgment of Pyongyang and the untenable position of Washington.

The economic outcome most attractive to Russia is not for market forces and globalization to prevail, but for regional planning to occur as states respond to the North's peculiar transition without trust in modern economic forces. Only through a regional arrangement is there much hope for South Korean investment or North Korean trade growing much. Russia counts on suspicions in the North toward China and South Korea to lead to preference for as close economic ties with Russia as possible. Resisting easy cross-border ties with China and the South, the North could well look to big energy pipelines and transportation corridors linked to Russia for more control. To save the Russian Far East, Russians consider it essential to protect and develop their ports and corridors, identifying the future of North Korea as critical to a regional approach for Russia's coastal axis.[22]

Russians praised Kim Dae-jung's trip to Pyongyang in 2000, Koizumi's trip to Pyongyang in 2002, and China's shuttle diplomacy to Pyongyang and beyond in 2003–05. All of these initiatives were taken with Moscow's encouragement and gave a boost to multilateralism. In contrast, they took exception to Bush's "axis of evil" charge in 2002 and the way Bush started the crisis nine months later, steps that forced a showdown which sidelines Russia. On the left many argued that the United States was to blame for the crisis, refusing to accept an independent regime in the North. Having proven in Iraq that it would attack if a country was not protected by nuclear weapons, the United States had given the North no choice. According to this logic, the only hope for a settlement is that the United States will be forced to forego an attack in Korea because it is tied down in other wars.[23]

Navigating between the United States and China, Putin found more in common with China during the course of the nuclear crisis. Russian writings on China's handling of the six-party talks and China's relations with North Korea and the United States were overwhelmingly positive.[24] There was frequent mention of how Sino-Russian relations were drawing closer. An image emerged of a patient, pragmatic China that was showing Russia the way to handle North Korea and to face a complex crisis. If in the 1990s many Russians doubted China's motives or raised warnings about the future, the common cause shared by the two states at a time of renewed anxiety about U.S. behavior muted such criticisms.

If when Koizumi visited Pyongyang in September 2002 and thanked Putin for contributing to the summit Russian media praised Japan's approach, the tone changed as the nuclear crisis unfolded. In 2003 the media regretted that the United States had pressured Japan and it had backed down. Later as Japan dwelt on the issue of its abducted citizens and eventually discussed imposing economic sanctions, Russians doubted its constructive contribution to the multilateral talks. Yet, there was often an underlining assumption that Russia and Japan had a similar outlook on regional integration, favoring the development of a north-south corridor rather than east-west linkages to China. Expecting that Japan would be troubled by moves toward unification, some Russians, nonetheless, predicted that this would make it more eager to improve bilateral relations.

Under Putin four things have changed that make it easier to contemplate Northeast Asia regionalism. First, at the initiative of Kim Dae-jung and then as a result of the showdown between George Bush and Kim Jong-il, North Korea emerged as a focus of both strategic and economic calculations for finding a multilateral approach. Second, a sharp rise in energy prices and a frantic effort by China and, to some extent, Japan to secure future supplies has given Russia, flush with cash and an image of sustained growth, a privileged status. Third, Putin has succeeded in reasserting central control over local authorities, overcoming the divisions that made coordinated policy toward Northeast Asia states difficult. Fourth, US unilateralism and Putin's maneuvering to cooperate while searching for balance have raised the stakes for regionalism. Strategizing about Russia's important place in an emergent region no longer seems far-fetched. Yet, these factors that boost Russian hopes must be set against a backdrop of continued weakness that is still not adequately taken into account in circumstances where wishful thinking often prevails.

Two trips at the end of 2005 by Putin showcased Russia's search for a place in regionalism. In mid-November he traveled to South Korea for the APEC summit and a separate meeting with host Roh Moo-hyun, followed by his first summit in Japan in five years. The results, coming on the heels of Russian leadership in expanding the role of the SCO and its presence at the fifth round of the six-party talks in Beijing, clarified Moscow's aspirations and the still considerable barriers it faces in Northeast Asia. In mid-December Putin flew to Malaysia for the ASEAN summit, a meeting with Malaysia's president, and at the host's invitation, an opportunity to speak to the first East Asian Summit. Having unsuccessfully sought entry into the new regional grouping, which comprised ASEAN + 3 and the newly added members Australia, New Zealand, and India, Putin made the case for inclusion at the 2006 meeting and in other ways sought to raise Russia's voice in the process of region-building. This visit marked a new priority for Southeast Asia. As ASEAN struggled to deflect great power pressures to steer it in one direction or another, Putin saw room for his country's diplomacy to become part of the mix.

Compared to 1997 when after some delay Russia managed to gain a spot in APEC, its case was bolstered by a number of newly recognized assets. First, its economy had rebounded with six years of sustained growth and a recent surge in trade with many partners in Asia, especially China. Putin brought to both Tokyo and Kuala Lumpur large numbers of Russian business leaders and officials, making the case that investors had a lot to gain if obstacles such as Japan's preoccupation with the territorial issue were set aside. Yet, on December 7 Japanese Foreign Minister Aso Taro spoke of Russia's need to resolve the Northern Territories issue in order to establish new bilateral relations that "would provide a means by which Russia would be accepted as a full-fledged member of Asia."[25] As a decade earlier, Tokyo reserved for itself the right to stand in the way of Moscow's regional aspirations as a lever to resolve their bilateral dispute no matter what might be the economic lure. Moreover, differences within Southeast Asia over the scope of regionalism blocked Moscow's entry into the East Asian Summit and could continue to do so, given that its economic lure far from home remains quite limited.

Second, skyrocketing energy prices and ambitious Russian plans for expanded production in Sakhalin and new oil and gas pipelines from Siberia raised their profile in a new era of energy insecurity. Since 2002 China and Japan had battled over the terminus of a planned oil pipeline from Western Siberia, and Putin's visit to Tokyo renewed the competition despite China gaining the edge in December 2004 with the decision to build the line first to its border with a Chinese extension to the Daqing refineries and only later at a date unknown to build as far as the Pacific ocean. The meeting with Roh brought together two leaders interested in a regional energy regime. Whether pipelines would eventually cross North Korea or oil and gas would reach South Korea by tankers, Putin was dealing from a position of strength in seeking massive investments in his country's primary assets for Northeast Asian regional cooperation.

Third, Russia's tightening strategic partnership with China and growing arms shipments, including to Malaysia, added to its status as a participant in the six-party talks in reasserting its role in strategic matters across Asia. Putin pressed for further recognition, for instance in still uncertain preparations for a multilateral security organization to succeed the six-party talks. If the East Asian Summit was to become an exercise in balancing powers, such as the inclusion of India as a counterweight to China, then Putin wanted his country to become part of the calculus.

Fourth, Putin made his trips as a long delayed strategy for the development of the southeastern tip of the Russian Far East appeared to be taking shape. There was a talk of a forward-looking plan for special economic zones, new processing plants and energy-intensive industries to take advantage of the expected energy abundance after pipeline construction, and, for the first time since the collapse of the Soviet Union, major investments by the Russian state in infrastructure. With China eagerly pursuing business interests in the Russian Far East, Putin faced the challenge of reaching beyond bilateralism that could fuel anxieties about "quiet expansionism" in search of region-wide economic integration.

At the end of 2005 Russia made its strongest case for acceptance in emergent regionalism, but it faced a difficult environment. The North Korean nuclear crisis after a September 19 joint statement by the six parties had become exacerbated, leaving Russia as the most marginal of the six parties facing an uncertain wait. Sino-Japanese and Japanese–South Korean political relations were deteriorating, creating a divisive climate. Russo–U.S. relations had worsened over clashing approaches to Ukraine, Georgia, and Central Asia and Putin's retreat from democracy. The United States was particularly concerned about Russia's ambivalent position on Iran's quest for nuclear weapons. Suspicious of regionalism becoming a mechanism for China to gain hegemonic power, the United States did not welcome a greater role for Russia that was throwing its weight behind China as well as opposing universal values as in the new alliance with Uzbekistan and support for it within the SCO after its massacre of protesters.

With Southeast Asia becoming an arena of intensifying great power competition—the United States treating it as a battlefront in the war against terrorism, India at last flexing its great power potential, and China and Japan competing with different designs for regionalism—, Putin was trying to reassert Moscow's influence more than a decade after Gorbachev had abandoned the alliance with Vietnam after withdrawing support for its occupation of Cambodia. Of course, Indonesia is the prize due to its large population and plentiful natural resources. After a hiatus caused by the Asian financial crisis and domestic political divisions, the new President Yodhoyono was again flexing his state's power. Selling weapons gave Russia a foothold; yet it had little else to offer so far from its borders. In addition, regionalism was a joint ASEAN pursuit in which all interested outside parties had to defer to the organization's consensus-building processes. The United States and Japan had too many partners in the region, such as Singapore, to give Russia much hope as long as it retained an image of obstructing their objectives.

Unresolved Problems in Thinking about Regionalism

So far, hopes for Northeast Asia have failed to focus realistically on persistent problems. The idea of Putin becoming a critical mediator because of his personal ties with Kim Jong-il floundered when it became obvious that Russia has few cards to play compared to any of the other participants in the six-party talks. Dreams of an "Iron Silk Road" revitalizing the Trans-Siberian Railroad faced the stark reality that this is not the shortest distance across Eurasia and that Russia's investment climate is not reassuring to those interested in the oil industry or container shipping to Russian Far East ports. In the July 2004 election for the mayor of Vladivostok and then the February 2005 reappointment of the governor of Primorskii krai, we see no sign of centralization as a means to tackle corruption and misadministration. Finally, the fact that China champions regionalism and could be poised to gain a dominant position may make Russians reconsider thoughts that they will gain by limiting the U.S. role. Instead, strategic thinking should be preparing the way for finding an endgame in the Korean nuclear crisis, a jumpstart to South Korean interest in a regional approach to reintegration of the peninsula, and a renewed effort to win Japanese cooperation as well as that of international investors in the risky, long-term projects essential if Russia is to use energy as a springboard to more regional cooperation. Yet, to fault Putin alone for narrowly focusing on raising Russia's voice would mean overlooking the difficult environment for pursuing a different strategy.

Russia has expected other states to accept the Russian Far East as is rather than to remake it to attract their interest. Lately, this reasoning has been buttressed by optimism that a regional energy regime will become a driving force for integration, perhaps raising the total of oil to Asia from 3 to 30 percent of Russia's exports and forming a gas network of comparable importance. Yet, despite many summits replete with planning for joint energy development, many projects have yet to win approval or funding. In 2004 Putin and Roh may have dreamt together about five transcontinental lines to the Pacific—oil, gas, a new Trans-Siberian–Trans-Korean railway linkup, electricity, and optic fiber—, but a mission by the head of Gazprom to Pyongyang in early 2005 proved that there are no shortcuts to overcome the many problems. Hopes in the Russian Far East for a development plan approved by Moscow were blocked in 2003 by officials who warned that market principles were not advancing and again in 2005 when, despite rumors of success in a year-long competition, of six special economic zones designated for the country not one was located in the Far East. This vote of no-confidence along with the naming of a new presidential representative for the region indicated that Moscow was waiting until criminality in the way of business would be brought under control. Moscow firms were still struggling to take control and shuttle traders were still being ousted in favor of more substantial organizations, but these changes did not necessarily improve the climate for competition. Fearful that as in the early 1990s special economic zones would become a conduit for massive tax evasion, Moscow was not ready to open its window on the Pacific to regionalism even in strictly economic terms. After all on October 27, 2005 the Audit Chamber chief remarked that Russia was continuing to lose vast amounts of fish and timber to illegal exports, bringing losses in state funds as well as environmental damage from predatory exploitation.[26]

Although China was Russia's closest partner in regionalism, trust was limited. In the face of claims by Russia that the SCO was becoming a world pole of strength,[27] fear of Chinese penetration of Central Asia was leading Russia to prefer barriers to economic integration. China accepted Russia's place in the six-party talks over North Korea, but China was in a dominant position and was likely to press for economic integration that left the Russian Far East on the periphery. At the East Asian Summit and ASEAN + 3 China was serious about economic regionalism advancing rapidly, while Russia seemed to have in mind a limited geopolitical approach, highlighting multipolarity based on equality among states with security in the forefront. Putin appeared to be looking for a breakthrough with Japan and other countries, but he was not having notable success. Russia could tail China in its moves toward regionalism, but it would be left mostly with bilateralism. The reality was that Russia was not prepared for regionalism as it continued to be guided by antiquated thinking about balance of power and limited foreign penetration into its territory.

Limiting strategic thinking to one country at a time is not an answer to Russia's exposed Far East and weak economic and demographic position in Northeast Asia. It should be a champion of some sort of regionalism based on an accurate assessment of the long-term trends in the area. Given the assertive unilateralism of the Bush administration and the unconcealed ambitions of Putin to reassert influence in the lands of the former Soviet Union, as well as in parts of the Middle East and Northeast Asia, closer ties to China fit the logic of traditional strategic thinking. In November 2004 Putin and Hu Jintao agreed on the final demarcation of the Sino-Russian border. At the same time, Putin indicated that gas and oil from the Sakhalin-1 project would largely go to the Chinese market. While Japanese taxes had paid for perhaps $1 billion of the development costs, China would be the chief beneficiary.[28] Although Putin had selected the Pacific route for the much-discussed oil pipeline from West Siberia and that could have been seen as a blow to China and benefit to Japan, if Japanese assistance were not forthcoming for development of the region's natural resources a decision could be made after completion of the first of two sections to channel the oil instead to China, initially by train. Russia was prepared to use its energy card on behalf of a regional strategy that could put Japan on the spot. Emboldened by the energy market, its leaders were confident that they had more leverage.[29] China was in eager pursuit, and Putin would not deny it without greater incentives from other powers.

The SCO represents a form of regionalism with relevance for Northeast Asia too. It puts national and even regime security first, while resisting outside pressures whether over human rights or over economic reforms. This is regionalism steeped in the past, dictated by state rather than business interests and redolent with the language of the cold war. When Russia and China joined in naval military exercises, ostensibly under the auspices of the SCO, in August 2005, the message was that they, no less than the U.S.–Japanese alliance, would set the terms for strategic outcomes in Northeast Asia as well as prevail in Central Asia. This clashes with the promise of broad regionalism under discussion in the East Asian Summit.

After assuming the ambassadorship to Japan Losyukov explained in late 2004 that as a Eurasian country Russia would use its position in Asia as well as Europe to raise its international stature. In light of the dynamism of the APR, in which the United States, China, and India as well as Russia and Japan are facing rapid changes, there are increasing opportunities for economic and political integration. Given unstable elements and shared concern over seedbeds of international terror, religious extremism, separatism, and cross-border crime as well as energy security and the problems of the Korean peninsula, Losyukov sees the need for a multilateral approach. He stresses that apart from some countries in the CIS, China is the most trusted partner of Russia. Through a spirit of mutual compromise, the two have settled their territorial dispute. This is the reality that now must be faced by Japan as well as the United States. He added that Japan and Russia have the potential to transform their relations, already boosted by new defense exchanges and nearly two years of 40–50 percent growth in trade, but certain politicians in Japan are calling instead for an extremely dangerous rollback in overall relations. From this perspective, Russia is prepared to proceed with extended compromise talks along the model taken with China and to work with Japan toward increased integration within a multilateral framework or, if Japan were to insist on a kind of ultimatum on a quick decision to return the four islands then a dangerous state for the region would follow.[30] Presumably, the response could include Sino-Russian cooperation to resist Japanese nationalism, energy supplies focused on China rather than Japan, and reluctance, likely to be shared with North Korea, to include Japan in the multilateral talks focused on the future of the Korean peninsula. Losyukov's unusual diplomatic warnings reflected new strategic thinking in Russia. Yet, it showed more impatience than understanding in trying to draw Japan closer, as a long-term outlook would suggest.

Alexander Panov was interviewed at the time of the publication on November 26, 2004 of his memoirs in Japanese. He suggested that Japan return to the Irkutsk agreement, which was rejected by the hard line that followed Koizumi's rise to power. Drawing a parallel with problems that were faced in Sino-Russian relations, he argued that if Japan rethinks its political and economic approach to Russia strong leadership on both sides and mutual concessions can lead to a territorial agreement.[31] In the face of delay inside Japan in focusing on a forward-looking approach to Russia, these appeals suggested the potential for progress if both sides prepared for making difficult concessions ahead. Yet, in 2005 there were no such preparations. Instead when Putin went to Tokyo in November Russian coverage stressed that economics would proceed in lieu of territorial negotiations. Without moves toward normalization with Japan, one cannot expect a strategy toward the region as a whole that does not rely heavily on China.

South Korea and Russia have edged closer since the low point in relations in 1997–98. The visit by Roh Moo-hyun to Putin's dacha in the fall of 2004 revealed a joint sense of how to proceed in the six-party talks. Moscow would welcome it if Seoul were less beholden to the United States and more assertive. Yet, the two sides are reluctant to embrace tightly, since Russia counts on North Korea's acceptance of its sponsorship role and South Korea is wary of arousing further U.S. distrust. Russian analysts argue that their country is most in favor of a united Korea, and this message resonates well with South Koreans.[32] Putin and Roh recognized that the economic ties between their countries remain at a low level. After high hopes in the early 1990s because of large-scale assistance in connection to normalization of relations and again in the mid-1990s as South Korea seemed to show the most interest in projects in Vladivostok and Nakhodka, Russia's strategy for the region has failed to impress Korean business. Indeed, the narrowness of Russia's business interests, despite pretensions for a major role in North Korea's recovery, leaves it handicapped in normal moves toward regionalism. Strategic thinking compensates with other claims to raising Russia's profile, even as it continues to bypass the essential economic and governance transformation for a normal role.

Refusing to abandon its claims to influence in areas in the vicinity of its eastern borders, Russia turned first to China, then to North Korea, and finally to a regional strategy that combined the two while accepting South Korean collaboration and leaving the door open to Japan without openly challenging the United States. China's multipolar approach beckoned in the mid-1990s, the sunshine policy favored by South and North Korea was appealing at the end of the decade, and the logic of the six-party framework gained favor in 2003–05. Although there were misgivings in hitching Russia's regional policy to China's rise and North Korea's defiance, the prospects outweighed the alternatives of passivity or irrelevance. In August 2005 Presidential Representative Konstantin Pulikovsky, who had been assigned to cultivate personal ties with North Korean leaders, called in Pyongyang for increased bilateral economic cooperation. In contrast to the rapidly rising totals for trade with China and South Korea, North Korean trade with Russia remained around $150 million.[33] Russia was demonstrating that it did not side with U.S. efforts to pressure the North and was anxious, despite many signs to the contrary, not to let its economic presence fall far behind that of the other two neighboring states. This was crisis reasoning in the absence of regionalism.

While there are signs of increased strategic thinking about Northeast Asia as a whole, the current transitional situation has postponed the need to make the difficult decisions but not the importance of preparing the analytical foundation for them. Riding the tail of North Korea as it flails around in search of regime survival is not likely to suffice once the nuclear crisis is resolved. Relying on China as the bulwark for Russia's regional voice cannot be satisfactory as China's power continues to gain dominance along the Russian Far East borders. The logic of Japanese–Russian cooperation in regionalism keeps growing even if the two sides show no signs of finding a path toward normalization.[34] Pursuit of South Korea also should be intensifying. Transformation of governance in the Russian Far East lies at the heart of any promising regional strategy. The case for a strategic outlook is strengthening.

Proponents of regionalism in Russia rank security first, economics second, and culture last among the forces that matter. As before, Moscow considers itself a major force in resolving traditional security questions in Asia. The six-party talks give it a role since 2003 that it had coveted for a decade, and it remains keen on the establishment of a multilateral security framework that balances power in Northeast Asia in a manner Moscow can exploit. Instead of a united, full-scale struggle against terrorism and WMD, this is a message about the need for compromises with no one country or alliance able to gain a preponderance of power. Moscow is banking on a security settlement to end the nuclear crisis justifying its agenda as the basis for regionalism.

Discussions of integrationist processes explain economic ties in ways quite foreign to champions of globalization. Opening borders and attracting foreign investment into competitive market economies are themes left in the background, at best. Rather, the thrust is on state-centered projects to develop energy and transportation networks.[35] The essence of integration is infrastructure and managed trade—the flow of natural resources under the guidance of officials more than of human resources managed by entrepreneurs. This inevitably leads to concentration on "scientific" indicators of conditions favorable to Russia, such as resource locations and seaport locales, not to more sensitive matters such as state capacity and support for business interests. Thus, top-down and economics second suggest a type of regionalism quite different from what others describe.

When it comes to matters other than so-called objective forces, the emphasis is on non-interference in each other's affairs. This means that differences are to be addressed by understanding each other's distinctiveness and rejecting any temptation to apply human rights concerns. Perhaps, the only cultural glue is the call for using regional cooperation in resistance to global cultural forces, especially American ideas.[36] With this civilizational reasoning coupled with reticence about economic openness and preoccupation with a balance of power to check global forces, regionalism in Russian eyes threatens to become an echo of communist-era thinking.

Conclusion

In 2005 new developments gave Russia reason to take a fresh look at prospects for regionalism. Plans for the inaugural East Asian Summit led the countries of ASEAN + 3 to debate what should be the role of the new organization they were establishing and which additional countries should be invited. Unlike the EU, where the rules were largely in place and reflected Western values, the East Asian Summit could be shaped anew and is bound to reflect principles appealing to Russian leaders, such as noninterference in the affairs of other states. Yet, given the secondary emphasis on security in ASEAN + 3 and Japanese reservations about Russia joining forces with China, the path into the East Asian Summit would seem to require a shift in Russian tactics. This creates the temptation to turn instead to smaller groupings where China could press its case and where global values and openness to global economic forces are irrelevant.

In his December 14, 2005 speech at the East Asian Summit Putin made a clear appeal for Russia to be accepted as a member. He stressed the great significance of the new organization for integrating the Asia–Pacific region, which is the leader in global development. He praised its integration based on equal partnerships and suggested that it could unite and coordinate existing multilateral forums including APEC, the SCO, and ASEAN. Emphasizing the dual role of strengthening security and development, he claimed that Russia would contribute to a regional security system and energy supply security. With some expecting that Australia, instigated by the United States, would try to block Russia's entry based on different thinking about security, Putin appeared to be seeking to forge a regional triangle with China and India as well as a gateway to the Muslim world through ASEAN that would combine Eurasian and Pacific power.[37]

Increasingly, Russians have accepted an argument that, driven by ideology, the United States is destabilizing various regions, including Northeast Asia and Central Asia, contrasting the motives of their country in favor of peaceful coexistence and a balance of power that prevents any one state from dominating.[38] While Japan has accepted United States dominance for its own ends, China and North Korea too, with South Korea in sympathy, are also intent on balance. They welcome Russia's role, whereas the United States has tried to exclude it. The priority in regional cooperation is to form a geopolitical framework that obliges the United States to accept a limited role. Given this preoccupation, there is room for Russia to play a large role in Northeast Asia. The growing linkage between energy and geopolitics also means that Russian oil and gas are not simply another commodity; they are prized as a factor that can shape the way security concerns are addressed. Such reasoning obviates the need for facing the fundamental problems in integrating Russia into a dynamic region.

The problems in Northeast Asia have old roots and draw Russia back to old ways of thinking. Also Russia's weak foothold inclines it to the countries that are eager for it to be active in the region, the two communist-led states with agendas focused on old problems beginning with divided countries. Neither the United States under George W. Bush nor Japan under Koizumi has made an appealing case for Russia to try a different orientation, but Putin has not given them much encouragement of late. Domestic reform is stalled and with it the rationale for a foreign policy aimed at a different regional configuration in keeping with globalization. Little analysis prepares the way for strategic thinking about Asian regionalism in synch with globalization. This would require more forthright coverage of the failings of Russia's governance and the threats to international security. With China and North Korea beckoning Russia toward a more confrontational type of regionalism, integration processes remain little explored.

Thinking necessary for a long-term regional approach does not yet show the way forward. In the Gorbachev era progress in bilateral relations and the need to overcome lingering suspicions may have justified the lack of a regional approach, and Putin may also be able to point to international factors limiting the chances for regionalism. Yet, even if Putin has done better than early Yeltsin and even late Yeltsin in coordinating steps toward Northeast Asia, he falls short of Gorbachev in linking the regional and the global and still has not resolved the fundamental uncertainties in strategizing about how to fit Russia and especially the Russian Far East into an emerging region. Putin is eager to bring Russia into the East Asian Summit and to convert Russia's role in the six-party talks into security and energy regionalism, but reliance on China, North Korea, and the SCO fails to reassure Japan and the United States. In the absence of a positive investment climate and trust in preventing the proliferation of WMD, Russia will arouse too many suspicions to become a reliable regional partner.

Putin's meeting with Koizumi at the G-8 summit in St. Petersburg in July 2006 provided another chance to clarify Russia's energy polices and priority for Japan witⁿn Asia. Yet, just as the overall summit left unsettled Russia's relations with the U.S. and its entry into the W.T.O, there were no state guarantees that could have led Japan to begin to fund the energy pipline to the Pacific and development of oil fields. Putin was now firmly in charge of a recentralized energy powerhouse boosted by record oil prices, but he was wary of committing to international deals that could limit Russia's options. Cooperation also proved incomplete over the July 4 North Korean multiple missile launchings that has alarmed Japan as well as the United States. While Japan pressed for a strong Security Council rresolution, Russia backed China's insistence on a statement that lacked teeth, even if it still infuriated the North. The basic direction of regional policy remained rejection of U.S. leadership and objectives, wariness of Japan, and reliance on China.

Notes

1. M. A. Troitskii, *Transatlanticheskii soiuz 1991–2004* (Moscow: Nauchno-obrazovatel'nyi forum po mezhdunarodnym otnoshenii, 2004); Gennady Chufrin, ed., *Russia and Asia-Pacific Security* (Stockholm: SIPRI, 1999).

2. Gilbert Rozman, *Northeast Asia's Stunted Regionalism: Bilateral Distrust in the Shadow of Globalization* (Cambridge: Cambridge University Press, 2004).

3. F. Joseph Dresen, ed., *Russia in Asia—Asia in Russia: Energy, Economics, and Regional Relations: Conference Proceedings* (Washington, DC: Kennan Institute Occasional Paper #292, 2004).

4. *Chosun ilbo*, August 18, 2005.

5. Dmitri Trenin, *The End of Eurasia: Russia on the Border Between Geopolitics and Globalization* (Washington, DC: The Carnegie Endowment for International Peace, 2002).

6. *Perspektivy razvitia Rossiiskikh regionov: Dal'nii Vostok i Zabaikal'e do 2010 goda* (Khabarovsk: Institut ekonomicheskikh issledovanii, Dal'nevostochoe otdelenie RAN, 2002).

7. K. Vnukov, "Russia-China: Enhancing Partnership and Cooperation (On the outcome of Russian President Vladimir Putin's visit to China)," *Far Eastern Affairs*, Vol. 32, No. 4 (2004): 53–56.

8. S. V. Sevast'ianov, "Modeli mezhdunarodnogo sotrudnichestva v Severo-Vostochnoi Azii: rol' mezhpravitel'stvennykh i nepravitel'stvennykh organizatsii" (Moscow: MGIMO avtoreferat, 2002).

9. M. Kapitsa, "Problemy mira i bezopasnosti na Dal'nem Vostoke," *Problemy Dal'nego Vostoka*, No. 5, (1987): 3–12.

10. V. L. Larin, *Kitai i Dal'nii Vostok Rossii* (Vladivostok: Dal'nauka, 1998).

11. Alexander Lukin, *The Bear Watches the Dragon: Russia's Perceptions of China and the Evolution of Russian-Chinese Relations Since the Eighteenth Century* (Armonk, NY: M.E. Sharpe, 2003); Semyon Verbitsky, Tsuyoshi Hasegawa, and Gilbert Rozman, eds., *Misperceptions between Japan and Russia* (Pittsburgh: The Carl Beck Papers in Russian & East European Studies, University of Pittsburgh, 2000).

12. Gilbert Rozman, "Moscow's Japan-Watchers in the First Years of the Gorbachev Era: The Struggle for Realism and Respect in Foreign Affairs," *Pacific Review*, Vol. 1, No. 3 (1988): 257–75; Gilbert Rozman, "Chinese Studies in Russia and their Impact, 1985–1992," *Asian Research Trends*, No. 4 (1994): 143–60.

13. Gilbert Rozman, "China, Japan, and the Post-Soviet Upheaval: Global Opportunities and Regional Risks," in Karen Dawisha, ed., *The International Dimension of Post-Communist Transitions in Russia and the New States of Eurasia* (Armonk, NY: M.E. Sharpe, 1997), pp. 147–76.

14. Fiona Hill and Clifford Gaddy, *The Siberian Curse: How Communist Planners Left Russia Out in the Cold* (Washington, DC: Brookings Institution Press, 2003).

15. Brad Williams, "The Criminalisation of Russian-Japanese Border Trade: Causes and Consequences," *Europe-Asia Studies*, Vol. 55, No. 5 (2003): 711–28.

16. Gilbert Rozman, "The Crisis of the Russian Far East: Who Is to Blame?" *Problems of Post-Communism*, Vol. 44, No. 5 (September/October 1997):

3–12; Gilbert Rozman, "Troubled Choices for the Russian Far East: Decentralization, Open Regionalism, and Internationalism," *The Journal of East Asian Affairs*, Vol. 11, No. 2 (Summer/Fall 1997): 537–69.

17. Sherman Garnett, ed., *Rapprochement or Rivalry? Russia-China Relations in a Changing Asia* (Armonk, NY: M.E. Sharpe, 2000).

18. Gilbert Rozman, ed., *Japan and Russia: The Tortuous Path to Normalization, 1949–1999* (New York: St. Martin's Press, 2000).

19. G. Toloraia, "Koreiskii poluostrov i Rossiia," *Mezhdunarodnaia zhizn'*, (December 2002): 63–72.

20. Artyom Lukin, "Russia and Multilateral Cooperation in the Asia-Pacific Region" (Vladivostok: unpublished manuscript, 2004).

21. Evgeny Bazhanov, "Russian Debates about Korea" (Moscow: unpublished manuscript, 2005).

22. *Zolotoi rog*, July 22, 2003, p. 2.

23. Aleksandr Brezhnev, "Trubnyi glas iz Pkhen'iana," *Zavtra*, October 2003.

24. Gilbert Rozman, "The Russian Response: Local and Regional Concerns" (Princeton, NJ: unpublished manuscript, 2005).

25. www.mofa.go.jplannounce/fon/aso/speech0512

26. *Moscow Times*, October 28, 2005.

27. *Izvestiia*, November 1, 2005.

28. *Sankei shimbun*, December 11, 2004, p. 1.

29. "Puchin daitoryo yokuru ni oyabazu," *Sentaku*, December 2004, pp. 46–47.

30. A. Losiukov, "Puchin daitoryo no honichi to kongo no Nichiro kankei," *Ajia jiho*, December 2004, pp. 4–19.

31. *Tokyo shimbun*, November 24, 2004, p. 24.

32. V. A. Medvedev, et al., *Koreiskii vopros: integratsionnye protsessy v Severo-vostochnoi Azii* (Moscow: Gorbachev Fund, 2005), p. 18.

33. *Itar-Tass*, August 16, 2005.

34. Gilbert Rozman, "A Chance for a Breakthrough in Russo-Japanese Relations: Will the Logic of Great Power Relations Prevail?" *Pacific Review*, Vol. 15, No. 3 (2002): 325–57.

35. *The Role of Trans-Siberian Railroad in the Development of Cooperation between Pacific Rim Countries* (Vladivostok: FENU Publishers, 2003).

36. Andrei P. Tsygankov, *Whose World Order?: Russia's Perception of American Ideas after the Cold War* (Notre Dame, IN: Notre Dame University Press, 2004).

37. http://www.kremlin.ru, December 14, 2005.

38. Aleksandr Voronstov, "Iadernii krizis na Koreiskom poluostrove v mezh-dunarodnom kontekste," in N. Simoniya, ed., *Polveka bez voiny i bez mira: Koreiskii poluostrov glazami Rossiiskikh uchenykh* (Moscow: IMEMO, 2003), pp. 219–20.

Contributors

EVGENY BAZHANOV is vice president of the Diplomatic Academy and director of the Research Institute of Contemporary International Studies, Foreign Ministry of Russia. From 1970 to 1985 he served as a diplomat in Singapore, the United States, and China, and from 1985 to 1991 he was an adviser on foreign policy for Mikhail Gorbachev. He is the author of 25 books and over 1000 articles on politics and international relations.

ALEXEI BOGATUROV is dean of the School of Political Affairs at Moscow State Institute of International Relations (MGIMO), Russian Foreign Ministry where he has taught since 1991. His most recent monographs (co-authored) are *Systemic History of International Relations. 1918–2003* (2004) and *World Politics: Theory, Methodology, Applied Analysis (2005)*.

JOSEPH P. FERGUSON is vice president of the National Council for Eurasian and East European Research. He received his Ph.D. from the Johns Hopkins University, and was in residence at Princeton University as a post-doctoral fellow. He has published numerous articles and essays on the international relations of Eurasia and Northeast Asia.

ALEXANDER LUKIN is director of the Center for East Asian and Shanghai Cooperation Organization Studies at Moscow State Institute of International Relations (MGIMO), Russian Foreign Ministry and research associate at the Institute for European, Russian, and Eurasian Studies of the George Washington University. A recent book is *The Bear Watches the Dragon: Russia's Perceptions of China and the Evolution of Russian-Chinese Relations since the Eighteenth Century* (2003).

VASILY MIKHEEV is a corresponding member of the Russian Academy of Sciences (RAS) and director of the Center for China, Northeast Asia and Central Asia Studies at the Institute of World Economy and International Relations (IMEMO), RAS. His most recent monographs are *Northeast Asian Globalization* (2003) and *China: Risks, Threats and Challenges to Development* (2005).

ALEXANDER PANOV is the Russian ambassador to Norway. He has worked in many posts in Tokyo and Japan-related positions in the Russian Foreign Ministry, serving as ambassador to South Korea, deputy minister on the Asia-Pacific Region and then ambassador to Japan. His publications in Japanese include *From Distrust to Trust (1992)* and *Blue Sky after the Thunder (2004)*.

GILBERT ROZMAN is the Musgrave professor of sociology at Princeton University, where he has taught since 1970. His most recent monograph is *Northeast Asia's Stunted Regionalism: Bilateral Distrust in the Shadow of Globalization* (2004). He also co-edited *Korea at the Center: The Dynamics of Regionalism in Northeast Asia* (2006).

KAZUHIKO TOGO served in the Japanese Foreign Ministry from 1968 on Russia, the United States, Europe, international law and economics. After serving as ambassador to the Netherlands, he retired in 2002. He taught at universities in Moscow, Tokyo, and Leiden. In 2004–06 he has been engaged in teaching and research in Princeton. His recent publications include *Japan's Foreign Policy 1945–2003: The Quest for a Proactive Policy* (2005).

DMITRI TRENIN is a senior associate of the Carnegie Endowment for International Peace and director of studies at its Moscow Center. He is the author of *Russia's China Problem* (1999), *The End of Eurasia: Russia Between Geopolitics and Globalization* (2002), and *Integration and Identity: Russia as a New West* (forthcoming).

Index